PHENOMENOLOGY AND THE NON-HUMAN ANIMAL

CONTRIBUTIONS TO PHENOMENOLOGY

IN COOPERATION WITH THE CENTER FOR ADVANCED RESEARCH IN PHENOMENOLOGY

Volume 56

Scope

The purpose of this series is to foster the development of phenomenological philosophy through creative research. Contemporary issues in philosophy other disciplines and in culture generally, offer opportunities for the application of phenomenological methods that call for creative responses. Although the work of several generations of thinkers has provided phenomenology with many results with which to approach these challenges, a truly successful response to them will require building on this work with new analyses and methodological innovations.

PHENOMENOLOGY AND THE NON-HUMAN ANIMAL

At the Limits of Experience

edited by

CORINNE PAINTER
Washtenaw Community College, Ann Arbor, Michigan

and

CHRISTIAN LOTZ
Michigan State University, East Lansing, Michigan

Springer

A C.I.P. Catalogue record for this book is available from the Library of Congress.

ISBN 978-1-4020-6306-0 (HB)
ISBN 978-1-4020-6307-7 (e-book)

Published by Springer,
P.O. Box 17, 3300 AA Dordrecht, The Netherlands.

www.springer.com

Printed on acid-free paper

for Socrates, the feline member of our family

Contents

SECTION IV: AT THE MARGINS OF PHENOMENOLOGY

Acknowledgments

The editors of this volume would like to thank Emporia State University (Emporia, Kansas) for supporting this project with a grant, which provided monetary support for our research. We would also like to thank the contributors to this volume, for their insightful and provocative essays, which challenge each and every one of us to rethink our relationship with our non-human animal neighbors. Finally, we would like to thank our animal friends, who, in their own way, and without knowing it, were the inspiration for this volume.

1

Introduction

Phenomenology and the Question of the Non-Human Animal

Corinne PAINTER and Christian LOTZ

As Max Horkheimer wrote sixty years ago,

> Modern insensitivity to nature is indeed only a variation of the pragmatic attitude that is typical of Western Civilization as a whole. Only the forms are different. The early trapper saw in the prairies and mountains only the prospect of good hunting; the modern businessman sees in the landscape an opportunity for the display of cigarette posters. The fate of animals in our world is symbolized by an item printed in the newspapers of a few years ago. It reported that landings of planes in Africa were often hampered by herds of elephants and other beasts. Animals are considered simply as obstructers of traffic.[1]

The Frankfurt School in general and Horkheimer in particular connects these observations to a "speculative theory of reason," according to which he claimed that ever since the re-installment of modern rationality in the 18th Century, all entities have ceased to be acknowledged for their intrinsic value. He claimed, that is, that entities are no longer viewed as worthwhile and significant in their own right, but instead, simply as objects of dispositional power that are thus evaluated on the basis of instrumental reason, i.e., on the basis of their practical value for "some other thing." In this way, what started as a project of realizing genuine (philosophical) reason and value in our world finally turned towards itself, with the dawn of modern rationality. The (misguided) emancipation of reason from nature, as Horkheimer argues, turned into the *rational and organized oppression of nature*, which, since human beings are a part of nature, forced human reason to turn against itself, and in so doing reveal itself as a most dangerous and destructive substance. Indeed, in its very attempt to liberate itself from nature, reason became the destructive force that guides the history of the Western world, the monstrous effects of which we bear witness to regularly. Not surprisingly, "this principle of domination," as Horkheimer (and Adorno) put their bold claim, "has become the idol to which everything is sacrificed."[2] Sadly,

C. Painter and C. Lotz (eds.), Phenomenology and the Non-Human Animal, 1–11.

what Max Horkheimer noticed in 1946, shortly after WWII, while facing what the European (left and right) intelligentsia diagnosed as *the failure of Western Civilization as a whole*, seems, still, to be true, even sixty years after Horkheimer published this diagnosis in his *Eclipse of Reason*.

As most of the recent literature in environmental philosophy, animal rights, eco-philosophy, and animal welfare has uncovered and repeatedly pointed out – though usually without explicit reference to the overall speculative and idealist background that rules Horkheimer's philosophy of history – our current practices of relating ourselves (1) to our "natural" selves, (2) to the natural environment, and (3) to non-human animals, imply a whole range of destructive tendencies, which are not only visible in our eating practices, in our agriculture and food production, and in our industrialized way of treating non-human animals, but also in our linguistic practices, in our mentalities, and in our overall attitudes towards life, death, and meaning. Accordingly, what almost all authors working in these fields uniquely propose and attempt to do is to re-think precisely these relations: they try to re-conceive our relations to ourselves, to the environment, and to "the other," where this latter category includes non-human animal others. Moreover, fully aware that these problems are not merely local or regional problems, but global ones, these thinkers acknowledge that a proper diagnosis and treatment must consider all aspects of life, including, especially, history, culture, society, and politics. Consequently, we find in all academic fields – from agricultural technology and bio-engineering to the social sciences, psychology, and even literature – a wealth of critical reflections on these pressing topics, about which even the most skeptical thinkers and early cultural critics (such as Horkheimer) would have been pleasantly surprised if they were alive today.

In this connection, the philosophical literature on animal rights, animal welfare, and ecological philosophy has literally exploded during the last three decades. Almost every university library has made space for special sections on environmental philosophy (broadly construed), and new texts are being produced regularly. Given this fact, it is rather astonishing that philosophers who work in various classical Continental traditions, such as German Idealism, Marxism, Existentialism, Phenomenology, Hermeneutics, and (Post)Structuralism, have struggled to position themselves forcefully within this scholarly space, wherein their contributions lag behind those that are rooted in other traditions, particularly the Anglo-American Analytic tradition. For although things look different in the field of environmental philosophy, to which the phenomenological tradition has contributed significantly,[3] in relation to the general literature on non-human animals, we find only a handful of publications that are primarily written from an explicitly European or Continental perspective.[4] The editors and contributors to this Volume acknowledge this lag, and hope to "make up for lost time" (so to speak).

Interestingly, the main reason for the lack of phenomenological contributions to the literature on the non-human animal is – paradoxically – also likely to account for the wealth of phenomenological considerations of nature and environment. The reason has to do with what we find in the canonical and classical authors working in this tradition: whereas authors working in other contexts and traditions do not seem to be focally interested in framing their analyses in relation to their historical-cultural-social-natural environments, classical European authors routinely – as a matter of course – attempt to think through contemporary questions from a point of view that is *defined by* and *carried out in terms of its relation to* their traditions and, thus, their environments. For example, as Husserl famously put it in his *Crisis*, understanding ourselves in our contemporary being just means to "reflect back" on the tradition that we have inherited, and to see our place in relation to nature, culture, and world.[5] Furthermore, according to Heidegger, philosophical practice requires an *Abbau* – a destruction – of the history of philosophy, precisely because of its refusal to acknowledge its dependence on world.[6] Even Foucault went so far as to define the "ontology of ourselves" and the question of what and who we are as an *archaeological and genealogical project*, which could therefore not be adequately addressed without proper analyses of nature and environment.[7] And the list of European thinkers who advance similar claims and structure their analyses accordingly, is much longer, of course.

Notwithstanding the significant achievements concerning these "environmental themes," such attentive concern did not often spill over into *explicit* considerations of the non-human animal or of the human-animal relation. For, whereas most of the classical authors did not offer central analyses of non-human animals or of the underlying ontological presuppositions that tend to guide our assumptions when thinking about the distinction between the human and the animal,[8] all phenomenological authors reflected intensively on our relation to the overall environment and nature; indeed, the phenomenological tradition from Husserl on developed new notions of nature, perhaps most notable amongst them, Husserl's and Heidegger's reflections on the surrounding world and Husserl's and Merleau-Ponty's reflections on the intersubjective constitution of nature. These critical examinations were then picked up in the 70s by left thinkers both in the United States and on the Continent, probably because of their connection to the Marxist tradition.[9] Finally, the concept and rich analyses of the "lived Body," especially as it was first developed by Husserl and further developed by Merleau-Ponty, is probably *the* ground-breaking discovery of phenomenology that ultimately led to a full rejection of Cartesian epistemology, the latter of which provided the foundation for the modern conception of rationality and nature, as it was criticized by Horkheimer (and others). However, in contradistinction to the many focused efforts to rethink the general concept of nature and environment, which (as we pointed out) was historically grounded in the tradition of European thought, the project of rethinking our relation to the non-human animal seems to require a more autonomous and historically independent development of ideas, thoughts, and arguments. This volume is an attempt to contribute to this project, the contemporary significance of which should not be underestimated.

In this connection, virtually all phenomenologists have helped develop alternatives to the sharp subject-object distinctions that underlie almost every philosophical theory up to the 20th Century, many of which still determine the leading epistemologcial theories of contemporary philosophy, especially within the Anglo-American tradition. Perhaps the most visible effect of the development of these alternatives may be seen in the terms "world" and "worldhood," particularly as they were explicated by Heidegger in his analysis of worldhood. Heidegger's analysis lays bare a unique feature of what phenomenologists call "world," which is worthwhile to mention in this context: the fundamental definition and essence of world *on all levels*, which necessarily includes nature, culture, and history, is *shared* and *communal*. In addition to the introduction of the "lived Body," the *communality and publicity of world* – even, or especially, nature – is the second revolution that occurred within phenomenology at the beginning of the last century. In this connection, Husserl went so far as to claim that the very *objectivity* of "things out there" in the spatio-temporal world is intersubjectively constituted. "The other Ego," as he writes in his *Cartesian Meditations*, "makes constitutionally possible a new infinite domain of what is 'other:' an *Objective Nature* and a whole Objective world, to which all other Egos and myself belong."[10] Consequently, if animal others are also "Egos," which simply means that they have a *unified, experienced perspective* on the world, then we must come to the conclusion that humans and animals not only partially or "accidentally" live alongside each other; rather, we fundamentally *share* with each other the *objectivity* of what we call "world." Put simply, to live in a world that is "there" *for* everyone – including non-human animals – intentionally implies and *presupposes* "a community of Egos existing with each other and for each other."[11] Undoubtedly, most commentators of Husserl's phenomenology have overlooked this *radical* "trans-species" spirit of Husserl's thought in the 5th *Cartesian Meditation*.[12]

This volume should be seen in the light of this innovative and, it might be said, revolutionary spirit. All of the volume's contributors, though from diverse backgrounds, try to make (more) sense of what it means to share a world with others, and in so doing, they attempt to discover what it means to *be with* non-human animals and to *exist for* non-human animals.

The authors writing in this volume locate themselves within the phenomenological movement in a broad sense, offering reflections from a number of phenomenological perspectives, including: from a Heideggerian perspective (Kuperus), from an anthropological-philosophical perspective (Oele), and from a Foucaultian perspective (Carlson). In addition, they reflect on marginalized topics, such as empirical psychology (Ruonakoski, Lohmar) and literature (Mensch). Still further, in addition to reflecting ontologically on the question of the non-human animal by criticizing human exceptionalism (Toadvine), the ethical dimension of this question is exemplarily addressed by thinking through the notions of intentionality and empathy (Brown, Painter). As a result, this volume goes beyond the traditional scope of phenomenology, as developed by Husserl, Heidegger, Sartre, and Merleau-Ponty. For, rather than exclusively developing the classics (though this is also done), the authors in this volume are united in their attempts to expand the limits of phenomenological philosophy, especially since they recognize what we pointed out above, namely, that phenomenological contributions to the urgently important contemporary debate regarding non-human animals is lagging behind contributions from other traditions. With this in mind, the contributions are divided into four sets of reflections: [1] Section One: *Phenomenology, Ontology, and Anthropology,* deals with anthropological considerations from a phenomenological standpoint. The editors of this volume consider this an important set of reflections, since in opposition to the German discourse of the 20th Century, philosophical anthropology has not (yet) become prominent in the Anglo-American world.[13] [2] Section Two: *Phenomenology, Psychology, and Language*, is concerned with the connection between phenomenological philosophy and the empirical sciences, particularly phenomenology's connection to psychology, whereas [3] Section Three: *Phenomenology and Ethics*, moves beyond the descriptive level, wherein attempts to properly describe the non-human animal are done within the context of offering prescriptive and normative analyses of the human-non-human animal relation. Here, the development of an ethical perspective from a phenomenological point of view is acknowledged as a most pressing issue, and, at the same time, as a uniquely difficult task, especially given that (so far) the phenomenological tradition tends to approach philosophical problems on an ontological or a descriptive basis and not from an ethical standpoint. Finally, [4] Section Four: *At the Margins of Phenomenology,* goes beyond the core of phenomenology by presenting considerations on "disabled otherness" from a Foucauldian perspective and on "alterity" from a literary and theological perspective.

I. Phenomenology, Ontology, and Anthropology

Gerard Kuperus (University of San Francisco), in his contribution *Attunement, Deprivation, and Drive: Heidegger and Animality*, elucidates Heidegger's analysis of non-human animals and his thesis about their "world-poverty." He argues that Heidegger's analysis of the poverty of the non-human animal is central for his understanding of the distinction between human and animal, since it rests upon his non-traditional claim that whereas animals are deprived of attunement and moods, and thus deprived of full "worldhood," humans are defined precisely in terms of these phenomena. According to Heidegger, the non-human animal world is somehow "closed" while the human world is "open," which is evidenced most especially by Dasein's experience of "profound boredom." As Kuperus shows, profound boredom, while seemingly akin to the animal's poverty in world, constitutes, paradoxically, Dasein's fundamental attunement, according to which Dasein finds its richest possibilities for existence, insofar as it can distance and free itself from its general mindless captivation in the world. Since this possibility is not available for the non-human animal, he is forced to remain captivated and absorbed by his drives and instincts, whereas humans can distance themselves from their environment and therewith create new possibilities for themselves, including a form of appreciating and "being with" animals.

Marjolein Oele (University of San Francisco) covers both traditional and new ground in her contribution, *Being Beyond: Aristotle's and Plessner's Accounts of Animal Responsiveness*. As acknowledged above, the German tradition in philosophical anthropology is not well known in Anglo-American debates; fortunately, Oele's essay is a step towards changing this situation. Following her elucidation of Aristotle's account of touching, she examines Helmuth Plessner's philosophy of biology, focusing on his understanding of "responsiveness" and its relevance for the contemporary debate. As Oele argues, in contradistinction to other approaches to non-human animals, which do not pay serious attention to the robust manner in which animals *live* in their environments, she shows that organisms not only react to their environments in a very specific sense, but they *respond* to it. With the support of Aristotle's interpretation of touching and Plessner's theory of organisms, Oele develops a general conception of the "responsiveness of life," which is most impressive. However, According to Oele, while it turns out that Aristotle employed highly sophisticated notions of self-reflexivity and self-affection, which he attributed to all living beings, he ultimately failed to solve the problem of the "*localization*" of this "touching" and "responsiveness;" for, according to Aristotle, as touching and responsiveness do not seem to belong to a special sense-organ, though they must be conceived as somewhere "inside" the animal body, they nonetheless may not be associated with any particular organ of sensibility. This obstacle, which renders it difficult to understand this essential feature of the animal body, according to Oele, is overcome by Plessner's notion of "*positionality*," which he (Plessner) characterizes as the relation between a living organism and its environment. In this way, although Plessner may be said to "improve upon" Aristotle's account of the responsiveness of the animal body, by solving (and perhaps eliminating) the "localization" problem, both Aristotle and Plessner seem to converge in their (non-Cartesian) assumption that the animal body is "non-localized" in a spatio-temporal sense, due to the fact of its inner reflexivity and its transitive nature. As Oele shows, animal bodies, thus, have extremely rich modes of being in nature.

Ted Toadvine (University of Oregon), in his essay *How Not to be a Jellyfish: Human Exceptionalism and the Ontology of Reflection*, begins his considerations of "human exceptionalism" by pointing out that we have yet to find a philosophical solution to recent attempts in philosophy to break down the metaphysical thesis that there is a *difference in kind* between human and non-human animals. By drawing from Heidegger, Scheler, and Agamben, Toadvine argues that the "animal-human distinction goes to the heart of the phenomenological method." As Toadvine points out, the human being seems to be the only entity that can ask for truth, which includes the request for truth regarding the distinction between human and non-human animals. Consequently, as Toadvine shows, we need to reconsider the phenomenological method itself, since this will make appropriate investigations of the non-human animal possible, and in this way allow us to avoid charges of human exceptionalism, according to which the claim is advanced that the human species is the final, most unique, and best product of evolution (or creation). According to Toadvine, the most promising ideas on this matter come from Merleau-Ponty, who radically tries – at least in his later work – to overcome all ontological distinctions and, even, to disconnect reflection from exclusive humanness, thereby reintegrating the concept of reflection into being itself. Indeed, as Toadvine (paraphrasing Merleau-Ponty) puts it, "animality and humanity are given only together,… such that we cannot draw a sharp ontological boundary between human and nonhuman animals nor arrange their relations hierarchically."

II. Phenomenology, Psychology, and Language

Dieter Lohmar (University of Cologne), in his essay *How Do Primates Think? Phenomenological Analyses of Non-language Systems of Representation in Higher Primates and Humans*, argues against traditional philosophical claims (such as Kant's), which maintain that non-human animals are unable to refer mentally to objects that are not immediately present. Indeed, Lohmar rejects, on phenomenological grounds, the prejudice that non-human animals are unable to think, arguing that thinking, understood as the representation of something absent (Lohmar here follows Husserl's sixth *Logical Investigation*), ultimately must be ascribed to *all* primates, and not just to humans (who are members of the primate group, Lohmar reminds us). In addition, his discussion and extensive use of empirical research shows that almost all other activities that philosophers have traditionally used for distinguishing human and non-human animals, such as various modes of communication, deception, tool use, production and transportation, as well as social cooperation, also fail to establish any significant distinction between primate groups. The same holds true for "object permanence," which refers to the thesis that an individual is able to have an idea of an enduring object even when the object itself is not immediately present, and for the representation of future events, both of which are evidenced by a mass of animal research that establishes their capacities to perform these acts. The most central claim of Lohmar's overview targets our traditional view of the centrality of language for operating with metaphysical distinctions. In this connection, Lohmar claims that language is not the primary system of representation, as was (and still is) traditionally thought, since it sits "on top" of other representational systems, including the faculty of emotion, of imagination, and of *phantasmata*, all of which are faculties that humans and other primates regularly employ. Interestingly, though Husserl himself did not spend much time explicitly treating this theme, Lohmar's central thesis finds its ground (and confirmation) in Husserl's genetic phenomenology. Lohmar gives further force to his thesis by analyzing daydreams, which he characterizes as an "old mode of thinking" that has been around for all of "thinking history." This "old mode of thinking" involves "scenically imagining" objects (including characters of persons) that are immediately absent and not represented via language, and is engaged in by all primates, according to Lohmar.

Erika Ruonakoski (University of Helsinki) also deals with psychological themes in her contribution, *Phenomenology and the Study of Animal Behavior*. In her essay, Ruonakoski argues that there can in fact be a genuine dialogue between phenomenology and the study of animal behavior, primarily inasmuch as it can be a helpful tool for investigating and clarifying the relationship between the scientist and the research subject. Using the phenomenology of Merleau-Ponty, Ruonakoski establishes that no matter how abstract, highly theoretical, and scientific our research into animal behavior might be, it is nevertheless the case that the human experience of the animal is the necessary point of departure for our investigations, and that, if properly acknowledged and appreciated, it can serve as a "gradual awakening" to the different-but-similar modes of being of the non-human animal, on the basis of which the animal's world can be viewed as the human world too, wherein meaningful behavior – both animal and human – is constituted and witnessed. In addition, Ruonakoski argues that phenomenology can likewise benefit from the discoveries of theorists working in other traditions, such as the hard and soft sciences, given that their empirical findings can challenge the phenomenologist's ontological presuppositions, thereby offering ever new possibilities for understanding the non-human animal, as well as the human-animal relation. Finally, then, Ruonakoski shows that phenomenological and non-phenomenological researchers can be co-beneficiaries of a very productive relationship, the consequences of which are improved studies of, as well as increased possibilities for, meaningful communication between humans and animals.

III. Phenomenology and Ethics

Charles Brown (Emporia State University), in his paper *The Intentionality and Animal Heritage of Moral Experience: What We Can Learn from Dogs about Moral Theory*, argues that a phenomenological conception of the intrinsic rationality of moral experience can help us to overcome the traditional overly rationalistic framework with which we typically operate in our culture. Brown focuses on a new conception of the self, which allows us to integrate emotion, particularity, and animality into moral philosophy. Intentionality is the central bridge that, according to Brown, can lead us to appreciate the *intrinsic* moral dimension that characterizes relationships between humans and animals. In this connection, Brown argues that humans share with non-human animals an emotional world within which animal others *care about the same things that humans care about,* as he illustrates with reference to his canine companion, Lily. We are, in Brown's words, "co-witnessing" each other. In addition to showing the strength of phenomenology in comparison to traditional "monistic" and overly rationalistic conceptions of morality, Brown's contribution can also be taken as a sort of "corrective" to the discipline of phenomenology, insofar as phenomenological analyses have traditionally neglected the natural sciences, especially Darwinian biology, which Brown successfully incorporates into his own insightful analysis of the moral world and of the way in which both human and non-human animals participate in this world on the basis of a "proto" moral openness to the world.

Corinne Painter (Washtenaw Community College), in her essay *Appropriating the Philosophies of Edmund Husserl and Edith Stein: Animal Psyche, Empathy, and Moral Subjectivity*, joins Brown in his attempt to consider the ethical aspects of the investigation of non-human animal nature, by examining the central role that empathy plays in the human-animal relation. With the help of Edmund Husserl and Edith Stein, Painter argues that the "animal other" is reached through the experience of empathy, which, she maintains, can ultimately lead to an ethics of care that crosses species boundaries. As she points out, Husserl characterized what he referred to as the "personalistic attitude" as a mode within which we encounter others – including non-human animal others – through care and concern. Most centrally, using Stein's phenomenological description of empathy, she shows that the concept of empathy is misunderstood if it is conceived as a form of "feeling one with the other" or as a (possible) result of specific act; rather, empathy, she argues, has an *a priori* status and should be conceived as the very *condition* of being related to others, including animal others. In this way, she shows that empathy does not rely upon our ability to overcome the difference between the one who empathizes (the "empathizing agent") and the one who is the subject-object of empathy (the "empathizing patient"); rather, as Painter argues, it *preserves* the foreignness of the other in her otherness. Drawing upon this understanding of the phenomenon, empathy successfully captures the undeniable access we have to the foreign subjectivity of the animal other, with whom we share meaningful relationships and experiences, even while appreciating the foreignness that characterizes these relations. On this basis, she shows that there is a sort of "moral kinship" between animals and humans, which, if respected, provides the appropriate phenomenological ground for an ethics that respects all moral subjects.

IV. At the Margins of Phenomenology

Licia Carlson (Harvard University) pushes the ethical perspective of the human-non-human animal relation to a still new dimension. In her essay, *The Human as Just An Other Animal: Madness, Disability and Foucault's*

Bestiary, from the standpoint of a linguistic phenomenology, Carlson analyses how the concept of "being human" not only functions as a rule of exclusion (in the Foucaultian sense) in regard to non-human animal others, but also implies a general rule of exclusion that defines our relation to "disabled" human others. The conflict at issue here, according to Carlson, appears between these two exclusions and may be expressed in the following question: "How does challenging the associations between the cognitively disabled and non-human animals obscure or deny our animal nature and perpetuate negative views about non-human animals?" In order to provide an appropriate answer, Carlson turns her attention to Foucault's early work on madness, since we can find there a new way of looking at the distinction between what is traditionally conceived as human and what is typically held as not human. Carlson contends that Foucault's work can serve as the basis for a genuinely critical examination of often oppressive forms of treatment for various "others" – human and non-human – that fail to properly respect these others in their particularity.

Finally, James Mensch (Saint Francis Xavier University), through the reading of a contemporary novel, explores the link between phenomenological analysis and literature in his contribution *The Intertwining of Incommensurables: Yann Martel's Life of Pi.* In his essay, Mensch examines the connection between two seemingly opposed "alterities" that, paradoxically, define human beings: *their animality and their divinity*. By investigating the two very different accounts that Pi tells in his attempt to explain how he comes to be the sole survivor of a shipwreck (his entire family as well as the ship's crew are killed), Mensch launches into a detailed elucidation of the novel's main character, "Richard Parker" (Pi), who, during his time on the ship, takes on the character of a tiger, thereby displaying his animal nature, but who, at the same time, tries to deny his animal nature by placing himself above animals. In this way, Richard Parker (Pi) comes to see that humans are really the most dangerous animal, refusing to accept their own animality, while also refusing to see their divinity, both of which are central aspects of human identity. Although we usually separate "humanness" from animality and divinity, as Mensch points out, "both the animal and the divine show themselves in the madness that moves life in strange but saving ways, the very madness without which no species would survive."

Though the authors contributing to this volume (as we earlier acknowledged) come from diverse backgrounds (due to the fact that phenomenology itself is a pluralistic endeavor), and display different focal interests in their contributions, they all claim that a redefinition of our being-in-the-world is needed in the contemporary discourse, and that this requires a reconsideration of our *being with* and our *being for* others, particularly non-human animal others; for only then may we establish a world that is worth living for every living being. The sharp distinction that we have grown all too comfortable making between "human" and "not-human" – in large measure thanks to the tradition of Western philosophy – is to be reexamined and possibly overcome, according to these authors, and this is precisely what they have attempted to do, each in their own way, in their essays. What this means for us today might be expressed in these beautiful yet chilling words of Jacques Derrida: "The animal looks at us, and we are naked before it. Thinking perhaps begins there."[14]

Notes

1. Horkeimer, Max. *Eclipse of Reason.* (New York: Continuum Press, 1999), p. 104.
2. Ibid., 105.
3. For an especially strong overview of phenomenological considerations of environmental philosophy, see: *Eco-Phenomenology: Back to the Earth Itself*, eds. Ted Toadvine, & Charles S. Brown (Albany: SUNY Press, 2003). In addition, check the impressive list of titles in SUNY's series on environmental philosophy.
4. Two excellent (fairly recent) volumes are: *Animal Others. On Ethics, Ontology, and Animal Life*, ed. Peter Steeves (New York: State University of New York Press, 1999); and *Animal Philosophy: Essential Readings in Continental Thought,* eds. Matthew Calarco & Peter Atterton (London: Continuum Books, 2004).
5. Husserl, Edmund. *Edmund Husserl: The Crisis of the European Sciences and Transcendental Phenomenology*, tr. David Carr. (Evanston: Northwestern UP, 1970), p. 17.
6. Heidegger, Martin. *Being and Time*, tr. John Macquarrie and Edward Robinson. (San Francisco: Harper Publishing Co., 1962), §6.
7. Foucault, Michel, "What is Enlightenment?" in *Foucault, Michel:, Ethic, Subjectivity and Truth, Essential Works of Foucault 1954–1984*, ed. Paul Rabinow. (New York: The New Press, 1997), p. 315.
8. This is with the notable exception of a handful of philosophers working in the European tradition who did reflect (in some way) on animals. For an overview of these thinkers' reflections on the animal theme, see the essays collected in Calarco & Atterton, eds., *Animal Philosophy* [full citation information given in note 4]. This volume, of course, hopes to participate in this new and fresh project.
9. A connection to the Marxist tradition can be seen by attending to Marx's thematization of the relation between human beings and nature (though, as contemporary scholars will tell us, his analysis was speciesist).
10. Edmund Husserl. *Cartesian Meditations. An Introduction to Phenomenology,* tr. Dorion Cains. (Dordrecht: Kluwer, 1999), p. 107.
11. Ibid., p. 107.
12. Such a "mistake" would probably not be made by the authors contributing to this volume.
13. The most prominent thinkers within this tradition are Max Scheler, Helmuth Plessner, Hans Jonas, and Arnbold Gehlen.
14. Derrida, Jacques. "The Animal That Therefore I Am (More to Follow)," in *Critical Inquiry*, 2/28, pp. 369–418.

2

Attunement, Deprivation, and Drive

Heidegger and Animality

Gerard KUPERUS

With the German *Stimmung*, which can be translated as "mood," or, better, as "attunement,"[1] Heidegger describes the being of the human being as "being-there" (*Dasein*). This *Dasein* is always in a mood or attunement. For it can be (not) in the mood for something; it can be in one of its moods; it can be moody; or, *Dasein* can be in a bad or a happy mood. In *Being and Time*, Heidegger argues that, because of our moods, our world is "never the same from day to day."[2] Even scientific research does not know reality in an absolute manner, since the attunement of the researcher opens up the world it investigates: "even the purest θεωρια [theory] has not left all moods behind it."[3] Although this perhaps appears as a limitation, our attunements, in fact, make the world accessible in the first place: they open up the world to us.[4]

In his 1929–30 lecture course, the *Fundamental Concepts of Metaphysics*,[5] Heidegger describes the opening up of the world through our being attuned, in opposition to the poverty in world that, according to Heidegger, characterizes the being of the (non-human) animal. While our constant *attunement* constitutes our very accessibility to the world, the animal, in contrast, is poor in world, as it can only *behave towards* the objects that it encounters. Put simply, it lacks the kind of opening up of the world that is made possible through our – specifically human – attunements.[6]

In this essay, I discuss the poverty in world of the (non-human) animal, as analyzed by Heidegger. Interestingly, Heidegger himself admits that this is a somewhat obscure statement, and that it only seems to have meaning in relation to the *Dasein* of the human animal: the animal is poor in world, yet it is not completely deprived of world.[7] Although Heidegger's analysis in his lecture-course pertains primarily to the concept of world, he does provide an interesting analysis of the difference between the human and non-human animal, particularly in that he does not simply describe the human being as an animal with logos, or as an animal with rationality, nor does he describe humans as political animals, as is often done within the tradition. Alternatively, it is precisely the *ability to be attuned* that constitutes the particularity of human existence, according to Heidegger.

C. Painter and C. Lotz (eds.), Phenomenology and the Non-Human Animal, 13–27.

In his lecture course, Heidegger discusses three different forms of poverty and deprivation: the above mentioned poverty in world of the non-human animal, second, the poverty in being of contemporary *Dasein*, and, third, the deprivation of world in the fundamental attunement of profound boredom. In what follows, I will discuss these three forms of poverty or deprivation, where the goal is to offer a preliminary analysis of Heidegger's distinction between the human and the non-human animal.

I. Poverty in World: The Being of the Animal

In the second chapter of his lecture course, Heidegger draws his well-known distinction between the human being (*Dasein*), the animal, and the stone, on the basis of their respective having and not having of world. Heidegger states that the stone is "worldless," that the animal is "poor in world," and that the human being is "world forming."[8] The thesis that the animal is poor in world is the "point of departure" for Heidegger's analysis, and results in a comparison between, on the one hand, the stone and the animal, and, on the other hand, the animal and the human being.[9] The animal's existence is said to lie between the stone and the human being. But what does it mean to be "between" them? What does "poverty in world" mean? The poverty in the world of animality is, as Heidegger indicates, the most obscure of these three theses, and – as we will see – has a meaning *only* in comparison with the other two.

Heidegger starts his analysis with a comparison between animal and man, which he characterizes as a comparison between poverty and wealth. He claims that the animal possesses "less in respect of what is accessible to it, of whatever as an animal it can deal with, of whatever it can be affected by as an animal, of whatever it can relate to as a living being."[10] The world of the animal is limited: the bee's world, for example, is limited to its hive, blossom, and other bees. But it is not only that the domain of the animal is quite small, rather, "the extent and manner in which an animal is able to penetrate whatever is accessible to it is also limited."[11] This means that the animal is not able "to know" things around it. The human animal, instead, has a world that is much richer: it is greater in range, and it is able to extend this range. Human animals can explore new areas, while the bee will only busy itself with its hive, blossom, and other bees. We are also able to penetrate much deeper in our world than the animal can. This difference in depth can be found, for example, in the idea that the bee "does not know the stamens of these blossoms *as* stamens, it knows nothing about the roots of the plant and it cannot know anything about the number of stamens or leaves..."[12] These examples of possible relations to being fall outside the range of possibilities for the bee, especially as it falls outside the possibilities of animality to have access to beings *as such*. The human being, in contrast, can penetrate into the range of the "as such:" we can experience beings *as beings*. The human being's range is, compared to the animal's range, not only fundamentally different in the sense of this accessibility to *beings as beings*, but is also larger and can be extended: it is a penetrability that can "penetrate ever more deeply in this penetrability."[13] Hence the world-formation of man is "the extendibility of everything that he relates to."[14] In other words, both horizontal (a wider range) and vertical (deeper penetration) expansion is possible, whereas for the animal, in contrast, no horizontal or vertical expansion is possible. There can be expansion for the animal, but only within its own very limited range. In this vein, the bee can, for example, explore a new field with blossoming flowers, but it cannot explore a whole new area. This differentiation in penetrability between the non-human and human animal can be characterized as a difference in the accessibility of beings.

How then is animal existence characterized in contrast to *Dasein's* possibility to relate to beings as such? Heidegger defines the animal's poverty in world as deprivation: "What is poor here by no means represents merely what is 'less' or 'lesser' with respect to what is 'more' or 'greater.' "[15] This does not mean that a hierarchy is set up between the animal and the human being, or between different animals, which would mean that the animal "is less" in its being poor. To be poor, instead, has to be understood here as a "*being deprived* [*Entbehren*],"[16] which is not to be conceived as a mere lack or deficiency, since it pertains to the very *way in which* it is poor. This "way" pertains to the lack of attunement of the animal, or to "how it takes this deprivation [...] *the way* in which it is *in a mood* [*zu Mute*] – *poverty in mood* [*Ar-mut*]."[17] As the translators suggest, with the expressions "*zu Mute*" and "*Ar-mut*," Heidegger here refers in the German to the mood of the animal, or rather, to the animal's lack of mood.[18] In this way, deprivation – poverty in world – is, as Heidegger argues here, not to be understood as "poor" or "meager" (like the poor flow of water in a river), but rather, as "poverty in mood."

Poverty in mood, or lack of attunement, is described as (a form of) captivation (*Benommenheit*). The organism "drives itself towards its own capability for ..."[19] Any capability, for Heidegger, requires a drive (*Trieb*): there is no capacity without a drive, and only "something that is capable, and remains capable, is alive."[20] The drive and capability of the animal requires some sort of a unity, which cannot be characterized as personhood, but is an absorption in itself: the animal "intrinsically retains itself and is intrinsically absorbed in itself."[21] This absorption is characterized as captivation, which is a necessary condition for the animal: it "can only behave insofar it is essentially captivated."[22] The animal is constantly driven by instincts, such as the instinct to collect and store food. To illustrate this, Heidegger mentions the bee – apparently, one of his favorite examples. According to Heidegger, while the bee flies towards a particular scent, towards which it is driven "for the purpose of collecting and storing food,"[23] he questions whether the bee knows what it is doing, and he refers, in this regard, to a scientific experiment within which a bee's abdomen is cut away. As the bee is fed during this experiment, it keeps sucking from a large bowl of honey, and because its abdomen is cut away, the bee loses the honey and never "becomes full." Since the bee keeps sucking honey "even while the honey runs out of the bee from behind,"[24] this proves, for Heidegger, that the bee is by no means able to recognize the presence of too much honey; it simply keeps sucking it into its body, following the mere instinctual drive to collect honey.

Normally – when there is no cruel biologist cutting away its abdomen – the bee will stop sucking when it cannot take anymore, when it is full. At this point, another drive will immediately occupy the bee, namely, the drive to bring the honey to its hive. Now, with the honey running out from behind, it "is simply taken [*hingenommen*] by its food."[25] This instinctual being taken "towards …" "excludes the possibility of any recognition of presence."[26] It is a "specific inhibition" in which the animal does not have a comportment towards beings, but merely behaves (*benehmen*), without any apprehending (*vernehmen*).[27] The "possibility of apprehending something as something is *withheld* [*genommen*] from the animal;"[28] it is taken away from it in its being captivated (*benommen*). The animal is thus taken (*hingenommen*) and captivated by beings, such that it cannot come to a reflective stop; it can only behave through a behaving towards beings. The instinctual drivenness, as Heidegger conceives it, is "a being driven from one drive to the other."[29]

Heidegger describes this captivation as taking place in a ring that encircles the animal, and is "constituted by the reciprocal drivenness of its drives."[30] Within this ring, nothing appears simply *as something*. Heidegger illustrates this by appealing to female insects that eliminate the male partner after copulation. For Heidegger, this implies that the other animal (at least in this case) is never simply there as another living creature, but is there either as sexual partner, or, when the sexual functionality disappears, as prey. The animal, therefore, does not grasp a being *as such*, but grasps all beings merely in terms of its own behavior.

The encircling ring – the surrounding environment to which the animal has access – is, as Heidegger calls it, a "disinhibiting ring."[31] While the animal does have access or openness to the world within this ring, this access is characterized as drivenness and instinctual behavior. It is – as Heidegger argues – the "*encirclement* which makes possible the behavior in which the animal is related to other things."[32] However, this relatedness is not a *genuine comportment towards beings*; rather, the animal "opens itself up to what is other in approaching it."[33] In the above mentioned examples, we can see that this approach is always an approach of something as … (prey, partner, etc.), within which that which is approached never is understood *as such*. This openness as approach is a disinhibition [*Enthemmung*]; a not being able to stop, a mere movement from one drive to the other. The disinhibiting ring is, therefore, not to be understood as "a kind of encapsulation;" instead, the animal opens up a sphere: "the animal surrounds itself with a disinhibiting ring."[34] The ring is thus not laid down by an external force, as it were, but is constituted from out of the animal itself. The life of the animal is "the struggle [*Ringen*] to maintain this encircling ring or sphere."[35] Accordingly, the animal is being taken as such; its driven existence is an open absorption in the ring, which is constituted and maintained by the animal itself.

II. Human Poverty

In the preceding pages, I discussed Heidegger's analysis of the animal's poverty in world, according to which the animal is captivated in a ring within which it is driven and within which it behaves towards objects. Within this ring, the animal is opened up and captivated. In what follows, I will discuss how Heidegger describes the existence of *Dasein* as it is captivated in the everyday, and how its loss of captivation in the form of profound boredom relates to the poverty in world and to the captivation of the animal. The guiding questions in this regard are how Heidegger distinguishes our everyday captivation from the captivation of the animal, and how the deprivation experienced in fundamental boredom differs from the deprivation of the non-human animal.

Heidegger criticizes contemporary *Dasein* for constantly occupying itself with the beings that surround it, within which – one could say – *Dasein* forgets itself. *Dasein* is absorbed with all kinds of responsibilities, tasks and appointments. In completing these, we have become an indifferent one, "a no one," inasmuch as we busy ourselves with the beings that surround us, with the "present-at-hand" and the "ready-to-hand." We occupy ourselves with those things that we can handle with our acquired skills. We are – as one could say – lost in the things. Our identity has been lost in the beings with which we occupy ourselves. We have become – as Heidegger himself expresses it – an "undetermined I."[36]

It seems, at first glance, that the situation of contemporary *Dasein*, determined as an "undetermined I," is closely related to the poverty of the animal. The animal is driven towards beings and *Dasein* is occupied with beings. As discussed above, Heidegger states that all capacities involve drives. Such a general formulation seems to be applicable both to animal and to human beings, as they both have capacities, which are enabled through drives. However, Heidegger draws a clear distinction between the *behavior* of the animal, characterized as *drive*, and the *comportment* of the human being, characterized as *action*. Human comportment is a "doing and acting," while the behavior of the animal is a "*driven performing* [*Treiben*]." An "instinctual drivenness, as it were, characterizes all such animal performance."[37]

However, the distinction between behavior and action remains quite indeterminate. Is the comportment of the human being, within which its "behavior" is an acting upon beings, radically different from the animal behavior as drive? The animal only *behaves towards* beings, while *Dasein* can know things *as such*. Yet, Heidegger's claim is that in our everyday occupation and acting upon beings, we are absorbed and forget both about the "as such" of the beings upon which we act, as well as about our own being. This oblivion seems to bring us closer to the animal world, as we merely "behave towards" beings, without knowing them "as such." Heidegger nevertheless maintains that there is a fundamental difference between the animal behavior and the acting of *Dasein*.

As discussed in the introduction, Heidegger describes the human animal as a being-in-the-world that always involves an attunement or mood. Attunements open up the world. The animal, on the other hand, is described as a poverty in mood and is said by Heidegger to lack *Dasein's* kind of accessibility to the world. The only relation the animal has to the world is through behavior. As opposed to this deprived world of the animal, even the deprivation of *Dasein* is determined as mood or attunement. In order to shed more light upon the concept of attunement, I shall turn my attention towards Heidegger's analysis of profound boredom.

The first part of Heidegger's lecture-course starts with an analysis of deprivation or poverty, in the form of boredom. Boredom is an attunement directly related to our captivation through "the everyday," the immediate and prevalent occupation with everyday life that entails an attempt to avoid boredom. In his analysis of boredom, Heidegger distinguishes three different forms: (1) becoming bored *by* something, for example, while waiting for the next train, (2) being bored *with* something and the passing of time belonging to it, for instance, at a dinner-party, and (3) *profound boredom*. I will leave the first two forms of boredom aside and focus on profound boredom, which is characterized as "it is boring for one" [*es ist einem langweilig*].[38] In this case we are not *bored with* or *bored by* "something," but, rather, we *experience indifference*, i.e., the emptiness of our existence. The "it" of "it is boring for one," "is the title for whatever is indeterminate, unfamiliar," which is nothing else than "one's own self that has been left standing, the self that everyone himself or herself is."[39] We are thus familiar with this "it," as it is *who we are*. We are, on the other hand, estranged from this familiarity, which has become an "it." Our own self vanishes: "Name, standing, vocation, role, age and fate as mine and yours disappear."[40] All these parts of our identity, of who we are, emerge into the "undifferentiated no one." We, i.e., contemporary *Dasein*, have become no one. *Dasein* has disappeared into the everyday, which, earlier in the course, is described as a being held captive (*gefangen*).[41] We are imprisoned by the beings that surround us. Earlier I described Heidegger's use of the word "*benommen*," which characterizes the captivation of the animal. The imprisonment of contemporary *Dasein* is, on the other hand, captured with the word *gefangen*. This choice of words is significant, since it suggests that, in contrast to animals, who are simply *taken by* that towards which they are driven, we are *held captive*. While our everyday existence is in general perhaps not so different from this animal existence, Heidegger's language already suggests that human beings have the possibility to escape the captivation of their everyday existence, while animals do not have such a possibility in their "being taken."

Such an escape is offered in the attunement of profound boredom, which is a loss of the power that we experience in our everyday being.[42] It is an elevation beyond "the particular situation in each case and beyond the *specific beings* surrounding us there."[43] The particular situation within which we find ourselves attuned, and the specific beings that surround us do not simply leave us empty; rather, they do not have any particular value to us. We could suggest that in profound boredom we are not even bored with the beings that surround us, but that "all and everything appears indifferent to us."[44] In this "being left empty" things do not disappear, but they show themselves as a whole in their indifference. Heidegger characterizes this as "*Dasein's being delivered over to beings' telling refusal of themselves as a whole*."[45] The beings that surround *Dasein*, which in its everyday existence keep *Dasein* busy, do not tell anything, they refuse themselves as a whole. This telling refusal of beings as a whole is a lack of possibilities; there are no possibilities offered. This "being left empty" is indeed the first moment of profound boredom.

It is perhaps not easy to conceive this attunement, especially since Heidegger does not give any examples, in contrast to the first two forms of boredom, for which he does provide examples. One is not bored as one has to pass time, nor is one bored by the conversation or behavior of others during a social gathering; rather, one is bored in a more fundamental way. The lack of examples in the description of profound boredom might in fact give a hint here. In this attunement of profound boredom we are not being bored by, or being bored with *something*, as in the two examples that were given earlier; rather, *all things lose all meaning*. In profound boredom, things are *indifferent*, instead of *boring*. In response, we are, as we will see, necessarily thrown upon ourselves.

When boredom arises, we mostly struggle against it. When we are bored (in the mundane sense) we try to escape it and put it to sleep, by trying to relate to something that has meaning for us – something that can drag us from this uncanny attunement into a more pleasant one. Heidegger describes profound boredom in a radically different way, namely, in the sense that this attunement seems to be attractive. In this connection, Heidegger writes: "it would almost be presumptuous to close ourselves off from what this attunement wishes to tell us."[46] Profound boredom, in this way, is a "telling refusal" that brings with it a "being held in limbo," a *Hingehaltenheit*, i.e., a being held back, a being in the state of a stance, or a being brought to a halt. This being held in limbo is the telling refusal that "is in itself a *telling*,"[47] inasmuch as it points to the very possibilities of the activity of *Dasein*. This is not a speaking about, or a dealing with, possibilities, "but in its telling refusal it *points to them* and makes them known in refusing them."[48] Precisely in not telling, the moment of "being left empty" tells us something as a "dawning."[49] What is announced in this dawning are the unexploited possibilities of *Dasein*: it shows *Dasein* in its possibilities. In still other words, the indeterminate character of profound boredom takes away the concrete possibilities and forces us to contemplate on our very determination. The telling refusal is, then, a lack of possibilities that entails an understanding that this attunement must tell us something about our very existence and about our possibilities.

The above described situation of the everyday, within which *Dasein* has become undifferentiated as a "no one," is reversed in the attunement of profound boredom. When it is boring for one, the undifferentiated I becomes bored by that which has made her into this "no one." The beings that have made one undifferentiated, become undifferentiated *for* one: "Beings as a whole refuse themselves tellingly, not to me as me, but to the *Dasein* in me whenever I know that 'it is boring for one.' "[50] A call is – so to speak – made, to that which is forgotten in one's occupational existence, i.e., one's very existence in the world.

The "impoverishment" or emptiness described by Heidegger here is, thus, not only a deprivation or poverty, but – paradoxically – brings with it a certain wealth, we could say. For, indeed, in the deprivation of world, new possibilities are given, new possibilities are "calling." Consequently, this poverty points to that which "properly makes *Dasein* possible."[51]

The reversal of the situation of the "undifferentiated I" into the indifference of the beings can also be found in the notion of "entrancement."[52] Here the metaphor of captivation in the sense of imprisonment (*gefangen sein*) comes again into play. While Heidegger uses the words *Bann* and *Gebanntsein*, translated as "entrancement" and "being entranced," the verb *bannen* can also mean to ban or excommunicate. Accordingly, *Gebanntsein* can mean being excommunicated.[53] We can understand this as a being banned from that which *Dasein* ultimately can be and is: *Dasein* has been excommunicated from its very possibilities, because of its occupation with or imprisonment in the beings that surround it. In profound boredom, this situation is reversed when *Dasein* is excommunicated from those beings that have kept it imprisoned.

The meaning of entrancement, on the other hand, should not be forgotten here either. To be banned from the everyday is not possible without *Dasein's* being entranced. To be entranced in the situation is to show the ultimate possibilities of *Dasein*, which is not possible without banishment from beings. It is precisely the double meaning, of entrancement and excommunication, which plays a decisive role here: In order to be entranced in this profound attunement, on the basis of which access to beings *as such* is gained, *Dasein* needs to be freed from the beings with which it is occupied in the everyday. As such, this attunement involves a negative experience of excommunication, within which *Dasein* is ultimately bored with the everyday.

What, however, is that which entrances *Dasein* in such a way that *Dasein* is bored through and through by the beings that surround it? What is this strong force that attunes one in such a way that the everyday is banned, that one's power in the everyday is given up by letting oneself be overpowered by this boredom?[54] The ban from the everyday, and entrancement into the moment of vision, is caused by an entrancement of time: "*what entrances* is nothing other than the *temporal horizon*."[55] The time of the clock, the time of measurement has stopped flowing in the "it is boring for one" (*es ist einem langweilig*: one has a long while). It is not time that has stopped that entrances, but it is "rather the time beyond such flowing and its standing."[56] "Entrancing time" is the temporality of *Dasein*, it is "the time which in each case *Dasein itself as a whole is*."[57] It is thus not that point in time at which boredom arises – that point where time comes to a standstill – but it is "the whole expanse of the entire time of Dasein"[58] that entrances, and, at the same time, excommunicates us from everyday beings. This time that entrances and bans, the very temporality of *Dasein*, is that which constitutes not merely finitude, but essentially makes *Dasein* possible.

Heidegger's critique of the tradition of metaphysics comes to the surface of his text here: *Dasein* is not to be understood as something present-at-hand, but, instead, as temporal. The temporality constitutes its very essence. *Dasein's* freedom in this respect is its possibility to free itself, to open itself up to itself. It should be emphasized here that this freedom as openness, which shows our own existence as essentially temporal, is not to be understood as a ready-to-hand answer. It does not lead to the ultimate truth; rather, "this path leads straight into the dark."[59] While our occupation in the everyday creates a "safe haven," profound boredom opens us up as genuinely temporal beings.

Heidegger characterizes the path into the dark as a particular and specific attunement that involves emptiness as "the very *absence of any essential oppressiveness* [Bedrängnis] *in our Dasein*."[60] Emptiness is thus "not a pure nothing," but "lack, deprivation, need."[61] Heidegger, interestingly, uses here the word "*Entbehrung*," which is the same word he uses (as we have seen) to describe the animal's poverty of world.[62] I suggested above that this lack of any essential oppressiveness in contemporary *Dasein* is quite close – as close as we can get, maybe – to the animal world. For indeed, Heidegger describes us here as "servants of slogans, adherents to a program,"[63] which is a characterization that seems close to the characterization of the bee as a servant of its drive to collect honey. At the very least, we can say that Heidegger's criticism of contemporary men, of which "none is the custodian of the inner greatness of *Dasein* and its necessities,"[64] points towards lack, need, and deprivation. What is missing in our occupation in the everyday is the *Geheimnis* – the mystery – in our *Dasein*, and thus, "the inner terror that every mystery carries with it and that gives *Dasein* its greatness remains absent."[65] This mystery is, as Heidegger implicitly argues, a possibility *only of Dasein* (it gives *Dasein* its greatness), and thus it may be this possibility of *Dasein* that draws the most distinct limitation with the animal being.

The particular boredom Heidegger is describing here is caused by a specific being left empty, a "fundamental emptiness,"[66] and although this may be covered over or hidden by a "contemporary restlessness," it is also shown in the occupational existence in the everyday: whereas we concern ourselves, according to Heidegger, only with learned competencies that can be instilled, that which cannot be instilled, that which brings terror, is set aside. Boredom, now, arises from out of *Dasein* itself, it gives a sign, it announces itself as a telling refusal, "the telling absence of any oppressiveness."[67] This refusal of oppressiveness does not announce something that can be understood in advance, and it is therefore not a need that oppresses. Rather, the mystery in our *Dasein* is announced in this being left empty. Accordingly, the "most extreme demand" is made upon man here: "*it is that Dasein as such is demanded of man, that it is given to him – to be there.*"[68] This is the resolute disclosedness of *Dasein* itself, an openness towards its very existence. In this moment of vision (*Augenblick*), *Dasein* is brought before its own *Dasein*. *Dasein* is opened up here not as "something that one takes for a drive in the car, as it were, but something that man must specifically take upon himself."[69]

In its everyday occupation *Dasein* is blind to its own being-there; however, the fundamental attunement of profound boredom can grant vision, announced as a lack in the form of a need, the "most profound need,"[70] as Heidegger argues. In the everyday, we are imprisoned or held captive (*gefangen*)[71] by the beings that surround us. We are banned from this captivity, though, in the fundamental attunement of profound boredom. This excommunication is at the same time an opening up as resolute disclosedness, a rupture of the captivation, i.e., a liberation of imprisoned *Dasein*. Indeed, the moment of vision demands the "innermost necessity of the freedom of *Dasein*;"[72] in order to be free, one first has to be excommunicated from those things that hold one captive.

III. Conclusion

In the preceding pages, I analyzed Heidegger's conception of contemporary *Dasein's* poverty as a lack of oppressiveness – a lack of urge (*Drang*) – and the poverty of the animal as a deprivation of world. The animal's poverty consists in the idea that it can only *behave* in an instinctual drivenness, while *Dasein* can *comport* itself towards beings; it can experience beings *as beings*. An example of the lack of comportment in animal life is the female insect that can only *behave towards* other animals, such as the male insect, which it takes either as prey or as sexual partner, while it cannot grasp the animal *as animal*, disconnected from any kind of behavior. Every relation of the animal involves behavior, while comportment towards another being *as being*, is impossible for the animal.

An important question in this respect is whether human beings in their everyday existence are radically distinct from this instinctual behavior. Heidegger critically analyzes contemporary *Dasein* as occupied in the everyday, wherein it is absorbed by the beings that surround it. *Dasein* uses, manipulates, and acts upon these beings, and in doing so it loses itself in this everyday existence, within which it lacks any oppressiveness. Interestingly, it is in the everyday that *Dasein* feels at home; for the occupation with beings that surround it is a drive (*Trieb*) to be at home, a drive away from the uncanny feeling of homesickness that is experienced in the experience of profound boredom. This "home" is already different from the world of the animal, however, as we – in contrast to the animal – can apprehend the beings that we act upon *as beings*. Home can be understood here as that which we apprehend. Apprehending is, as shown above, something impossible for the animal: for it can only be captivated (*benehmen*); it cannot apprehend (*vernehemen*).

Heidegger's lecture course is original, in that it does not simply rehearse traditional accounts of the human-animal division, by describing human beings as rational animals, or as animals with language (*logos*), as has been done throughout the history of philosophy. As we have seen, instead of defining human beings as rational animals, Heidegger defines the human being as attunement: "*Dasein as Dasein* is always already attuned in its very grounds. There is only ever a change of attunement."[73] While the animal is drivenness from drive to drive, *Dasein* is a being attuned from attunement to attunement. On this view, the difference between *Dasein* and animal is, then, primarily a difference between comportment and behavior, where the animal's incapacity to be comported lies in its lack of the possibility to experience beings *as beings*. The animal, in Heidegger's analysis, keeps going, without ever coming to a stop; the animal merely behaves and is not attuned. Human beings, in contrast, do not merely *move toward*, but can *keep a distance*; they are not absorbed in their worlds as the animal is. We humans *can* come to a stop in our otherwise driven existence.

Heidegger describes the most radical halt as the fundamental attunement of profound boredom. In this fundamental halt, caused by a lack of oppressiveness, we lose our drive of the everyday. This lack of drives leads us straight into the dark, where we do not feel at home, into feelings of "being left empty" and "being held in limbo" (*Hingehaltenheit*).

It is striking that Heidegger describes this situation as deprivation, since, for *Dasein* deprivation is not a lack of attunement, but rather, an emptiness as a mood of poverty.[74] Deprivation as mood is quite distinct from the animal's deprivation of world, however. For, as I suggested above, in the comparison of the respective worlds of animal and *Dasein*, the deprivation of the animal is, actually, a poverty in mood, a lack of mood. Although Heidegger never actually writes explicitly that the animal cannot be attuned, by describing animality as, on the one hand, being *taken by and absorbed into* its drives, and human existence as, on the other hand, always *being attuned and as having the ability to be fundamentally attuned*, Heidegger implicitly suggests this.

In its being captivated (*benommen*), the animal is taken by (*hingenommen*) and absorbed in (*eingenommen*) its drives. Dissimilarly, although *Dasein* also becomes captivated in the everyday, *Dasein* is still not merely taken by beings, but *acts upon them*. This suggests that *Dasein* always keeps a distance and that in its becoming absorbed in its occupation with the beings that surround him, *Dasein* can also free itself from its captivation, by being banned from the everyday. In this situation *Dasein* is driven through an entrancement, which turns out to be the very temporality of *Dasein*, i.e., its very essence. To experience oneself in one's possibilities through a complete loss of the concrete possibilities that surround one in the everyday, is something that is inaccessible to the animal. While *Dasein* is captured in its everyday occupation with the beings that surround it, the animal is not imprisoned, but "taken by," which leaves no room for escape. It can only *behave towards* those beings, as determined through its drives.

The captivated animal is described as living in a ring that is constituted and maintained by the animal itself. *Dasein* also seems to have such a ring, yet it has quite a different accessibility to this ring. For its world – the ring – can be expanded both in width and in depth. *Dasein's* relation to the world is thus characterized as "a peculiar transposedness to the encompassing contextual ring of living beings."[75] This does not place human beings on the same level as the animals, however, as we are held captive "in a quite specific way." We exist in the midst of beings, which captivate us "not on the basis of any particular influence or impression. No, we are captivated from out of our essence."[76] This essence, for Heidegger, seems to consist in the ability to be constantly attuned. So, while the animal is absorbed in its being driven and therefore incapable of experiencing anything *as such*, *Dasein's* openness is "a being held toward," within which the world opens up in a particular way through the attunement that provides this openness in the first place.

Heidegger's descriptions of the everyday existence of *Dasein* and of animality initially give the impression that the two forms of being are rather close, while in his actual analysis a clear distinction is drawn. This conclusion can be explained by the fact that Heidegger is very critical of contemporary *Dasein*, who leaves aside any provocative, or metaphysical questions, and takes up only those things that can be easily instilled. This means that *Dasein* leaves aside the question concerning the essence of its own being: to avoid this question, it hides in the everyday, trying to avoid any homesickness, such as that which the experience of profound boredom brings. Accordingly, *Dasein* is described as always already attuned and capable of keeping a distance towards the beings that surround it; it can grasp beings as beings and, therefore, it can experience their very existence. Such an experience requires a loss of world, a deprivation as mood. A loss of world seems to be impossible for the animal, as it is absorbed in the beings that are accessible to it, and as such it cannot escape this absorption. The animal loses itself in its particular way of being open, so to speak. It is therefore poor in world: it has some access, but no possible attunement within which it is confronted with its own essence. *Dasein's* loss of world, on the contrary, is not a deprivation of world, but brings new opportunities for human *Dasein* (which are impossible for animality).

In conclusion, we can say that whereas the animal is always already deprived of world, *Dasein's* possibility to be deprived (paradoxically) brings *Dasein* its richest possibilities; indeed, it gives *Dasein* "its greatness."[77] What I here refer to as *Dasein's* "richest possibilities" is precisely what creates the abyss between the captivation of the animal and the entrancement of *Dasein*. The animal is, in its own drivenness, absorbed, without having any possibility to free itself, given that there is no possibility to stop its drive and to be *fundamentally attuned*. For Heidegger, the animal can only behave *towards beings*; its attunement is never such that it may be characterized as a mood according to which it relates to a being *as a being*, or, even, to its own being.

Notes

1. *Die Stimmung* first of all refers to the tuning of a musical instrument, and *die Stimme* is the human voice. For this reason, I prefer the translation "attunement" above "mood." Heidegger sometimes uses the term in conjunction with *bestimmen* (to decide, determine, or ascertain), or *Die Bestimmung* (determination, destination, or vocation). As we will see, one's attunement can contain a certain call that can determine one's destination.
2. Martin Heidegger, *Being and Time*, trans. Macquarrie and Robinson. (NY: New York, Harper and Row, 1962), p. 177. [German Text: *Sein und Zeit* (Tübingen, 1993) (based on 7th edition, 1953), p. 138].
3. Ibid.
4. In this sense, attunement is perhaps a harmony or tuning with the world. It is also worth mentioning that in his lecture course, Heidegger does not use the concept *Befindlichkeit*, which in *Being and Time* seems to be equated with *Stimmung*.
5. Martin Heidegger. *The Fundamental Concepts of Metaphysics, World, Finitude, Solitude*. (IN: Bloomington, 1995). Hereafter, cited as *FCM*, followed by appropriate page number(s).
6. The animal is a "poverty in mood [Ar-mut]" FCM p. 195. In his interpretation of Heidegger's lecture course, Alasdair MacIntyre misses this point entirely when he takes the poverty of the world of the animal as "a lack of possibility to grasp the world as a whole" (p. 47.) see: Alasdair McIntyre. *Dependent Rational Animals*. (Chicago and La Salle: Open Court, 1999). McIntyre ties the notion of "poverty in world" to the non-language possessing animal (p. 50). Yet, in describing *Dasein* as a being always attuned, Heidegger attempts to overcome the traditional way of thinking of the human animal as an "animal with language, or reason." Poverty in world is, therefore, not – as McIntyre suggests – a poverty in language or reason, but *a poverty in mood, or attunement*.
7. *FCM*, p. 195.
8. Ibid., p. 177.
9. Ibid., p. 185. It is questionable whether we can transpose ourselves into a stone or into an animal. Heidegger touches upon this problem in §43 (and he will later, chapter 4, part 2, discuss it in greater detail), where he discusses the accessibility of life: "How are living beings as such – the animality of the animal and the plant-character of the plant – originally *accessible*? [Heidegger's emphasis] Or, is there no possibility of any original access here at all?" (*FCM*, p. 179). The question concerning our accessibility to the stone (the non-living being that does not have access towards anything) is left aside entirely. David Krell argues in this regard that the question of accessibility is a central problem: "World" – the concept through which Heidegger defines the animal, the stone, and Dasein – is, according to Krell, the " 'accessibility' to the beings in one's surroundings" (p. 116). See: David Farrell Krell. *Daimon Life, Heidegger and Life-Philosophy*. (IN: Bloomington, 1992).
10. *FCM* , p. 193.
11. Ibid.
12. Ibid.

13. Ibid.
14. Ibid.
15. Ibid., p. 195.
16. Ibid. Derrida, in *Of Spirit*, discusses Heidegger's language of poverty in detail and suggests the further development of a language of alterity in the analysis of animality: "it has an *other* relationship." Although Heidegger does avoid anthropocentrism, Derrida claims that he still takes "the measure of man," since the animal is defined as lacking the kind of world that *Dasein* has. Jacques Derrida. *Of Spirit, Heidegger and the Question*, trans. Geoffrey Bennington and Rachel Bowlby. (IL: Chicago, The University of Chicago Press, 1989), p. 49.
17. *FCM* , p. 195.
18. This translation can be justified by Heidegger's use of the word *Zumutesein*, which means "to be in a mood." Nevertheless, there might be another meaning of the words *Mut*, *zu Mute,* and *Ar-mut* in play here. To use these words for mood is a rather unconventional usage in 20th-Century German. For *Mut* is mostly translated as "courage," and *Zumutesein* might also refer to *Zumutung*, which means "to demand." This would imply here – since Heidegger discusses the deprivation of the animal – that the animal is poor in *being challenged* (i.e., in facing a demand), and that the animal is poor *in courage.* Heidegger, however, talks (in this context) also about the *poorness of man*, which implies that contemporary *Dasein* is poor in the sense of not being challenged, insofar as Dasein does not have the courage to face a demand.
19. *FCM* , p. 228.
20. Ibid., p. 236.
21. Ibid., p. 238.
22. Ibid., p. 239.
23. Ibid., p. 241.
24. Ibid., p. 242.
25. Ibid.
26. Ibid.
27. This experiment makes one wonder what would happen to a human being if it could take in an infinite amount of food. Does a human being stop eating before it has a feeling of fullness? Some treatments of obesity, such as gastric stapling, attempt to instill a feeling of fullness by reducing the size of the stomach. In other words, the drive to eat is (it turns out) reduced by a boundary that does not come from any apprehension, but from a feeling that is perhaps similar to the feeling of the fullness of the bee. In developing new methods to treat obesity (for example, through hormones), researchers often use rats to experiment upon. In such experiments it seems to be presupposed that our drive to eat is similar to that of animals. Hence, there is a question regarding whether our limitations in our drive to eat are different from the limitations in the bee's drive to collect honey.
28. *FCM* , p. 247.
29. Ibid., p. 249.
30. Ibid.
31. Ibid., p. 255.
32. Ibid., p. 254.
33. Ibid.
34. Ibid., p. 255.
35. Ibid.
36. Ibid., p. 143.
37. Ibid., p. 237.
38. Ibid., p. 134.
39. Ibid.
40. Ibid., p. 135.
41. Ibid., p. 128.

42. Ibid., p. 136.
43. Ibid., p. 137.
44. Ibid.
45. Ibid., p. 139.
46. Ibid., p. 136.
47. Ibid., p. 140.
48. Ibid.
49. Ibid., p. 141.
50. Ibid., p. 143.
51. Ibid.
52. Ibid., § 32.
53. The dictionary entrance for the verb "bannen" is: "1. banish, expel; put under the ban; excommunicate [...]" *The New Cassell's German dictionary*, based on the editions by Karl Breul, (NY: Funk and Wagnalls Company, 1958).
54. *FCM* , p. 136.
55. Ibid., p. 147.
56. Ibid.
57. Ibid.
58. Ibid., p. 148.
59. Ibid., p. 150.
60. Ibid., p. 163.
61. Ibid., p. 162.
62. For example, ibid., p. 195.
63. Ibid., p. 163.
64. Ibid.
65. Ibid.
66. Ibid., p. 164.
67. Ibid.
68. *FCM*, p. 165. Also, on p. 195, Heidegger discusses the lack of *Mut* (courage/mood) of the animal. It seems to be, though, that both *Dasein* in its lack of oppressiveness, and animality in its lack of courage, have this lack of *Mut* to take up this most extreme demand (*Zumutung*).
69. *FCM*, p. 165.
70. Ibid., p. 166.
71. Ibid., p. 128.
72. Ibid., p. 166.
73. Ibid., p. 68.
74. Ibid., p. 195.
75. Ibid., p. 278.
76. Ibid.
77. Ibid., p. 164.

3

Being Beyond: Aristotle's and Plessner's Accounts of Animal Responsiveness

Marjolein OELE

"O Leben, Leben: Draußensein"
(R.M. Rilke, *Last Note*, December 1926)

A volume that uses the term "non-human animal" immediately draws our attention to the complexity that is at stake in any analysis of animal life. Necessarily, such an analysis involves our "human animal" interests that, consciously or subconsciously, may stand in the way of an "open" view of the animal being. That our own evolution still evokes controversial debates is in large measure due to the fact that it puts to the test the very distinction between "human animals" and "non-human animals." Yet, some philosophers have found a way to philosophize about animal life, not by avoiding discussion of this distinction, but by offering a wider perspective, namely, that of a philosophy of biology. One of the 20th Century philosophers who has engaged himself with such a project is Helmuth Plessner. His "philosophy of the organic" searches for an underlying rationality of biological forms that is not merely anthropomorphic, but aims at doing justice to life in its biological diversity. In his *Die Stufen des Organischen und der Mensch*,[1] he establishes that living beings are related in a particular way to themselves and to their environment, and that it is this relationship that allows for the various basic properties of organisms. Interestingly enough, a much older philosophy of biology, namely, that of Aristotle, also attributes substantial significance to the way that living beings respond to their environment. In particular, Aristotle's discussion of the phenomenon of *touching* as described in *De Anima* offers insight into this responsiveness, as touching is described there as fundamental in grounding an animal's bodily life. At the same time, Aristotle's considerations of touching, however, raise difficulties with regard to the *localization* of touching in the animal body. This paper aims to clarify Aristotle's discussion of touching and its importance for the animal being. Secondly, it tries to show how Plessner's philosophy of animal life continues the discussion of life as responsiveness, and how it offers an interesting reply to Aristotle's *aporia*,[2] precisely by questioning the concept of localization in living beings.

C. Painter and C. Lotz (eds.), Phenomenology and the Non-Human Animal, 29–37.

I. Primacy of Touching in Aristotle's *De Anima*

Aristotle's analysis of touching is prominently present in his writings concerning animal beings in *De Anima*. According to Aristotle, the touch [ἁφῆ] is not just any sense, like the others, but is far more fundamental for life as such: "So touch and taste are necessary for an animal, and it is clear that without touch it is impossible for the animal to be, but the other senses are for the sake of well-being" (III.12. 434b23-25).[3] Whereas the other senses contribute to the enhancement of life,[4] touching (which also includes taste for Aristotle)[5] is of a more basic nature: it grants the animal its life, indeed, its very being. For Aristotle, an animal does not need to possess any sense but this one (III.13 435b8). Thus, the significance of touching goes far beyond describing just an aspect of an animal's existence, and extends to its entire being: touching is constitutive of its life. Without touch, there is no animal body. Without touch, there is no sensitive life. Also, "without touch there can be no other sense" (III.13 435b2-3).[6] In short, touching is both a necessary and a sufficient condition for the possibility of being an embodied animal being.

Yet, the constitutive character attributed to touching appears to be in plain contradiction with the vulnerability and dangerous exposure that is implied with the sense of touch. This vulnerability is apparent in various ways: in contrast to other senses, such as seeing and hearing, whose objects are often at a relatively safe distance, the objects of touch are not only dangerously close but involve direct contact and a passive undergoing. Consequently, as Aristotle notes, if there is a question of an "excess" of tangible objects, not only the sense of touch, but the whole living being is destroyed (III.13 435b7-19). In the case of the other senses, however, excess would only destroy the sense-organs, but not the entire living being. In addition, touching is not restricted to one part of the body, but its risky exposure pertains to one's *entire body* – which is again in contrast to the other senses that are safely limited to relatively small parts of our bodies.

Nevertheless, the constitutive character of touching and its vulnerability may not be as contradictory as they appear. As Chrétien writes in his commentary on touching in Aristotle: "every sensible and sensitive life is a life at risk, and it would not be sensitive if it would not be at risk."[7] In other words, the vulnerability associated with touching is nothing else than the *very condition* of a sensitive life. A successful resistance to or allowance of what touches one is paradoxically only possible *precisely because* of one's exposure.[8]

This openness to one's environment is not limited to animals, but is also present in other organisms, such as plants. Plants, too, are affected [πᾶσχοντα] in some way by tangible things (II.12 424a33-34); for it is this affection that provides the basis upon which they grow or reproduce themselves. However, the affectivity associated with life acquires a new level in the animal form of life, as its body *reacts* with a sensation: an animal *senses* its being acted upon. This reaction implies that an animal's body incorporates a bodily "reflection" upon the kinds of things that it encounters.[9] This also includes a bodily reflection upon the nutritive faculty shared with plants, insofar as touching also includes taste, understood as "the sense of nutrition."[10]

The sensations perceived by touching are multiple, and include discriminating qualities such as "hot and cold, dry and wet, hard and soft" (II.11 422b27-28). These tangible qualities, it should be noted, are also "the distinctive characteristics of body *as body*," according to Aristotle (II.11, 423b27-28).[11] Thus, what is discriminated and sensed by the sense of touch is not just "other" or "different" than one's body, but expressive of an animal's body *as such*. The touch's sensation thus *reflects* what the body is, as it brings to the fore the body's own constitution.

Interestingly, the body's own constitution also plays a crucial role in sensing the objects of touch. Whereas the other senses are themselves actually deprived of the qualities they sense (II.11 424a4 ff.), the sense of touch is itself actively involved in sensing. The body itself functions as measurement, as it senses "what is hotter or colder, harder or softer," etc. than it (II.11 424a4-5). Thus, the body is not "neutrally" invested in touching, but always actively engaged and interested in what arrives upon it,[12] and yet, its bodily character does not diminish its sensitivity and discriminatory power, but, on the contrary, the versatility of touching appears to make it *more sensitive*.[13]

The interest that the body takes in its affections remains, however, *dependent upon* its affections. As Aristotle puts it, there is "no sensation of the sense[-organs] themselves" (II.5 417a3-4), which means that *the body needs to be touched* in order to sense: without this, no sensation occurs. Chrétien speaks in this regard about the *transitive* nature of sensibility,[14] which refers to the idea that sensibility is not inherently reflexive: it does not find an origin in itself on the basis of which it can turn back into itself. Rather, it is always operating *beyond* itself, as a response *to* something. Said differently, the sensible body is irreducibly dependent upon the given. It is therefore the touch that *gives* the animal its sensitive body. Simultaneously, this gift draws the animal body always outside of itself, as it finds itself in its responsiveness. It is this phenomenon of life's always being-outside-of-itself and being-in-transition that is so beautifully illustrated by Rilke's characterization of life as "*draußensein*."[15]

The responsiveness expressed in an animal's sensation is, however, always its *own*. Particularly in the case of touching, where the body itself functions as measurement, an animal's own body is at stake: it compares its *own* qualities as body with that which touches it. The animal's body reacts, therefore, with feelings of pleasure and pain. In this way, sensitive responsiveness implies appetite, and thereby desire, spiritedness, and willing (II.3 414b2-10).

What this account of touching in Aristotle has shown so far is that the animal's bodily, sensitive life is dependent upon touching. Thus, in order to live its life as a sentient being, the animal must be touched, and, accordingly, the animal must be open to this touch. However, an animal's body is also actively involved in measuring what is touched, so much so that it experiences pain and pleasure while sensing. The question this raises is the following: if touching involves both a crucial "being beyond" as well as the body as tangible, living, desiring body, where is touching localized? That its transitional character raises difficulties with regard to the *localization* of touching, is, in fact, pointed out by Aristotle himself: "But it is an impasse [ἀπορίαν] whether it [touching] is one or more than one sense, and what the sense organ [αἰσθητēριον] that is perceptive of touch is..." (II.11 422b20-21).

Touching is unique, insofar as it raises this impasse; indeed, of none of the other senses do we inquire into its unity and into the nature and the localization of its sense-organ.[16] For, unlike the other senses, since touching includes making multiple distinctions, is spread out over the entire body, and includes taste, its unity is not necessarily guaranteed. Moreover, a sense-organ in the sense of a specialized body-part is not obvious in the case of touch, whereas in the case of hearing, for example, air, according to Aristotle, is the medium for bringing sounds to our ears. But what is the equivalent of the ears in the case of touching? Aristotle answers mysteriously that its sense-organ is *inside* [ἐντὸς] (II.11 423 b23-24), and that although the body's flesh [σᾶρξ] is also involved, it is so only as the *medium* of touch (II.11 423b26-27).

This solution is uneasy, to say the least, and in many ways simply continues the *aporia*,[17] as it is difficult to grasp what is meant by a sense-organ that is characterized indeterminately as "inside." It is equally difficult to understand the status of a medium that belongs to the body, which is at the same time *beyond* the body in its interactive, mediating role. Nonetheless, the aporetic character of the localization of touching indicates something important: that in its responsiveness the animal's body has a particular *doubleness*. It itself is the body that senses, while it is itself also a medium – a transitory region. Its affections are part of it, but it also adopts a particular *distance* in regard to those affections – it views them from its "inside." Thus it seems that, in its response to touching, the doubleness of the body resists localization of itself. Is this resistance to localization a marginal phenomenon, or characteristic of animal life as such? As will be shown in the following reflections upon the work of Helmuth Plessner, nothing less than grasping life as such is at stake in answering this question.

II. Plessner and the Positionality of Animals

The Aristotelian discussion of touching has opened up a crucial aspect of animal life, namely, its relationship to its body and its environment. A systematic and original examination of this relationship can also be found in Plessner's *Die Stufen des Organischen und der Mensch*, a text rather unfamiliar to the Anglophonic philosophical world.[18] Driven by resistance to the modern, dualistic Cartesian perspective, which views life either as physical, bodily extension or as immaterial, spiritual thought, Plessner searched for an alternative view of life, which tried not only to be faithful to the way living beings[19] present themselves (their *Erscheinungsweise*),[20] but also to successfully account for their "development, self-regulation, organization,"[21] etc. By contrasting the way that inanimate beings appear in distinction to animate beings, Plessner notes a remarkable difference: an inanimate being "appears according to its spatial boundaries as a centrally organized unity of attributes."[22] Accordingly, by giving an account of all of its aspects, the object as a whole can be described. In contrast, in perceiving a living being, the latter appears to escape being adequately described on the basis of a similar totalizing grasp.[23] For example, regardless of its position or its activity – sleeping, eating, purring, or chasing a ball – a cat's presence to us goes beyond a determination of its particular qualities, its activities, its habitat, in short: its spatial-temporal qualities. What remains unrecognized in such a totalizing grasp is the *relationship* that a living being has to its environment by "arising in it, depending on it, yet opposing itself to it."[24] An organism distinguishes itself in a particular way from the environment, while interacting with it: it *bounds* itself in a specific manner.

Plessner uses the term "positionality" to capture this characteristic phenomenon of life.[25] In the case of lifeless things, the boundary is only the virtual "in-between" (*Zwischen*) between body and contiguous medium. This means that the boundary is the point at which one thing stops, e.g., the medium, and the other begins, e.g., the thing.[26] Its boundary is identical with its contour or outline, and as such, it is nothing but "pure transition, from one to the other, from the other to the one..."[27] In the case of living things, however, the boundary belongs to the body itself,[28] and the *body itself establishes this transition*.[29] Thus, in living beings, the body is related to itself in its relationship to its boundary. The relation to its boundary is in this way "two-directional"[30] and thereby acquires a double aspect: "it is, through its relationship to its boundary *both directed out beyond the body and back into it again*."[31]

The relationship between body and body, however, implies a reflexive structure. In order to maintain the relationship between body and body, therefore, the body must relate to a "central point,"[32] which functions as the center of the bounded "bodily-area,"[33] making it into a *system* within which parts (i.e., organs) can function as parts of a whole.[34] Although the body itself occupies space as "bodily area," its center is not itself spatial.[35] It transcends spatiality, while yet controlling the spatiality of the body: "relative to the body which is its body, it is nowhere and everywhere."[36]

Although positionality is a foundational characteristic of all living beings, it is "relatively submerged in the life of plants."[37] Indeed, only in animals does it come fully to the fore. Plants have an *open* form of positionality, which implies that they are *directly* incorporated into their environments and that they remain dependent upon them.[38] For example, many plants are to a great extent dependent upon environmental factors, such as wind and insects, to transfer their pollens and reproduce themselves.[39] An animal's form of positionality, on the other hand, is *closed*, which implies that it is only *indirectly* incorporated into its environment, and that it is an independent segment of its corresponding bio-cycle.[40] Positionality is here manifested in a very clear way: an animal is open to its environment, and thus its boundary is receptive. Nevertheless, in order to protect itself its body must be closed off, and thus the animal body must have the boundary as part of itself.[41]

Since it includes its boundary in itself, the animal body is subjected to two antagonistic rhythms: "one unidirectional with, the other opposed to the environment."[42] It is this very antagonism that mediates the organism with itself, by producing a closed whole and organizing it.[43] This antagonism can only be sustained when there is a center that stabilizes and organizes both the periphery and the core. "It is stabilized and made explicit in animal life through the *mediation* of a central organ that carries the sensorimotor functions, and which thus makes *action* possible."[44]

Consequently, according to Plessner, the closed form of positionality in animals explains the basic properties of their animal life. As has just been established, its positionality accounts for its sensorimotor functions. In addition, the fact that animals are dependent upon organic nutrition, i.e., that they must live off the living,[45] can also be traced back to their positionality.[46] Whereas a plant is so open to its environment that it becomes, in some way, a "passage through" (a *Durchgang*),[47] as can be illustrated by its ability to live off both the organic and the inorganic, an animal is more independent and requires complex forms of nutrition that are akin to it. Furthermore, an animal's positionality accounts for its drives and wants. Because of its closed form, its independence maintains itself over and against its environment, even while it is *also* a part of this environment. By being closed back, and yet open, it seeks fulfillment from its environment while remaining always essentially unfulfilled.[48] Consequently, an animal's drives are "nothing else but the immediate manifestations of this primary unfulfilledness."[49]

As can be established from this analysis of animals in Plessner's philosophy, a philosophy of animal beings finds its proper starting place in the concept of positionality, i.e., in the way that a living being, and most clearly an animal being, is related to its own boundary, and thereby to itself and its environment. In this way, an animal's biological life can be given a rational foundation, without depriving it of the flexibility and variety that each species realizes.

III. Comparative Notes and Conclusion

Aristotle's and Plessner's approaches in understanding animal life seem, at first sight, very different. Whereas Aristotle approaches animal life from the point of view of sensation, particularly, the sense of touch, Plessner, on the other hand, approaches animal life from a much more basic point of view, namely, by searching for a founding principle by way of which life – in its various forms – shows itself. According to Plessner, only then can particular characteristics, such as the sensori-motor functions of animals, be explained.

At closer inspection, however, Aristotle's and Plessner's accounts show a remarkable convergence. As was established, Aristotle's account of touching is not just focused on touching as one sense among others, on one aspect of an animal's existence; rather, he attributes significance to touching in relation to the foundation and preservation of the animal body as such. His approach of understanding the animal being is, in this regard, not so far removed from Plessner's query. Secondly, Aristotle's analysis of touching emphasizes the *transitive* nature of the animal's sensitive body, inasmuch as its own body and its sensations are irreducibly dependent upon what touches it. Again, this analysis shows similarities with Plessner's account of the fundamentally *relational* character of living beings, which comes to the fore most markedly in the closed form of positionality that is actualized by animal beings.

Furthermore, what is most remarkable is that both Aristotle's and Plessner's theories focus on the double nature of the body. In Aristotle, this double nature comes mainly to the fore as an *aporia*, when he discusses the problems of localizing the sensation of touch. That the touching body can function *both* as mediation *and* as sensation is the impetus for this difficulty. The answer to this difficulty – to distinguish a *medium* and an *inside* – only confirms the difficulty of establishing a definite localization for the body in its interaction. Plessner, on his account, offers a solution to this problem of the body's non-localization: according to Plessner, non-localization is an essential part of life as such, since life itself cannot be limited to the coordinates of spatiality. In contrast to things that stop where their boundaries end, an animal "takes its place"[50] within and against an environment. This place is not-localized, insofar as it cannot be determined by external coordinates. This is, simply put, the place of the organism. In taking its place, the animal body is related to the environment *via* its boundary, which is always its own, and yet, by having its boundary as part of itself, it is always essentially directed both beyond itself and also into itself again. It is this "double direction" that makes it difficult to distinguish an "inner" and an "outer" to the animal body.

In this way, both Aristotle and Plessner establish the importance of non-localization, and also the importance of the body's mediation. Although Aristotle's analysis is opaque with regard to the specifics of this view, the fact that an animal's body can function as a medium – through its *flesh* – is significant. This intermediary role of the body also returns in Plessner's analysis of positionality in animals, which acknowledges that the animal has its boundary as part of itself, and that its own body mediates its contact with the environment.

Finally, in their accounts of animal life, both Aristotle and Plessner attribute significance to the drives and wants that comprise such an inextricable part of an animal's life. Aristotle associates desires with sensation, and thereby makes desires part of the fundamental openness and vulnerability of animal life. Plessner, on his account, traces drives and wants back to the particular form of positionality realized by animal beings – closed off, yet open to their environment, and therefore always essentially unfulfilled. Although these accounts may show a different emphasis, the fact that both trace animal desire back to a fundamental transitivity and responsiveness to life is important.

What this comparative analysis of Aristotle and Plessner shows is how two different philosophies of biology approximate one another in their quest to account for the responsiveness proper to animal beings. What makes both Aristotle's and Plessner's philosophies so interesting is that both aim at offering a rationality for this responsiveness, without reducing this interaction to pure mechanism. As both philosophers show, an animal's responsiveness can only be explained by appealing to the animal body's transitive nature, which is always mediated by and through itself. Consequently, the animal body, as they describe it, escapes localization, while always taking its place as a living, sensitive, driven being.

Notes

1. Helmuth Plessner. *Die Stufen des Organischen und der Mensch; Einleitung in die philosophische Anthropologie*. (Berlin: De Gruyter, 1965). [first published in 1928]. Translations offered here are my own.
2. In his *On Touching – Jean-Luc Nancy*, Derrida emphasizes the aporetic character of Aristotle's analysis of touching. See: Jacques Derrida, *On Touching – Jean-Luc Nancy*, trans. C. Irizarry. (CA: Stanford, Stanford University Press, 2005), pp. 5–6.
3. Unless otherwise noted, I will use Joe Sachs' translation of Aristotle's *De Anima*. Aristotle. *On the Soul and On Memory and Recollection*, trans. J. Sachs. (NM: Santa Fe, Green Lion Press, 2001). For the Greek text see Aristotle. *On the Soul*, trans. W.S. Hett (Cambridge: Harvard University Press, [1936] 1995).
4. According to Chrétien, this "does not mean that the other senses are not protective or defensive of life, but means that they are not as necessary and constitutive of life as the sense of touch." Jean-Louis Chrétien. *L'Appel et la Réponse*. (Paris: Les Éditions de Minuit, 1992), p. 117.
5. For taste as a form of touching in Aristotle's *De Anima*, see, for example, III.12 424b18-19, where he claims that taste is a kind of touch, since it relates to food, and food is a tangible body.
6. Cf. also *De Anima* III.13 435a14.
7. Chrétien, *L'Appel et la Réponse*, 1992, p. 118.
8. Cf. ibid., p. 121: "One cannot defend oneself without exposing oneself."
9. This reflection is a *bodily reflection*, and by no means a *theoretical reflection*. Although it falls outside the scope of this paper, it is interesting to note how this reflection can again be doubled in the human being, where a reflection upon one's senses and one's taste may find realization in the quest for truth and morality.
10. Cf. Derrida, *On Touching – Jean-Luc Nancy*, 2005, p. 24.
11. Sachs' translation slightly modified; my italics.
12. Cf. also Chrétien, *L'Appel et la Réponse*, 1992, p. 117.
13. Cf. also ibid., p. 121.
14. Ibid., p. 141.
15. Ibid., p. 145.

16. Cf. ibid., p. 146.
17. Ibid.
18. In her interpretations of Plessner's work, Marjorie Grene has tried to make Plessner's philosophy more accessible. Cf. M. Grene, "Positionality in the Philosophy of Helmuth Plessner," *Review of Metaphysics* 20 (1966), pp. 250–277. Cf. also her *Approaches to a Philosophical Biology*. (NY: New York, Basic Books, 1968).
19. With regard to his view on human beings, he is aiming at uniting both their "Geistesgeschichte" and their "Naturgeschichte," so as to ground humans as both natural biological beings and mental, spiritual beings (Plessner, *Die Stufen des Organischen und der Mensch*, 1965, p. 6). In this way, one could say that his philosophy offers a "corrective" to Heidegger's analyses of *Dasein*, by way of grounding human existence in a "philosophy of living nature" (on this, see M. Grene, *Review of Metaphysics*, 1966, p. 250, fn. 1).
20. Plessner, *Die Stufen des Organischen und der Mensch*, 1965, p. 81
21. Grene, *Review of Metaphysics*, 1966, p. 253.
22. Plessner, *Die Stufen des Organischen und der Mensch*, 1965, p. 81.
23. Cf. ibid., pp. 81–82; and also, M. Grene, *Review of Metaphysics*, 1966, p. 252.
24. Grene, *Review of Metaphysics*, 1966, p. 253.
25. Plessner warns that this concept is not just a sheer spatial concept: Plessner, *Die Stufen des Organischen und der Mensch*, 1965, p. 157; see also, Grene, *Review of Metaphysics*, 1966, p. 254.
26. Plessner, *Die Stufen des Organischen und der Mensch*, 1965, p. 103.
27. Ibid.
28. Ibid., pp. 104–105.
29. Ibid., p. 103.
30. Grene, *Review of Metaphysics*, 1966, p. 257.
31. Ibid.
32. Plessner's term is *Zentralpunkt* (Plessner, *Die Stufen des Organischen und der Mensch*, 1965, p. 158).
33. Plessner's term is *Körpergebiet* (Plessner, *Die Stufen des Organischen und der Mensch*, 1965, p. 158).
34. Ibid., p. 158.
35. Ibid.
36. Grene, *Review of Metaphysics*, 1966, p. 163.
37. Ibid., p. 270.
38. Plessner, *Die Stufen des Organischen und der Mensch*, 1965, p. 219.
39. Ibid., p. 222.
40. Ibid., p. 226.
41. Ibid., p. 227.
42. Grene, *Review of Metaphysics*, 1966, 269; Cf. Plessner, *Die Stufen des Organischen und der Mensch*, 1965, p. 229.
43. Plessner, *Die Stufen des Organischen und der Mensch*, 1965, p. 229.
44. Grene, *Review of Metaphysics*, 1966, p. 270
45. Plessner, *Die Stufen des Organischen und der Mensch*, 1965, p. 234.
46. Ibid.
47. Ibid., p. 233.
48. Ibid., see also Grene, *Review of Metaphysics*, 1966, p. 269.
49. Plessner, *Die Stufen des Organischen und der Mensch*, 1965, p. 233.
50. Grene, *Review of Metaphysics*, 1966, p. 254.

4

How Not to be a Jellyfish

Human Exceptionalism and the Ontology of Reflection

Ted TOADVINE

In his popular environmentalist novel *Ishmael*, Daniel Quinn calls attention to the "creation myth" of our culture, according to which human beings are the *telos* of the evolutionary process. To illustrate this point, the character Ishmael, a telepathic gorilla, imagines an "anthropological" interview with a jellyfish undertaken a half billion years ago, prior to the evolution of land animals. In this imaginary dialogue, the jellyfish insists that it proceeds strictly on the basis of "observation, logic, and the scientific method," but comes to the conclusion that jellyfish themselves are the obvious pinnacle of the evolutionary process, the goal toward which this process has tended from its outset. The jellyfish's conclusions are intended to strike the reader as absurd, since the process of speciation has not stopped in the meantime; in retrospect, the jellyfish is only one species among many. But, according to Ishmael, humans are in no better a position to draw such a conclusion about their own place in the evolutionary process. Certainly, there is no *scientific* basis for such a claim, since the processes of speciation have continued unabated since our arrival on the scene, and there is consequently no reason to think our species is the last. Ultimately, the interpretation of the meaning or goal of the evolutionary process is not an empirical question but a philosophical one. The ubiquitous aggrandizement of humans as the "climax of the whole cosmic drama of creation" is therefore revealed to be nothing more than a cultural myth.[1]

Quinn's jellyfish story is intended to demonstrate the tenacity of our tendency toward "human exceptionalism," as well as to illustrate that the rejection of theistic worldviews is no guarantee of avoiding such dogma. But the message of the story is complicated by the fact that the imagined jellyfish is itself a "rational" creature with the capacity for language, as is Ishmael, the fictional gorilla who serves as mentor for the novel's human protagonist. The characters of the gorilla and jellyfish turn out to be humans in animal drag who can make their case against human exceptionalism only by ventriloquizing; they make use of the distinctively human capacities of language and reflection and thereby reinscribe the very difference they set out to deny. On the one hand, recent research suggests that the cognitive gap between humans and

C. Painter and C. Lotz (eds.), Phenomenology and the Non-Human Animal, 39–55.

other animals is much narrower than has formerly been supposed, with the growing consensus that our differences are a matter of degree rather than kind.[2] And even the age-old critique of anthropomorphism as a symptom of bias in scientific investigation is undergoing re-evaluation.[3] However, on the other hand, even if humans are a product of an evolutionary process, and even if our cognitive and communicative capacities differ only by degree from those of other animals, might not these differences still justify an exceptional status? Even if humans turn out not to be the only "rational" animal, taking this adjective broadly, might we not still be the only *philosophical* one?

From the standpoint of contemporary evolutionary biology, it seems that the answer would be negative: human capacities, including those of language and self-consciousness, are just as much a product of evolutionary selection as the traits of other animals. Even if humans have capacities that distinguish us from other species, these are no more or less exceptional than the distinguishing capacities of others. As Mary Midgley puts this point, "We are not the only unique species. Elephants, as much as ourselves, are in many ways unique; so are albatrosses, so are giant pandas."[4] Our uniqueness, then, regardless of the capacity that we might highlight to make it salient, is no cause for counting ourselves as special. If this tendency toward human exceptionalism lacks roots in scientific objectivity, perhaps we can seek its sources, as does Midgley, in our anxieties about the unacceptable parts of our own natures, which is why attempts to clarify our ambiguous uses of the term "animal" cannot fail to be "deeply and incurably emotional" (Midgley, 141). Since the drawing of the distinction between humans and other animals concerns the constitution of our own identities, it has been acknowledged that the drawing of this distinction is not – nor can it be – an entirely neutral or objective matter. For we define ourselves by an externalization of those qualities that we find unacceptable in our own natures, so that the distinction between human and animal is drawn not outside ourselves but *within us*, between "parts" of ourselves. Thus, as Giorgio Agamben notes, the division of animal from "man" must be located within "man" himself – for instance, as the internal schism of body from soul or of natural from divine – such that "man" must himself be understood as a "place …of ceaseless divisions and caesurae."[5]For Agamben, the central question of our "posthistory" is precisely that of our animality, posed most concretely by the ambivalence of our embodiment; "this body," as Agamben puts it, "that is irreducibly drawn and divided between animality and humanity" (12). "It is more urgent," Agamben argues, "to work on these divisions, to ask in what way–within man–has man been separated from non-man, and the animal from the human, than it is to take positions on the great issues, on so-called human rights and values" (16). Since humanism relies on an "anthropological machine," the business of which has been to suspend our nature between animal and human, terrestrial and celestial, a post-human political and philosophical stance is needed.

To weigh the contribution that phenomenology might make in this task, we must consider whether its own methodology is in principle caught up within the "anthropological machine," and what prospects might remain for it to twist free. From the perspective of phenomenological philosophy, which tries to lay bare the structure of experience as such, we must ask whether experience refers essentially to a subject whose experience this would be, and whether this subject is necessarily human. If so, any attempt to describe what it is like to be a non-human animal necessarily refers first to the experience of the human subject, from which this non-human experience would be derivative, and against which it is dialectically set apart. The question, then, is whether overcoming the "anthropological machine" would not also entail overcoming phenomenology as a philosophical method. If there is a sense in which phenomenology can twist free, such a transformation could not be a mere reversal; indeed, it is not enough to declare that humans are animals, whether rational or naked or technological. Rather, a double movement is required, which, on the one hand, opens a space for the positive description of the meaning of the animal's world as other than merely a modification of the world of the human subject, while, on the other hand – and this is perhaps the more complicated task – the human as such must be reconceived as neither opposed to nor reducible to the animal. This might also suggest another and deeper notion of "humanism." As a propadeutic to this larger question – i.e., the question of whether phenomenology is up to the task of twisting free from the anthropological machine – this essay will consider phenomenology's presentation of its own method, particularly the phenomenological reduction, conceived as a disengagement of thought from life. On the basis of this disengagement, phenomenology has traditionally accorded a certain ontological privilege to human beings. Understanding the human-animal relationship therefore requires an investigation of philosophical reflection itself, including its ontological dimensions. I will suggest that we can find the direction for such an alternative account of reflection, as an a-subjective expression of the *Selbstung* of Being, in Merleau-Ponty's final writings, where he describes an "*Ineinander*" or intertwining of animality and humanity according to which each is a variant of the other. This account of the human-animal relation is inseparable from a reconsideration, more generally, of the relation of life and spirit, and ultimately of the very method of phenomenology.

I. Ontological Exceptionalism in Phenomenology

Since its inception, phenomenology has shown an acute interest in research on animal awareness and has drawn from this research an interpretation of animal behavior in terms of intentionality, as can be seen especially in the works of Max Scheler, Aron Gurwitsch, and Maurice Merleau-Ponty.[6] By understanding animal behavior as intentional, the phenomenological method reveals that meaningful relations, rather than merely causal or mechanistic interactions, obtain between an organism and its environment. Edmund Husserl, taking the jellyfish as his example, recognizes that lower animals have an experience of nature, even if this experience of nature lacks the "higher horizons" that characterize the experience of the normal human adult.[7] This "jellyfish subjectivity" also deserves to be characterized as transcendental, since it is involved in constituting the sense of the world. According to Javier San Martín and Maria Luz Pintos Peñaranda, this extension of transcendental subjectivity to animals entails a re-conception of the very project of transcendental phenomenology, which demonstrates that it is not the other-worldly idealist approach portrayed by its postmodern critics.[8] Phenomenology, then, makes it first possible to recognize that animals not only *react* but also *respond*.[9] These insights have been extended by a number of recent writers, including the contributors to this volume, who have drawn on the phenomenological tradition to explore our kinship and reciprocity with other animals.[10]

But despite its value for describing the nonhuman animal lifeworld and its overlap with our own, does phenomenology actually avoid the problem of human exceptionalism, or does it simply reinscribe it on another register? This problem comes to the fore in the work of Heidegger, whom Agamben identifies as the "philosopher of the twentieth century who more than any other strove to separate man from the living being."[11] In *Being and Time*, for example, Heidegger treats life as a privative modification of *Dasein*. A description of animal life is reached by beginning with the fuller, richer experience of human being and proceeding by subtraction. If we are each, for ourselves, beings for whom being itself may be at issue, then the animal is by definition something less.[12] In his 1929–30 lecture course, *The Fundamental Concepts of Metaphysics,* Heidegger identifies this poverty or lack as the essential characteristic of animal being. The animal is captivated by its world and is incapable of escaping the limitations of its drives, which determine the structure and contents of its environment. The animal is oriented towards the objects of its drives, but never towards them *as* objects or *as* beings. So, the animal is open to the world around it, but open in a way that fails to "disconceal," to accede to being. Heidegger concludes that "Being open in captivation is the *essential possession* of the animal. On the basis of this possession it can be deprived, it can be poor, it can be determined in its being by poverty."[13] The animal, then, is "poor in world." However, we should take care not to interpret Heidegger's remarks as a justification for any *value* priority of humans over nonhuman animals, nor, in the words of William McNeill, as just "another essentialist or humanist 'theory' of the nature of animal life."[14] But, even if McNeill is correct to claim that in Heidegger's text there is "no sense in which Dasein may be said to be 'better' than any other living thing," it is nevertheless clear that Heidegger delineates an ontological boundary between animals and humans and accords to the latter what we might call an "ontological privilege."[15] Such an ontological privilege may not be the narcissism of the jellyfish that Quinn warns us to avoid, but can we deny that it amounts to a form of human exceptionalism nonetheless? Otherwise, why draw a boundary at precisely this point, dividing all living things along the axis of openness to being? Why is ontological access the measure of a being's being?

Although Heidegger's insistence on the ontological gap between the human and nonhuman animal has received considerable attention in recent discussion,[16] it must be noted that he is not the only phenomenologist to draw this sharp distinction. Nor can Heidegger's insistence on the radical distinction between human and animal be dismissed as a consequence of the peculiarities of his own interpretation of phenomenology; rather, the animal-human distinction goes to the heart not only of the phenomenological method but of philosophy itself. In its attempts to think through the relation of humans with other animals, and with nature more generally, philosophy confronts a fundamental ambiguity that has traditionally been expressed in terms of the contrast between life and spirit. In this connection, in his last work, *Man's Place in Nature*, Max Scheler wrote that "man is more of a problem to himself at the present time than ever before in all recorded history."[17] For Scheler, the problematization of the notion of "man" is not a failing but the very promise of the human spirit, of the "essential nature" that distinguishes us in kind from every other species. The notion of "man" is, for Scheler, deceptively ambiguous, given that we use this term to refer, on the one hand, to "the particular morphological characteristics of man as a subclass of the vertebrates and mammals" (*MPN* 12/6), while, on the other hand, the word "man" also "signifies a set of characteristics that must be sharply distinguished from the concept 'animal'," since it is these latter characteristics, those of Spirit or Mind (*Geist*), that Scheler takes as representative of our "essential nature" (*MPN* 13/7). Scheler willingly attributes to animals not only instinctual and habitual behaviors, but also practical intelligence, i.e., the capacity of "responding, without trial and error, to a new situation meaningfully" (*MPN* 33/29). Along with genuine intelligence, Scheler recognizes in animals "the capacity for generosity, help, reconciliation, friendship and similar phenomena" (*MPN* 37/34). Nevertheless, the goals of this intelligent behavior are set by the organism's drives, so that the animal never has the opportunity to choose between values as such. The animal's choices are always a function of its vital situation.

The human being, for Scheler, can neither be placed on a continuum with the animal, to differ from it only by degrees, nor be set off from the animal as different in kind thanks to some cognitive capacity. Rather, what definitively distinguishes "man" from animal is precisely the dimension of spirit, which is "opposed to life as such, even to life in man" (*MPN* 38-39/36). While the animal remains tied to the vital interests of its milieu, the human, through the dimension of spirit, is "open to the world." In Scheler's words,

> [the animal] lives, as it were, ecstatically immersed in its environment which it carries along as a snail carries its shell. It cannot transform

> the environment into an object. It cannot perform the peculiar act of detachment and distance by which man transforms an 'environment' into the 'world,' or into a symbol of the world (*MPN* 41/39).

This "peculiar act of detachment and distance" made possible by spirit is the foundation, according to Scheler, of objectivity, ideation, the construction of a world of ideas, and the orientation towards truth. Indeed, spirit motivates both philosophy and religion, since it reveals to us the contingency of this earthly existence and the transcendence of our spiritual being in relation to it. It is this distance that spirit opens between ourselves and the world that *necessitates*, for Scheler, our alienation from—and dominance over—nature:

> when man, becoming himself, broke with the methods of all preceding life to adjust or to be adjusted to the environment and embarked upon the opposite direction of adapting the revealed world to himself and to his own life of organic stability, when man separated himself from nature and transformed it into an object subject to domination and to the control of symbolic manipulation–at this moment man was also driven to anchor his own central being in something beyond this world. He who had placed himself so boldly above this world could no longer regard himself merely as a 'member' or 'part' of this world (*MPN* 88/90).

Scheler's account here is unremarkably traditional in its justification of human dominance over nature in terms of our spiritual difference in kind from it, and it is in reaction against such accounts that the current stress on our continuity with nature has become fashionable. But Scheler's account makes especially salient the link between our alienation from nature and the activity of philosophy itself. For Scheler, it is the wonder of our uncanny otherness from the natural world that inspires metaphysics, and the very orientation toward a world in its objective truth rests on a separation from and dominance over nature. In fact, for Scheler, the phenomenological reduction—the central methodological procedure for phenomenological philosophy—involves a suspension of our experience of reality that only the spiritual break with vital existence can make possible.[18] It is here that we arrive at the problem of the relation between humans and other animals in its true difficulty: the very assertion of our continuity with animals, proposed as a *true* assertion, already implies its own contradiction, since it is only by way of a radical difference from other animals that the human can accede to truth as such. The phenomenology of the nonhuman animal, if it wishes to come to terms with the specter of human exceptionalism, therefore requires an interrogation of the method of phenomenology itself, especially with regard to the relation between life and mind.

The work of Maurice Merleau-Ponty is, as a whole, a sustained interrogation of the relation of life and mind and the implications of this relation for the method of phenomenology. Not surprisingly, then, a number of recent authors have turned to Merleau-Ponty as the most promising inspiration for an eco-phenomenology.[19] Already in his first book, *The Structure of Behavior*, Merleau-Ponty rejects the schism between life and mind upon which Scheler's interpretation of the phenomenological reduction had relied, proposing that matter, life, and mind be understood instead as a series of structures or gestalts.[20] A gestalt, in Merleau-Ponty's usage, is a meaningful whole composed of internal relations and having emergent properties not attributable to its parts.[21] As gestalts, life and mind are ontologically continuous, and mind is conceived as being "founded" on the structure of life, which is, in its turn, founded on physical form. Reality may therefore be understood as a nested structure of such meaningful wholes, with each gestalt entering into multiply more encompassing gestalt relations with its environment. Since reality is constituted entirely by structural relations, there is no room in Merleau-Ponty's gestalt ontology for the decisive break that Scheler draws between life and spirit.

According to Merleau-Ponty's analysis, vital form is more than simply a complex physical system, as it introduces original and irreducible properties inexplicable at the physical level. While the equilibrium or tendencies of a physical form are a function of the forces of which it is composed, living systems are oriented toward virtual rather than real conditions, and the activity of the living system brings these virtual conditions into existence. Consequently, the organism is oriented toward a "milieu" or "environment" that is distinct from the world described by (our) physics. In the system formed between the organism and its environment, the tendencies toward equilibrium are fixed not by physical conditions but by the organism's own norms or preferences. Life is therefore oriented by the dialectic formed between its tasks or goals and the virtual environment within which these appear for it. This orientation by self-determined norms accords the living thing an individuality and freedom not present in physical structures, which is why life remains irreducible to its physical conditions. Consequently, the living thing, for Merleau-Ponty, has genuine *existence* in the sense of being-in-the-world.[22]

But just as the vital level of structure introduces original properties irreducible to the physical, the same may be said for the "human order." For the description of the vital level allows us to re-conceive the emergence of human consciousness from a level of perceptual involvement within which it remains oriented toward the physiognomies and sensible configurations of the world, rather than the "true" objects of the scientific realist. But the specifically human dialectic transcends this "lived consciousness." For animals, norms that orient the dialectical engagement with their environments are determined by the aprioris of their species, while humans have the capacity to vary their points of view and adopt an orientation toward the virtual as such, toward the "structure of structure" itself. This fundamental orientation toward the virtual is the basis for our capacity to go beyond created structures, to be expressive, and to orient ourselves toward a single "true" world, a universe. In a sense, this orientation must already be prefigured at the level of lived perception, but it nevertheless reorients this vital level of perception just as profoundly as the emergence of life reconfigures the physical.[23] It is within this context that Merleau-Ponty approvingly cites Scheler's remark that "Man is a being who has the power of elevating to the status of objects the centers of resistance and reaction of his milieu ...among which animals live entranced [*en état d'extase*]."[24] The ecstatic entrancement or immersion of animals within their milieu described here by Scheler, and apparently endorsed by Merleau-Ponty, anticipates Heidegger's similar description of the animal's "captivation" [*Benommenheit*] in the course he taught in the year following the publication of Scheler's text.[25]

While Merleau-Ponty's approach retains these echoes of the sharp divide between human and animal already sketched out in the work of his predecessors, in his own thinking the human-animal relation, or more generally, the relation between life and mind, remains a point of significant tension. We find throughout Merleau-Ponty's *oeuvre* two opposing tendencies that Étienne Bimbenet has described as the "archeological" and the "teleological;" the first oriented toward the primordial origins of consciousness in its lived perceptual situation, and the latter concerned with the development of consciousness toward rationality and objectivity as its telos.[26] Merleau-Ponty captures the difficulty of reconciling these two tendencies in his formulation of the "problem of perception" at the close of *The Structure of Behavior*,[27] and this problem orients his analysis in its sequel, *Phenomenology of Perception*, where he presents the return to "sense experience" [*le sentir*] as a means of rethinking the understanding in terms of both its "vital inherence" (the archeological tendency) and its "rational intention" (the teleological tendency).[28] Since this return to sense experience concerns the relation between specifically human perception and rationality, nonhuman animals receive no significant treatment in this text. The brief remarks Merleau-Ponty does make concerning animals reiterate his position in the earlier text; for instance, he notes that "our body does not impose definite instincts upon us from birth, as it does upon animals" (*PP* 171/169), and that, while "animal behavior aims at an environment (*Umwelt*) and centres of resistance (*Widerstand*).... Human behavior opens upon a world (*Welt*) and upon an object (*Gegenstand*) beyond the tools which it makes for itself" (*PP* 377/381).[29]

Those who have read Merleau-Ponty's account of perceptual reciprocity as providing the foundation for a kind of "biocentric egalitarianism" might dismiss these remarks as insignificant, as asides that show only Merleau-Ponty's failure to appreciate the implications of his own deeper insights. But this would be to overlook the peculiar ontological role that the human being plays throughout Merleau-Ponty's work as being's means of self-expression. In this connection, describing art as a process of expression, Merleau-Ponty recalls Cézanne's remark that "the landscape thinks itself in me ...and I am its consciousness."[30] When I contemplate the blue of the sky, Merleau-Ponty writes in *Phenomenology of Perception*, "it 'thinks itself in me,' I am the sky itself as it is drawn together and unified, and as it begins to exist for itself" (*PP* 248/249). The human perceiver is therefore a kind of "hollow" or "fold" within being, which is what Merleau-Ponty describes, borrowing a phrase from Valéry, as the "flaw" in the "great diamond" of the world (*PP* 240/241). This phrase is repeated in Merleau-Ponty's commentary on Sartre in "A Scandalous Author," where the contrast between the ontological situation of humans and nonhuman animals is clearly drawn: "Matter, sky, harvests, animals are beautiful. Man's attitudes, his very clothes, bear witness to the fact that he is of a different order. He is a flaw in the great diamond of the world" (*SNS* 57/45). "Man" can serve as an interruption in the plentitude of being precisely because of his constitutive negativity – which, even if Merleau-Ponty conceives of this as a hollow or fold rather than as a hole of absolute non-being – apparently distinguishes us from the continuity of natural being, which includes nonhuman animals. It is our expressive capacity and language in particular, as the excess of our existence over natural being, that provides the support for this circumscribed negativity and unveils that "miracle of expression" toward which all other beings tend (*PP* 230-1/229-30). It is therefore only through human expression, such as the paintings of Cézanne, that the truth of the world can be made manifest: "indeed only a human being is capable of such a vision which penetrates right to the root of things beneath the imposed order of humanity. Everything indicates that animals cannot *look* at things, cannot penetrate them in expectation of nothing but the truth" (*SNS* 22/16).

Yet a new and significant development in Merleau-Ponty's understanding of the human-nonhuman relation is brought to the fore in a brief radio address concerned with animal life that he presented in 1948.[31] Criticizing the classical understanding of animals (as well as children and "primitives") as either irrational mechanisms or privative analogues of adult human consciousness, Merleau-Ponty affirms that nonhuman animals "proceed to trace in their environment, by the way that they behave or act, their very own vision of things" and consequently cannot be denied a "kind of interiority" (*WP* 39/75). Merleau-Ponty continues to affirm here that the animal's way of "'giving shape' to the world" is characteristic of its species and lacks the coherence toward which the "healthy, civilised, adult human being strives" (*WP* 40/75-6, 37/72). Yet he also emphasizes the failure of humans to attain the coherence for which they strive, opening a space for human understanding to inform itself through a "liv[ing] alongside" the nonhuman animal (*WP* 37/72, 39/75). The "normal" person is therefore "invited …to rediscover within himself the whole host of fantasies, dreams, patterns of magical behavior and obscure phenomena" that remain a part of every consciousness and that "leave his knowledge of the natural world riddled with gaps, which is how poetry creeps in" (*WP* 37/73). Artistic expression, then, especially that of modern art, takes as its inspiration the irrational kernel of human consciousness and finds there a profound kinship with the child, the "primitive," and especially the animal. The kinship is manifest, Merleau-Ponty concludes, in the role that animals play as emblematic of the human, and even the superhuman, in the dreams of "primitives," the experiences of children and poets, and "the secret reveries of our inner life" (*WP* 40-42/76-77). The most mature form of human consciousness is therefore that which, having recognized such kinship, contests its own tendency towards a single, universal form of civilization and knowledge.

This discussion suggests a complication of the ontological relationship between humans and animals, perhaps going so far as to suggest a fundamental ambiguity in how we might understand the notion of the world "thinking itself in me." If the human is the point of being's self-enfolding and coming-to-consciousness, then how could this very enfolding involve, within itself, a second gap or hollow, namely, that of our animality and kinship with nonhuman animals? Here, we can measure the distance between Merleau-Ponty's account of our ontological status as being's self-expression and the modernist version of the representational subject as the mirror of nature. For being to "think itself within me" does not mean for me to re-present it to or within myself; rather, the "agency" here, if such language may still be employed, *lies with being*, which, through me, thinks itself. On this interpretation, my thoughts are not truly my own, and least so when such thinking discloses the unrepresentable, the unreflective origins of reflection. Thus, if we rediscover "in every object a certain style of being that makes it a mirror of human modes of behavior" (*WP* 33/69), this is not because we project our representations onto the object or discover its being in "our" image of it, but rather, because we find in each thing the very root of our own thinking, as this thinking originates within being. The advent of the animal in our dreams and myths is therefore *a trace of the nonhuman origin of all reflection*. On this reading, Merleau-Ponty's project would not prioritize the human subject as the bearer of the "image" of the world, but instead it requires a radical rethinking of the grounds of subjectivity as an effect of a deeper auto-affective or self-expressive relation within being as such.[32]

II. The Life of Spirit: Toward a Human-Animal Intertwining

The ontology that Merleau-Ponty begins to describe in his final writings, within which reflection is figured as the dehiscence and self-palpitation of the flesh of the world, is clearly an extension, in a non-subjectivist direction, of the earlier notion of the world thinking itself within me:

> What makes the weight, the thickness, the flesh of each color, of each sound, of each tactile texture, of the present, and of the world, is the fact that he who grasps them feels himself emerge from them by a sort of coiling up or redoubling, fundamentally homogenous with them; he feels that he is the sensible itself coming to itself.[33]

Here, Merleau-Ponty no longer treats mind as an ontologically distinct structure or region, nor does he attribute the power of reflection to human subjectivity; reflexivity is, rather, like language, a potency of being itself. Essences, ideas, are not representations for a consciousness but invisible hinges or folds within the visible, so that Being is "facticity and ideality undividedly" (*VI* 156/117). The coming-to-itself of the sensible or the turning back of the flesh of the world on itself, of which the body's auto-affection is the paradigmatic example, is the fundamental ontological operation that Merleau-Ponty terms "interrogation" or "questioning." The human being, the "being that questions himself," cannot assume responsibility for this questioning, since it is "borne by an infrastructure of being," and consequently the body's auto-affection and the reflexivity of thought are "the ultimate relation to Being" and "an ontological organ" (*VI* 160/120, 162/121). Our fundamental relationship with Being, therefore, becomes a relation of proximity to a "Being in dehiscence," splitting itself along a natural line, such as the line between the inside and outside of a living body (*VI* 170/128).

We may speculate that a version of this interrogation could be ascribed to animals, insofar as they are also perceiving beings. Such a move would extend to nonhuman animals a role as revelatory of being, as modes of being's own self-interrogation or self-expression. And, indeed, although *The Visible and the Invisible* remains silent on this point,[34]Merleau-Ponty's definition of life as "interrogative being" in his second course on the concept of nature in 1957–58 opens the way to this interpretation.[35] Whereas Sartre had defined human being in terms of nothingness, understanding this as the ontological meaning of our freedom and therefore of our disclosure of being, Merleau-Ponty refuses to oppose the pure positivity of the *blosse Sachen* with a pure negativity that would be human freedom. The investigation of life aims, then, to discern the role of an "operant non-being," a "non-difference-with-self" or "divergence" already within animal embryology. The implication here is that animal being cannot be on the side of the "great diamond," nature understood as positivity, while reserving for "man" alone the "flaw" that makes the coming-to-light of being possible.

To treat life itself as interrogative implies a new understanding of the ontological kinship of humans with animals. Although such an understanding is not proposed in *The Visible and the Invisible,* we know from brief remarks in the working notes that the unfinished portion of the text would have investigated a "man-animality *intertwining*" (*VI* 328/274).[36] Whatever clues we have for unraveling what this notion would have meant for Merleau-Ponty must be gleaned from his fragmentary notes for the 1959–1960 course on the concept of nature, "Nature and Logos: The Human Body."[37] There, Merleau-Ponty rejects Teilhard de Chardin's identification of reflection as the differentiating characteristic of human evolution, since this would amount to "establish[ing] man in a dimension where he no longer had any relation with life" (*N* 339/272). In other words, the prioritization of reflection, understood as "cephalization" or "cerebralization," would lead to the same error that we saw in Scheler, insofar as it relies on conceiving of our capacity for reflection as necessarily involving a break with nature and life. The alternative, Merleau-Ponty argues, is to recognize the body's auto-affection–e.g., its capacity to touch itself and to see itself–as "reflection in figural form" (*N* 335/268, 340/273). Such bodily reflection would not be the activity of a consciousness but instead "the coming-to-self of Being…the *Selbstung* of Being, without a notion of the subject" (*N* 335/268; cf. 340/273). From this understanding of the corporeal basis for reflection, Merleau-Ponty moves directly to affirm the *Ineinander* or intertwining of the human and animal: "From this it follows that the relation of the human and animality is not a hierarchical relation, but *lateral*, an overcoming that does not abolish kinship" (*N* 335/268; cf. *N* 340/273). Accordingly, if reflection is inherently corporeal and vital, then it involves not a break in the continuity of our relations with animals but an affirmation of this kinship.

Merleau-Ponty describes the move into reflection, in the passage just cited, as an "overcoming" or a "surpassing," *un dépassement*, but at the same time, he insists that this move is lateral rather than hierarchical. At several other points in the notes, he describes this transition as a "metamorphosis," which implies a transformation rather than a transcendence.[38] In this way, he aims to recognize a specific difference between humans and other animals in terms of reflection, even while resisting the tendency to promote this difference to a kind of exceptionalism. In this regard, the description of animal-human intertwining contrasts with Merleau-Ponty's earlier account in *The Structure of Behavior,* where he claimed that spirit or mind is the most comprehensive gestalt, insofar as it transcends while incorporating the lower gestalts of physical nature and life. While the characteristically human is still described by Merleau-Ponty in terms of spirit, now the emphasis is on spirit conceived as a certain manner of being a body, namely, on the "body *of* the spirit" in Valéry's terms.[39] Consequently, it is conceived as a certain divergence or variation of the more general interrogative tendency of life: "Body of Spirit, nature of Spirit. This does not impede that the content is very different from the animals–the human world from the animal *Umwelt*–but the spirit is as natural to man as Nature is to animals" (*N* 288/225).[40] This metamorphosis of life into spirit, or of animality into humanity, is comparable, Merleau-Ponty claims, to the emergence of life from physicochemistry, a comparison that again echoes his earlier description of matter, life, and mind as increasingly comprehensive gestalts. Here, however, the transformation is presented not as a transcendence toward a higher level of structure but as a lateral movement entailing no fundamental ontological discontinuity:

> Just as there is an *Ineinander* of life and physicochemistry, i.e., the realization of life as a fold or singularity of physicochemistry–or structure–so too is the human to be taken in the *Ineinander* with animality and Nature…. And this is why we are concerned with the body: before being reason, humanity is another corporeity (*N* 269/208).[41]

This relation of intertwining is not truly a surpassing, then, since we find, on the one hand, "strange anticipations or caricatures of the human in the animal" (*N* 277/214), while, on the other hand, the animality of the human remains a "permanent attestation," so that, finally, "animality and humanity are given only together" (*N* 338/271). It is precisely this "strange kinship" that the notion of flesh is intended to make cogent, since it provides a means for understanding the visibility of the invisible, that is, the vital inherence of spirit, in a way that treats the two as obverse and reverse or as part of a single ontological circulation. Just as the dual aspect of my body, splitting into sensible and sentient, figures being's dual aspect of visibility and invisibility, so life diverges along multiple lines, both human and nonhuman, neither remaining simply one nor becoming entirely multiple. Thus, we can neither draw a sharp ontological boundary between human and nonhuman animals nor arrange their relations hierarchically:

> one cannot conceive of the relations between species or between the species and man in terms of a hierarchy. There are differences of quality, but for this very reason living creatures are not superimposed upon one another, the transcendence of one by the other is, so to speak, lateral rather than frontal, and one meets all sorts of anticipations and reminiscences (*RC* 136-37/165).

The best means that we have for thinking this "strange kinship," Merleau-Ponty concludes, is through "mythical thinking" of the sort that he finds portrayed in a contemporary exhibit of Inuit masks, according to which the animal is a variant of humanity, just as humanity is a variant of the animal.[42]

Merleau-Ponty re-conceives the ontology of reflection in a way that maintains the continuity of spirit with life, suggesting a path by which phenomenology can break with the tradition of human exceptionalism. In a working note from *The Visible and the Invisible*, he writes:

> a sufficient reduction leads beyond the alleged transcendental "immanence," it leads to the absolute spirit understood as *Weltlichkeit*, to *Geist* as *Ineinander* of the spontaneities, itself founded on the aesthesiological *Ineinander* and on the sphere of life as sphere of *Einfühlung* and intercorporeity – The notion of *species* = the notion of interanimality. The intertwining of biology or psychology and philosophy = the *Selbstheit* of the world (*VI* 226/172).

Thus, it is through a deepening of the phenomenological reduction that one may be led to understand spirit as intertwined with life, as "wild spirit" [*esprit sauvage*] (*N* 290/227), emerging within life as a lateral metamorphosis. We may say, then, with Renaud Barbaras, that Merleau-Ponty's philosophy is fundamentally a phenomenology of life.[43] But to follow this thought through to the end, we must also consider its consequences for the very thinking of philosophy, now understood as only one of the many moments of the flesh's divergence and recuperation and, specifically, as a self-interrogation of flesh for which the very possibility of such interrogation is what is at stake. Merleau-Ponty recognizes that our intertwining with animality requires a new understanding of reflection, as we have noted, since treating the power of reflection as the distinguishing mark between humans and animals risks returning to a philosophy of consciousness that alienates humanity from life. If the relation of one hand touching another – the "touching-touched" relation – is "reflection in figural form, the inner of what is outer," then reflection can no longer be considered a capacity of the human being; it is rather the "coming-to-self of Being," which entails a lateral rather than an hierarchical relation between life and mind (*N* 340/273). Animal being is, on this view, just as much as human being, an interrogative fold within the world's flesh. Consequently, when, in *The Visible and the Invisible*, Merleau-Ponty defines philosophy as "the perceptual faith questioning itself about itself" and founds this questioning on a self-palpitation of the world's flesh,[44] he is admitting the possibility – perhaps even the necessity – of an ontological questioning at the level of life as such. In other words, he is announcing the possibility of an "animal philosophy."

Notes

1. Daniel Quinn. *Ishmael: An Adventure of the Mind and Spirit* (New York: Bantam Books, 1992), pp. 54–58.
2. See, for instance, Donald Griffin. *Animal Minds: Beyond Cognition to Consciousness*, rev. ed. (Chicago: University of Chicago Press, 2001); and Marc Beckoff, Colin Allen, and Gordon Burghardt, eds. *Cognitive Animal: Empirical and Theoretical Perspectives on Animal Cognition* (Cambridge, Mass: MIT Press, 2002).
3. See Elliot Sober. "Comparative Psychology Meets Evolutionary Biology: Morgan's Canon and Cladistic Parsimony," and Sandra D. Mitchell, "Anthropomorphism and Cross-Species Modeling," both in *Thinking with Animals: New Perspectives on Anthropomorphism*, ed. by Lorraine Daston and Greg Mitman. (New York: Columbia University Press, 2005).
4. Mary Midgley. *The Myths We Live By* (London: Routledge, 2003), p. 152.
5. Giorgio Agamben. *The Open*: *Man and Animal*, trans. Kevin Attell. (Stanford: Stanford U. Press, 2004), p. 16.
6. For an overview of early phenomenological appropriations of research on chimpanzee consciousness, see Lester Embree. "Chimpanzee Phenomenology: A Beginning for the Phenomenological Theory of Primate Ethology," presented at the Second Central and Eastern European Conference on Phenomenology, Minsk, October 10–12, 2003 (publication in conference proceedings forthcoming).
7. Edmund Husserl. *Zur Phänomenologie der Intersubjektivität. Texte aus dem Nachlass. Zweiter Teil (1921–1928)*, ed. by Iso Kern, *Husserliana 14*. (The Hague: Martinus Nijhoff, 1973), pp. 114–116. These passages are discussed in Javier San Martín and Maria Luz Pintos Peñaranda. "Animal Life and Phenomenology," in *The Reach of Reflection: Issues for Phenomenology's Second Century*, ed. by Steven Crowell, Lester Embree, and Samuel J. Julian. (Boca Raton, Fla.: Center for Advanced Research in Phenomenology, Inc., 2001; electronically published at www.electronpress.com), pp. 352–353.

8. See Javier San Martín and Maria Luz Pintos Peñaranda. "Animal Life and Phenomenology," p. 344 and *passim.*
9. For the importance of this distinction, see Jacques Derrida. "The Animal that Therefore I Am (More to Follow)," trans. by David Wills in *Critical Inquiry* 28 (Winter 2002), p. 400.
10. See, as examples: David Abram. *The Spell of the Sensuous* (New York: Vintage Books, 1996), and "Reciprocity," in *Rethinking Nature: Essays in Environmental Philosophy*, edited by Bruce Foltz and Robert Frodeman. (Bloomington: Indiana University Press, 2004), pp. 77–92; David Clark. "On Being 'The Last Kantian in Nazi Germany': Dwelling with Animals after Levinas," in *Animal Acts: Configuring the Human in Western History*, edited by Jennifer Ham and Matthew Senior. (New York: Routledge, 1997), pp. 165–198; Christian Diehm. "Natural Disasters," in *Eco-Phenomenology: Back to the Earth Itself*, edited by Charles Brown and Ted Toadvine. (Albany: State University of New York Press, 2003), pp. 171–185; Alphonso Lingis. "Animal Body, Inhuman Face," in *Zoontologies: The Question of the Animal*, edited by Cary Wolfe. (Minneapolis: University of Minnesota Press, 2003), pp. 165–182; and the essays collected in H. Peter Steeves, ed., *Animal Others: On Ethics, Ontology, and Animal Life*. (Albany: State University of New York Press, 1999).
11. Agamben, *The Open*, 39.
12. Martin Heidegger, *Sein und Zeit* (Tübingen: Max Niemeyer, 1963), pp. 49–50, 58; *Being and Time*, trans. by John Macquarrie and Edward Robinson. (San Francisco: Harper and Row, 1963), p. 75, pp. 84–85. See also, *The Open*, pp. 50ff. For an added elucidation of Heidegger's position, also see Kuperus "Attunement, Deprivation, and Drive: Heidegger and Animality," in this volume.
13. Martin Heidegger. *Die Grundbegriffe der Metaphysik* (Frankfurt: Klostermann, 1983), § 62, p. 391; *The Fundamental Concepts of Metaphysics* , trans. William McNeill and Nicholas Walker. (Bloomington: Indiana University Press, 1995), p. 269.
14. William McNeill. "Life Beyond the Organism: Animal Being in Heidegger's Freiburg Lectures, 1929–30," in *Animal Others*, op. cit., p. 198.
15. McNeill, "Life Beyond the Organism," p. 248n16.
16. In addition to the works by Agamben and McNeill already cited, see Jacques Derrida. *Of Spirit: Heidegger and the Question*, trans. by Geoffrey Bennington and Rachel Bowlby. (Chicago: Chicago University Press, 1989); "*Geschlecht* II: Heidegger's Hand," trans. by John P. Leavey Jr., in *Deconstruction and Philosophy*, ed. by John Sallis. (Chicago: University of Chicago Press, 1987), pp. 161–196; "Eating Well," trans. by Peter Connor and Avital Ronell, in *Points...Interviews, 1974–1994*, ed. by Elisabeth Weber. (Stanford: Stanford University Press, 1995), pp. 255–287; "The Animal That Therefore I Am (More to Follow)," trans. by David Wills, in *Critical Inquiry* 28 (Winter 2002): pp. 369–418; Michel Haar, *The Song of the Earth*, trans. by Reginald Lilly. (Bloomington: Indiana University Press, 1993); David Farrell Krell. "Spiriting Heidegger," in *Research in Phenomenology* 18 (1988): pp. 205–230; *Daimon Life* (Bloomington: Indiana University Press, 1992); John Llewelyn. *The Middle Voice of Ecological Consciousness* (New York: St. Martin's Press, 1991), especially Chapter 7; Dennis E. Skocz. "Wilderness: A Zoocentric Phenomenology – From Hediger to Heidegger," *Analecta Husserliana* 83 (2004): pp. 217–244.
17. Max Scheler. *Die Stellung des Menschen im Kosmos* (München: Nymphenburger Verlagshandlung, 1949), p. 10; *Man's Place in Nature*, trans. by Hans Meyerhoff. (Boston: Beacon Press, 1961), p. 4. Hereafter, this text will be cited as *MPN*, with German preceding English pagination.
18. See Scheler's discussion of the phenomenological reduction in *MPN* 53-55/51-54.
19. See Abram. *The Spell of the Sensuous*, op. cit., and "Merleau-Ponty and the Voice of the Earth," in *Minding Nature: The Philosophers of Ecology*, ed. by David Macauley. (New York: The Guilford Press, 1996), pp. 82–101; Neil Evernden. *The Natural Alien: Humankind and Environment*, 2nd. ed. (Toronto: University

of Toronto Press, 1993), esp. Chapter 2; Monika Langer. "Merleau-Ponty and Deep Ecology," in *Ontology and Alterity in Merleau-Ponty*, ed. by Galen Johnson and Michael Smith. (Evanston: Northwestern University Press, 1990), pp. 115–129; Don Marietta, Jr.. "Back to Earth with Reflection and Ecology," in *Eco-Phenomenology: Back to the Earth Itself*, op. cit., pp. 121–135. Concerning the relation with non-human animals more specifically, see Elizabeth Behnke. "From Merleau-Ponty's Concept of Nature to an Interspecies Practice of Peace," in *Animal Others*, op. cit., pp. 93–116.

20. I explore the relationship between Merleau-Ponty and Scheler on this issue in more detail in "'Strange Kinship': Merleau-Ponty on the Human-Animal Relation," *Analecta Husserliana* 93 (2006): 17–32.
21. Merleau-Ponty's Gestalt ontology may be fruitfully compared with that proposed by deep ecologist Arne Naess. I have examined Naess's ontology in "Gestalts and Refrains: On the Musical Structure of Nature," *Environmental Philosophy* 2, no. 2 (Fall 2005).
22. *La Structure du comportement* (Paris: PUF, 1942), 136–137; *The Structure of Behavior*, trans. by Alden Fisher. (Boston: Beacon Press, 1963), pp. 125–126. Hereafter, this text will be cited as *SB*, with French preceding English pagination.
23. See *SB* 189–192/ 175–176.
24. This citation from *Man's Place in Nature* appears at *SB* 191/176. Merleau-Ponty refers to pp. 47–50 of the 1928 edition of *Die Stellung des Menschen im Kosmos* (Darmstadt: Otto Reichl). In the 1949 edition, the cited passage appears on pp. 39–40. It is rendered in Hans Meyerhoff's translation as "[A spiritual being such as man] is capable of transforming the primary centers of resistance and reaction into 'objects.' (The animal remains immersed in them 'ecstatically')" (*Man's Place in Nature*, 37).
25. Martin Heidegger. *The Fundamental Concepts of Metaphysics*, §58b, 238 f.
26. Étienne Bimbenet, " 'Man is not a Reasonable Animal': Merleau-Ponty and the Issue of Anthropological Difference," presented at the 30th International Conference of the Merleau-Ponty Circle, Eugene, Oregon, 1 October 2005.
27. See *SB* 191/176, 241/224.
28. *Phénoménologie de la perception* (Paris: Gallimard, 1945), p. 65; *Phenomenology of Perception*, trans. Colin Smith. (London: Routledge, 1962; reprinted 2002), p. 62. Hereafter, this text will be cited as *PP*, with French preceding English pagination.
29. See also Merleau-Ponty's remark, in his discussion of intersubjectivity, that, unlike the gaze of the human being, "A dog's gaze directed toward me causes me no embarrassment" (*PP* 414/420).
30. "Le doute de Cézanne," in *Sens et non-sens* (Paris: Nagel, 1948; reprinted, Gallimard, 1996), p. 23; "Cézanne's Doubt," in Merleau-Ponty, *Sense and Non-Sense*, trans. Hubert and Patricia Dreyfus. (Evanston: Northwestern University Press, 1964), p. 17. Hereafter, this work will be cited as *SNS*, with French preceding English pagination.
31. In this series of seven radio addresses, the fourth is devoted to "Exploration du monde perçu: L'Animalité," *Causeries 1948* (Paris: Seuil, 2002), pp. 33-42; "Exploring the World of Perception: Animal Life," in *The World of Perception*, trans. by Oliver Davis. (London: Routledge, 2004), pp. 69-77.
32. And, to be fairer to Heidegger than we have been above, his thinking of animal being in *The Fundamental Concepts of Metaphysics* must also be read apart from the project of elevating the human representational subject. See William McNeil's comments to this effect in "Life Beyond the Organism," op. cit., pp. 212–213.
33. Merleau-Ponty, *Le Visible et l'invisible* (Paris: Gallimard, 1964), 153; *The Visible and the Invisible*, trans. by Alphonso Lingis. (Evanston: Northwestern University Press, 1968), p. 114. Hereafter, this text will be cited as VI, with French preceding English pagination.

34. The finished portion of the text makes hardly any reference to nonhuman life, save to differentiate the experience one has of the gaze of another human being from its "feeble echo" occasioned by the look of an animal (*VI* 102/73). See also a working note from February, 1959, where Merleau-Ponty describes animals, alongside things and madmen, as "quasi-companions" (*VI* 234/180). (Compare the similar remark from *Phenomenology of Perception* quoted in note 29 above.) In another working note, Merleau-Ponty distinguishes his position from a "hylozoism," since "The flesh of the world is not *self-sensing* (*se sentir*) as is my flesh" (*VI* 304/250). But, even if the flesh of the world is not sentient in general, what of the sentient flesh of nonhuman animals? Would not this sentience also be the expressive irruption of being's *écart*?
35. See "Animality, the Human Body, and the Passage to Culture," in Merleau-Ponty, *La Nature, notes, cours du Collège de France* (Paris: Seuil, 1995), p. 207; *Nature: Course Notes from the Collège de France*, trans. by Robert Vallier (Evanston: Northwestern University Press, 2003), p. 156. (Hereafter, cited as *N* with French preceding English pagination).
36. See also *VI* 222/168, 226/172, and 230-1/176-77.
37. Merleau-Ponty's summary of this course appears in *Résumés de cours, Collège de France, 1952–1960* (Paris: Gallimard, 1968), pp. 171–180; *In Praise of Philosophy and Other Essays*, trans. John O'Neill. (Evanston: Northwestern University Press, 1988), pp. 192–199. (Hereafter, this text is cited as *RC*, with French preceding English pagination). Merleau-Ponty's manuscript notes for the course, in a series of eight sketches, are published in *N* 263-352/203-84. Although the theme of "interanimality" already appears in the second course on the concept of nature (*N* 247/189; *RC* 134/163), the notion of an animal-human *Ineinander* or intertwining first appears in the final course.
38. See, for instance, *RC* 177/196: "The object of the last part of the course was to describe the animation of the human body, not in terms of the descent into it of pure consciousness or reflection, but as a *metamorphosis* of life, and the body as the 'body *of* the spirit' (Valéry)" (my emphasis). See also *N* 340/272, 277a/307n11.
39. Merleau-Ponty uses this expression at RC 177/196; N 284/222, N 288/255.
40. The contrast between "fusion with an *Umwelt*" and "projection of a *Welt*" is made again at *N* 284/222.
41. See also *N* 277/214.
42. See *N* 277a/307n11. Merleau-Ponty cites from Evelyn Lot-Falck's *Les Masques Esquimaux*, an exhibit catalogue to *Le Masque*, Musée Guimet, Paris, December 1959–May 1960, p. 9. This exchange or co-constitution of animality-humanity anticipates the concept of "becoming-animal" proposed by Gilles Deleuze and Félix Guattari, according to which human and animal enter into a single block of becoming, a kind of duet or counterpoint. For Deleuze and Guattari, such becoming, as we find it in musicians like Olivier Messiaen or painters like Francis Bacon, is always bi-directional: "The painter and the musician do not imitate the animal, they become-animal at the same time as the animal becomes what they willed, at the deepest level of their concord with Nature. Becoming is always double: that which one becomes becomes no less than the one that becomes" (*Mille Plateaux* [Paris: Minuit, 1980], p. 374; *A Thousand Plateaus* , trans. Brian Massumi [Minneapolis: University of Minnesota Press, 1987], p. 305). Thus, Bacon's slabs of flesh disclose a "common zone of undecidability" between human and animal, an open space within which each is in transition into its other. (See Ronald Bogue, *Deleuze: On Music, Painting, and the Arts* [New York: Routledge, 2003], p. 111.)
43. See Renaud Barbaras, "Phenomenology of Life," in *The Cambridge Companion to Merleau-Ponty*, ed. by Taylor Carman and Mark Hansen (Cambridge: Cambridge University Press, 2005), pp. 206–230.
44. See *VI* 139/103, 160ff./119ff.

5

How do Primates Think? Phenomenological Analyses of Non-language Systems of Representation in Higher Primates and Humans

Dieter LOHMAR

If we try to analyze the mental abilities of non-human primates (gorillas, orangutans, chimpanzees), we are confronted with the usual objections: we cannot know about the mental acts of animals because they are animals and not humans. Moreover, if we pretend to understand animals, we commit the mistake of anthropomorphisation [*Anthropomorphisiserung*], which is to say that we understand animals only by projecting the pattern of *our own human experiences* onto them. This might be the result of an obvious overestimation of the mental abilities of animals, from which owners of pets, above all, suffer. Anthropomorphisation is thought to be wrongheaded and misleading, because there is a deeply rooted prejudice that animals cannot think, cannot recognize, cannot decide, that they are not subjects with self-consciousness, that they are unaware of their history and their options, and that they only react to stimuli with instinctual, non-deliberated responses. We might call this the "bestialization" [*Bestialisierung*] prejudice. In any case, according to such a prejudice, we postulate an insurmountable gap between animals and humans, which in fact does not exist. I believe that we should not accept these extreme prejudices, and that we should instead determine, quantitatively, which prejudice might be the bigger misconception. Interestingly, in contrast to our ideas about our inability to understand animals, we are convinced that we are able to understand other humans, i.e., that we can know their mental acts on the basis of own experience. After all, humans can communicate with one another, so that in the case of misunderstandings we can correct our suppositions, whereas in the case of animals, this ability to communicate seems to be lacking, or so it is said.

In the first part of my article, I will discuss the function of an abstract system of representation. For humans, this function is best explained in terms of language. A system of representation enables us to have something in the mind (things or events) without having the corresponding intuition at the same time. In the case of language, words and expressions function as a means to intend [*intendieren*] objects and events, with the help of language symbols. However, as I will show, language is not the *only* system of representation that functions in the human mind, as there are other systems of representation that

C. Painter and C. Lotz (eds.), Phenomenology and the Non-Human Animal, 57–74.

are based on phantasmatic scenes, phantasmatic sensations, and on feelings. I will argue for this thesis on the basis of an appeal to dual-modal theories of the human mind, after which I will try to show that in human consciousness there are several systems of representation functioning at the same time. Indeed, human consciousness is organized poly-modally, and many of these systems, I will argue, also function in higher primates.

In the second part of the paper, I will discuss some of the mental achievements of primates, which have been discovered by contemporary primatologists and ethologists (who work in the context of behavioural science). Specifically, I will discuss object-permanence, communication, ideas of future and past, the consciousness of practical and moral obligations, the individual identification of other members of the group, the understanding of the ideas, feelings and will of others, the ability to engage in tactical deception (e.g., lying), the comprehensive social cooperation and political coalition engaged in, as well as the various tool-traditions of primates.

Finally, in the third part of the essay, I will analyze daydreaming, characterizing it as a special case of a non-language mode both of human thinking and of primate thinking. On this basis, I will try to show how some of the most important themes in the life of primates can actually be deliberated upon.

I. Systems of Representation in Humans and Animals

The question of how primates think seems to be misconceived in an important respect; for we ask this question even while we, ourselves, belong to primates. Thus it seems as if we want to know how we ourselves are thinking – at least this question should be easy to answer. For those of us working in the phenomenological tradition, however, we have appropriate respect and concern for this question; we certainly do not think that it is trivial by any means. In this connection, phenomenology claims that it is naive to suppose that our conceptual view of the world and of our consciousness is an appropriate base for a philosophical understanding of these phenomena.

One of the important advantages of phenomenology is that we take our conscious experiences – from a first person view – seriously, which means that we take the experienced activity of our consciousness – which is often interpreted as a mere accompanying subjective play of our conceptual thinking – as the original mode of the givenness of our thinking, perceiving, willing, and feeling. In the view of phenomenology, it is the fundamental activity of our mind that grants the intuition of all our objects. It is for this reason that even though our own experience seems to be only "our own" and allegedly private, we think it is a qualified basis for a scientific analysis of thinking in general.

Human conscious thinking acts usually occur within the medium of language and conceptual thinking, and thankfully there are already numerous useful phenomenological analyses of this activity. Following Husserl, the "*fundamentum in re*" of conceptual thinking is "categorial intuition," which involves a complex structure of acts of consciousness that enable the object of cognition to become intuitive. In close fusion with this intuitive act, there is a meaning-giving act that enables us to intend the intuitively given object of cognition (state of affairs [*Sachverhalte*]) with the help of words. Using the language mode of intending, we try to adjust the language expression to the primary intuition.[1] In reverse order, we are able to interpret sounds or murmurs as meaningful expressions, as well as words and sentences, and thereby, we are able to access the respective intuition and meaningful intention that may be the fundament of these expressions (this also works in the case of the "speaking" of machines or parrots). Accordingly, conceptual intentions in the form of language and the intuition of states of affairs belong together, although we can have them separately. This is the sense in which we may regard language as a system of the representation of things and states of affairs, which can also be intuitively given. Intuition, however, remains fundamental, originary, and independent in regard to language. For, indeed, we are able to think the same categorial contents that may have been intuitively given with the help of language, even in the absence of the appropriate intuition. This is the central function of a system of representation, which can be seen paradigmatically in the case of language.

But there are clear hints that language is not the *only* system of representation that is used by human consciousness. We already realize this in the very recognition of the distance between words and the intuition of states of affairs, which forces us to adjust the spoken sentence to the intuitive cognition and vice-versa. Consequently, there can be other, alternative systems of representation functioning in human consciousness at the same time. And while these alternative systems of representation are probably non-linguistic, they nevertheless must be (nearly) as powerful as the representation offered in language. One argument for this thesis is to be found in the evolution of man. In this connection, we would do well to note that the first hominids (australopithecus) changed their living space [*Lebensraum*] (rain forest / savanna) and extended their spectrum of diet (vegetarian / animal protein), which was only possible on the basis of an extended expert knowledge and because of their tool production, use, and preservation (much more extended than known in chimpanzees). *Homo habilis* already planned, executed, and coordinated big game hunting [*Grosswildjagd*]. *Homo erectus* settled the whole world 1.8 million years ago, therefore he must have had powerful systems of representation and communication that enabled foresighted thinking, stock holding of food [*Vorratshaltung*], and the creation of social institutions. Importantly, all these performances were possible without the use of an efficient phonetic language [*Lautsprache*], given that this facility (i.e., the facility of language) appeared only with *homo sapiens,* approximately 120–150.000 years ago. Consequently, there must have been a non-linguistic and yet powerful system of representation in human consciousness for nearly two million years.

If we conceive of thinking as the ability to refer to objects and states of affairs also in the absence of the intuitively given objects, then we realize that thinking is dependent on the use of a system of representation. In the case of language, we can clearly recognize some of the basic characteristics of systems of representation that enable thinking, namely, we must be able to produce the sensual carriers [*Träger*] of representation. For only if this production is possible, can I refer to objects and states of affairs in the absence of intuitive knowledge, since only then can I produce (at any time) spoken language. At the very least, I can produce the phonetic side of spoken language with the help of phantasma, conceived as a sort of "inner voice." This applies also to writing; for, generally, a sensual carrier of meaning can be used in a system of representation only if we can produce this carrier externally in sensuality or internally in phantasma, as a kind of quasi-sensuality. But these forms of representation are not necessarily linguistic. Importantly, this opens a possibility for understanding how animals might think. Or, to put this differently, we now see the possibility for understanding in which modes we (humans) think in the way that animals think.

What alternatives do we have for the carrier function of a system of representation? If we reflect upon the ideas that are to be found in our consciousness, we come to written or spoken words, gestures (particularly those that are immediately related to our body or to conventional sign language), phonetic signs [*Lautzeichen*], scenic imaginations, and feelings. (And this list is not exhaustive). What is perhaps most important to understand is that humans usually use more than one system of representation, indeed, probably more than two. In thinking, we always use a kind of poly-modal system of representation, and thus language is never the only functioning system. However, it is important for us to ask for a sharpened attention to the modes of thinking "underneath" [*unterhalb*] language. In my opinion, this research is quite possible to do within phenomenological philosophy, and I will attempt to do so here.

The thesis that in human consciousness there are two different but closely related processes that have the same mental performance has been posed already in 1975 by P. C. Wason and J. St. B. T. Evans.[2] The first process is characterized as a *low-level-system*, which is *phylogentically old*, *relatively simple*, *basically structured*, and *less trouble-prone* than other higher processes. It enables us to have quick perceptions and insights, and as such, it also enables quick and self-assured acting. This *low-level-system* is not language-based, and we share it in common with most of the higher organized animals, whereas the *high-level-system* rests on the use of language and concepts, and in this way the *high-level-system* is *relatively slow*, since it makes use of *complex rules* and *dependencies*. With the help of this conceptual system we are able to constitute new abstract objects and higher level concepts. However, most of our cognitive, emotional, and willing (volitional) performances, we are able to perform also within the *low-level-system* that we share in common with many higher animals.

In the above mentioned list of possible systems of representation, a certain evolutionary aspect is also included. However, while it is difficult to do justice to the evolutionary aspect in this limited space, I will try to shed some necessary light on it in the following discussion of some of the alternative systems of representation.

1. It is true that we (humans) usually think in the medium of language, but we also use phantasmatic scenes (for example in our daydreams) as ways of expressing wishes and concrete fears [*Befürchtungen*]. In daydreams, phantasmatic scenes serve as a medium of thinking within which we go through [*durchspielen*] our options for acting. These phantasmatic scenes occupy a great part of our awake life, even if we rarely reflect on this fact. Lying awake in the night, worrying about urgent problems or uncertainties, is a well-known form of scenic imagination. I might also refer here to empirical psychological investigations, which suggest that grown men think of sex every few minutes, where the mode of this thinking is definitely not conceptual. These experiences point out that in the scenic episodes of our conscious life, language seems to be forced into the background of consciousness in favor of non-linguistic scenic elements and pictures.[3] Nevertheless, we are able to think about our wishes and problems within the means of language and thus both modes of thinking are often mixed in daydreams. Humans, therefore, are using both systems at the same time and in mixed modes.

In addition, we know from studies of brain activity that most higher developed mammals can dream, insofar as they show the same pattern of neuronal activity combined with characteristic patterns of rapid eye movements as we (humans) do when dreaming. In these phases of sleep, their bodies show beginnings of actions and emotions that might be interpreted through us by way of comparing them with awake state actions and emotions. In this connection, most of us have seen a dog dreaming. Thus we may proceed under the assumption that the scenic-phantasmatic system of representation that is functioning in all primates during sleep is also functioning in awake states, just as is the case in humans.

2. It is true that we usually speak in language, but if it happens that we have to inform a person that does not understand my language about my urgent wish, for example, that he should drive me to the airport, something surprising takes place: we start immediately communicating with gestures and pantomimic performances that are accompanied by onomatopoeia. This is indeed a very revealing behavior; for the rapidity, the self-confidence, and the undubitable self-evidence [*Selbstverständlichkeit*] of this action, reveals to us that this mode of representation forms a deep layer in our ability to communicate. Furthermore, we might conclude that this gestic-pantomimic mode of representation is at all times functioning in our consciousness. Metaphorically speaking, it does not sleep. Indeed, we do not have to work hard to remember or rediscover this mode of communication; rather, it starts functioning immediately in the open communication situation that stands in for language, when language fails. Consequently, we can learn much of importance about our systems of representation by carefully examining this seemingly marginal behavior. Fortunately, one of the (many) merits of phenomenology involves staying aware of the

basic role that self-evident elements of our lives play, not only as fundamental constitutives of our world-constitution, but also as enigmas that we should clarify.

3. We might also interpret phantasmatically reproduced sensations, as well as feelings, as systems of representation. The basic presupposition for the carrier of a system of representation is that we can produce it at any time, even in the absence of the originary intuition of the object meant. Sensations that we first live through, as well as originarily given feelings, can be reproduced phantasmatically in the absence of the spring of this first intuition. The pleasant taste of a certain meal, for instance, can be enjoyed in the intuitive situation itself. However, this is not the only manner of enjoyment, for I can also think of the meal in a phantasmatic mode that allows me to nearly taste the meal. We might have this sort of experience when studying a cookbook richly illustrated, as when the different flavors develop phantasmatically in my mind, while turning the cookbook's pages. In this thinking, the phantasmatically reproduced sensations seem to "inform" me about the qualities that are expected (or hoped for) in this special meal. The same is true for feelings that we might have had in an original intuition of a successful action. If we think of the same action again, it is accompanied with the phantasmatic reproduction of the same feeling of success. In such thinking, the phantasmatically revitalized feelings (which may be accompanied with scenic phantasma) mean something: they mean that the action was pleasant and successful and that it is desirable to act like this again.

We know that most animals have sensations and also feelings. This is evident from the fact that most animals have a limbic system that proceeds the emotional aspects of consciousness. The limbic system forms a layer between the cerebellum [*Kleinhirn*] and cerebrum [*Grosshirn*], which is developed in all higher cerebralized animals. As such, primates, like humans, have this system of representation too.

Up to this point I have only pointed out some alternative systems of representation in human thinking, and I have discussed the way in which we ourselves experience them. Besides this, I have discussed some arguments that suggest that we might presuppose the same non-language systems of representation in primates. In so doing, I have so far only argued for the *possibility* that primates think in some of the "deeper" or "lower-level" modes of thinking in which we, humans, engage. But is this enough to suppose that primates *really* think? For example: Do we know what they are thinking about? The following section of this essay will address these questions.

II. What are Primates Thinking and Willing?

First, I feel compelled to mention that I am a romantic neither concerning the faculties of animals in general, nor concerning the faculties of primates in particular. Nor, however, am I a romantic concerning the faculties of humans. In this vein, there is a long list of faculties that were believed – for a very long time – to be exclusively human, which in turn served to establish a decisive difference between animal and man that, today, has been called into question. In the discussion that follows, I will concentrate on the mental abilities that are to be found in members of the primate group (gorillas, orangutans, chimpanzees), which is a group that is conventionally taken to stand "between" animals, who are traditionally thought to belong on one side of the divide, and humans, who are thought to belong on the other side.

1. Many philosophers believe that only humans can constitute objects and behave freely, while facing these objects. This conventional view interprets animal behavior as the mere result of instinctive reactions to various stimuli. On this view, animals react in an only *seemingly* wise way (for example, avoiding unpleasant experiences), but they cannot really refer mentally – or in a thinking, deliberative way – to absent objects. For Kant, this opinion is based on the conviction that animals do not have the facility of reason. In the transcendental deduction of his *Critique of Pure Reason*, Kant tries to demonstrate that the pure concepts of reason are necessary ingredients of all constituted objects, most primary amongst them, the concepts of substance and causality.[4] Also, Max Scheler, in his anthropology, takes the view that only man *has objects* and can act freely in regard to them.[5] As I will show, these opinions, though widely accepted, are incorrect in the case of many animals, particularly in the case of primates.

Jean Piaget introduces the concept of "object permanence" in his theory of the genetic psychology of children. "Object permanence" refers to the thesis that a living being is able to have an idea of an enduring object with lasting properties even when the object itself is absent. Piaget works out experiments with newborns and infants within which they are supposed to reach and to search for unseen objects. But given that this ability is based on the use of complex bodily movements that are difficult (if not impossible) to fulfill for human newborns, Piaget's experiments cannot be used to test the mental performances of newborns.[6] In response to this problem, today the mental facility of object permanence is tested both in humans and in animals with methods that depend neither on language nor on complex bodily actions. The method of eye-tracking, for example, allows us to determine mental facility by tracking the empirical-psychological insight that we watch longer for objects and events when we do not expect them [*Erwartungsverletzung*], than we watch for those that are expected. In an experiment within which a constantly moving black point vanishes behind a visual obstacle, we have discovered that a living being who can perform object permanence will expect it to move out behind the obstacle after a certain time, and that if this expectation is disappointed, the attention will hold on longer to the point at which the expected event should have occurred. In this way, we may establish that most mammals (as well as birds) can perform object permanence. These experiments also established comparable results for properties of objects, movements, and causal effects of events.

2. Many philosophers believe that only humans have the ability to communicate in language and therefore that only humans can communicate their thinking in the form of public communication. In contrast to this, animals are thought to have only limited abilities to communicate. While they can, for instance, give phonetic signals that have the function of warning the other members of the group, it is said that they cannot refer to present, past, or future events, objects, and intentions with the help of language (or through other, equally powerful means of open communication). However, this opinion is definitely incorrect regarding the abilities of primates, as certain training programs have established. In this regard, while the training of primates to use spoken phonetic language is extremely time-consuming and often does not lead to satisfactory results, in contrast, attempts to train chimpanzees in American Sign Language (ASL), as well as in the use of symbols in a tableau (e.g., Kanzi), has led to quite impressive results. With both methods we arrive at the result that primates are able to build sentences of up to two to three words. Interestingly, this corresponds (approximately) to the language abilities of two-year old children.[7] Moreover, in regard to these results we should keep in mind that the use of abstract symbols is dissimilar to the means of communication that are originary to chimpanzees (which is probably more powerful than this very artificial way). Indeed, about the primary way in which chimpanzees communicate, we hardly know more than that it exists.

3. Many philosophers believe that primates have no notion of past and future, and that they have no idea of practical rules and obligations that they may choose to obey or not. Following this opinion, animals are only reacting within the framework of instinctive forces, and as such, the rudimentary communication they are able to perform is also bound up in this framework. If this is true, it should not be possible for alarm calls to be used as a means of employing tactical deception, since this would require, amongst other things, self-consciousness. However, as will be shown, this received opinion is inaccurate, as is evidenced by investigations of the capacity for primates to engage in numerous forms of tactical deception.

Indeed, documentation of tactical deception in primates has a history of more than twenty years. The first collection of reports, "The St. Andrews Catalogue of Tactical Deceptions in Primates," was published in 1986, and reported 104 events of tactical deception. Since this time, reports have grown continuously (in 1990 there were 253 reports included).[8] This catalogue is organized in seven categories, which mirror the mental performances that are necessary to perform such deceptions.[9] A deception can consist in simply disobeying the obligation to communicate the discovery of food. This is an example often reported about subjects who are low in the hierarchy of the group, because if they report the food they will surely not participate in the meal. This kind of deception can be provoked by hiding food in a tube within which it can later be found by younger subjects whose rank in hierarchy is low. Sometimes in this situation, these subjects even behave inconspicously [*unauffällig*], by attempting not to show their excitement (creating an image), while other times they leave the place where they found the food only to come back later (distraction). Even these simple forms of deception show that primates have an idea of the future, given that they know the consequences that will follow if their discovery or their obvious excitement is registered by other group members. Moreover, it reveals that they are able to act freely in regard to the obligation to report the discovery of food to the group, by preferring and acting in regard to their own interest over the interests of those in charge of the group.

The creation of the inconspicuous misrepresentation (image) [*einen falschen unauffälligen Eindruck erzeugen*] shows that the deceiving primates are aware of the other group members' opinions about their knowledge and plans. This insight into the opinions of others presupposes that the subject is aware both of his outer appearance and of its effect on others (viz. their interpretations of his knowledge and intentions). This is an important aspect of self-consciousness. There are also situations reported within which a subject tries (for instance, by demonstratively limping) to give the bodily impression of being seriously hurt to a superior rival.[10] Chimpanzees are also aware of the effect of their mimic art and they can use this in order to manipulate their audience intentionally. Frans de Waal reports an event between two rivals within which the temporary winner, Luit, turns his back on the defeated but strong Nikkie. After a renewed provocation by Nikkie, Luit shows the characteristic nervous grin that signals anxiety, but in such a way that Nikkie can not see it. After that, Luit presses his lips together with his fingers until the revealing grin has vanished, and only after this, does he face him again to display superior behavior [*imponieren*].[11]

4. Most higher developed animals are individuals in the sense that they are able to recognize the members of their group and to know about their history and even their character (in the sense of their tendencies to act in certain ways). Behavioral science shows us that even sticklebacks have this facility. Groups of sticklebacks move in brooks [*Bächen*] and in other waters with a special method: they are vanguarded by a pair of fish that functions as a kind of reconnaissance patrol that announces danger to the group. This patrol is exposed to a relatively great danger, and if one of the two ever reveals itself as a coward (even once), the other refuses to cooperate with this individual in the future.[12]

5. Primates have insight into the minds of other members of their group and can include their intentions in their own plans and actions, as we can easily see in the examples of tactical deceptions, some of which were briefly outlined above. Besides this line of research, we would do well to acknowledge the research on so-called mirror-neurons, which is primarily done on macaque apes. This line of research suggests that in some regions of the brain there are neurons that are active, when the subject observes another animal's sensations, emotions, or bodily movements. In these cases, the pattern of neuronal activity is exactly the same as it is when the subject itself is performing the movements in question. We might (reasonably) interpret this in the following manner: the observing animal is *feeling the same thing* as the animal observed, with the help of a kind of simulation.[13]

6. For a long time it was believed that only humans can use tools. After having realized the extensive use of tools in other animals too, however, this belief in exclusivity was reduced to the facility of *producing* tools. But even this restricted opinion has now been overturned. For, today, not only do we know that chimpanzees can use upwards of thirty different kinds of tools, we also know that they can produce and transport tools as well. Importantly, both the use and the production of tools must be learned, and correspondingly, it must be taught, all of which can be – and, indeed, has been – observed in chimpanzees. The most impressive examples of this involve chimpanzees cracking palm nuts with the help of specially selected stones that are transported and sometimes also prepared for just this task.[14]

7. In many higher developed mammals that live in groups, different kinds of technical and social cooperation can be observed, including cooperative methods of hunting.[15] The impressive manifold forms of political cooperation and coalition in chimpanzees are convincingly described by Frans de Waal.[16] For instance, chimpanzees have been observed forming coalitions of two or even three members, so that they can come to dominate another group. Moreover, these necessary coalitions have a great variety of modes and sometimes quickly change, depending on circumstances.

8. Even today, it seems somewhat risky to speak about common obligatory rules in primates. Since most of the practical rules for behavior are bound tightly to the hierarchy in the group, this means that they are not conceived as *general* obligations but as only valid for the members in the lower part of the group hierarchy. Accordingly, these rules do not seem to meet our criteria for being *moral rules*, about which we (generally) think that they should hold universally. But even if these kinds of primate practical rules do not fit *our* conception of moral rules, they are nonetheless accompanied by punishment. In primate groups there are also practical rules that are enacted and sanctioned only by a part of the group, for instance, "mother-rules," which prohibit the instrumentalization of children.[17] There are also rules that are sanctioned by the whole community.

In chimpanzees, there is even a sense of justice, as was demonstrated by a recent experiment by Frans de Waal and Sarah Brosnan.[18] In this experiment, a machine exchanged playing pieces [*Spielsteine*] in two kinds of food, namely, in very popular grapes and in not so popular pieces of cucumbers. This machine could be manipulated by the experimenters in an arbitrary way such that at a certain point the machine started to prefer particular members of the group and thus behaved unjustly in favor of these preferred group members. After observing this unjust behavior, most of the capucine apes turned away from the attractive toy, suggesting that they "understood" something about what was happening and that they did not like it. There can even be observed what may be referred to as "just fury" in primates, when members of the group do not submit to the practical rules. For example, when it was discovered that the duty to communicate found food was not upheld, the swindlers were beaten up.[19]

Moreover, in early hominids, when bones of physically handicapped members are found – which supports the conclusion that the handicapped can survive in the group for a certain length of time – we may take this as a rather convincing "hint" that some sort of morality occurs in this group. Dissimilarly, if the same would happen in groups of primates we would probably hesitate to link this to "morality," and we would likely decide in favor of a "more simple explanation," preferably one that does not suppose mental abilities.[20] However, if we discover that a handicapped member in a group of primates has survived *because of* the help of other (non-handicapped) members, it is not clear that such a prejudiced judgment is warranted. And indeed, even though one might find skeptical objections against all of the theses proposed here, hoping to find more simple explanations that do not rely upon mental abilities, given that such skeptical objections may also be advanced against attempts to offer moral explanations for the social behavior of humans as well, and *for the same reasons*, such objections should be carefully scrutinized. In any case, I will not discuss such objections or counter-arguments against such objections here. Rather, I want, simply, to maintain that our tendency to accept skeptical objections in the case of primates, while refusing to entertain such objections in the case of humans, is likely to be grounded in the unjustifiable prejudice that I earlier referred to as "bestialization."

My admittedly limited aim in the context of this paper is to formulate and attempt to answer the following set of questions: How can highly cerebralized animals achieve all these mental performances, without the help of language? And which systems of representation do they use to perform these tasks? On one point we may be certain: it is not language; for we now know that there are alternative systems of representation that make the performance of these tasks possible.

Additionally, we know – or at least we believe that we do – that we (humans) accomplish these mental performances (usually) with the help of language. However, our theoretical considerations about possible systems of representation and their cooperation in human consciousness (which appear at the beginning of our analyses) have raised doubts in this regard, since it has been shown that more simple systems of representation (that we also use) may achieve the same performance without the means of language. This in turn suggests that the above mentioned discoveries in the mental abilities of primates indicates that they too are able to perform many of the same mental performances that we humans perform, without the means of language.

Consequently, it may just be the case that language-based thinking is only a superior layer of externally expressable representation, which lies superficially at the surface of the deeper and truly fundamental layers of representation. This hypothesis would imply that language has, with respect to our most esteemed mental abilities, no independent and originary contribution. To be sure, this does not imply that language does not enable us to refer abstractly to objects and cognition, such that we are able to speak about these objects in abstract concepts. Formally interpreted, such highly abstract concepts (e.g., necessity, universality, generality, etc.) reach a level that can only be achieved with language. But it might turn out that these "highbrowed" elements of a language system of representation only enable us to speak about cognitions that have already been achieved within the more simple systems of representation (for example, within scenic phantasma or feelings).

In order to explore this last suggestion, I will appeal to one of the authorities in modern philosophy, namely, Immanuel Kant. In his moral philosophy, Kant discusses the moral qualities of common rules (*Maximen*), which guide concrete actions. One such common rule is the rule of indifference, which states: "Do not help anyone who is in trouble." As is well known, Kant's categorial imperative demands that if such a common rule is to become (legitimately) a moral law [*objektive Gesetze*], it must be accepted as universally binding on all rational agents. Concerning the rule of indifference, Kant thinks that rational agents cannot accept this rule as universally binding, since a will that wills this law would be irrational and incoherent.[21] But it is important to ask, here, which mental operation is the basis of this insight. For, I can certainly imagine the rule of indifference becoming a common rule and in doing this, I see only indifferent faces and persons disinterested in the state of others. There is nothing *logically inconceivable* about such a state of affairs, even though a certain faint revulsion might arise in me. However, if I imagine myself in true need of another's help then I will no doubt want to get help, which will contradict my earlier will that allowed the common rule of indifference to become universally valid. In this way, scenic imagination, and the actual experience of conflicting wills and feelings, are modes in which the insight into the unacceptability of the rule of indifference really occurs. With language, therefore, I can only communicate about this experience, which always-already precedes the language.

This shows that the irreplaceable advantages of public speech must lie elsewhere. Thus, while systems of representation that are also means of public communication can have incomparably great advantages for the community, insofar as they allow us to pass on the invention of useful social institutions and technical tools to a whole group and to their descendants, these systems and their achievements do not constitute the only valuable form of communication, nor, as we have seen, do they stand alone without support from other systems. In this connection, Michael Tomasello speaks about a "ratchet-effect" of public communication,[22] within which he notices that the positive effect of collecting, conserving, and extending social and technical facilities with the help of language communication does not elevate the standards beyond those that are met by the fundamental mental performances that underlie and make linguistic performances possible. Just as this valorization of the qualitative contribution of language should not devalue the non-linguistic mental performances of humans, neither should it devalue the mental performances of animals, especially those of primates. It may even turn out that language is only a useful means in the "outer sphere" of public memory, wherein useful inventions that support the success of our species in an incomparable way are located. Nevertheless, this does not detract from the fact that most of the mental performances that we esteem in ourselves are as well performed by our brothers in the primate group, and that therefore they should not be overlooked or devalued, especially since it might be the case that the underlying mental performances that are highly esteemed in humans are *identically performed* by the human and the animal mind. If this is the case, what (primarily) makes humans stand out from the group of primates is their facility to speak in public, using general concepts, about their various mental achievements, many of which (as we have seen) turn out to be achievable by other primates, too.

III. Scenic Imagination in Daydreams as an "Old Mode of Thinking"

The phenomenological research that led me to consider the mental abilities of primates and the questions regarding different systems of representation is the phenomenology of weak phantasy (sensual phantasma).[23] While this seems a strange way to go about considering this theme, it was indeed during the course of my analyses of the manifold aspects of sensual phantasma, in conscious-wake states, that I became focally interested in the scenic organization of daydreams, thinking that it might well be interpreted as an "old mode of thinking," by which I mean a mode of thinking that has been around for centuries. But, lest I get ahead of myself, I shall start at the beginning of the story.

Sensual phantasma are products of imagination, which sometimes appear noticeable in normal perception but surprisingly (because they stem from imagination) do not cause a devaluing and reshaping of perception into "pure fancy." On the contrary, these phantasmatic elements contribute to the credibility of perception, indeed they make perception more convincing, insofar as the phantasma "fill-in" the aspects of perception that are either only present in a weak way or are absent altogether. A standard example of this function of "filling-in" is the strange taste in our mouth that occurs when we see *someone else* biting into a lemon. As it is *our own mind* that produces this affection I have named this process *phantasmatic self-affection*.

But insofar as phantasma are relatively weak, they are easily replaced by the corresponding sensual givenness. This points to the fundamental function of the sensual phantasma: they show *in advance* all the elements to be expected in sensually given intended objects [*vorscheinen lassen*]. We might even interpret this function as a projection of the usual sensual presentation of an object in my sensual field, such that my factual perception can be guided by this projection. Naturally, the phantasmatically projected elements of the object intended are oriented to the type (*Typus*) of this object, where the type is constituted on the basis of foregoing experiences.[24] But the projection of the elements of the type is also adjusted on the basis of the parts of the object that are already given. For example, visual phantasma adjust to the perspectival givenness of the object. Likewise, in the acoustic sphere it is possible that while I am reading a letter of a well-known person or an intimate friend, I can "hear" phantasmatically the characteristic voice of the writer in her tone, her temper, and her emotion. However, the function of the phantasma is not exhausted in filling in missing sensuality; for only because of the guiding function of the phantasma, which is oriented to the type of the object, am I able to perform the complex activity of perception, since I must know in advance which elements of sensuality belong to the presentation of the object and which do not. In this way, the anticipating phantasmatic projection, which is presented in accord with the type of the object, enables me to find exactly these usable elements of sensuality and to keep them together such that they form a coherent, meaningful presentation of the thing or event.

With respect to daydreams, daydreams are (usually) thought to present fears and desires with which we live in the everyday attitude, in the form of scenic representations that are aided by phantasma. Accordingly, daydreams are said to mirror the relevant order of events that lie somewhere between what should happen and what may (or should) never happen. It seems, in this connection, that in order to understand daydreams we do not need an extended psychoanalytical hermeneutics after all. But besides this, unlike usual nightly dreams, daydreams respect the identity, the causality, and the order of events in time. As such, they might reveal another mode of thinking that deals with everyday problems. Moreover, just as there are rarely elements of spoken language in nightly dreams, language is also usually missing in daydreams.[25] All of this suggests that the scenic mode of daydreams allows for an interpretation of them as an "old mode of thinking." In this connection, if I am worried in the mode of daydreaming – i.e., while daydreaming – then things, persons, and events arise there in a particular way within a scenic mode. In this way, the contents of my worries are presented in a certain manner, and sometimes there are also possible solutions presented; for example, in a happy and unexpected turn of the scene. In this way, daydreams present a non-language mode of thinking within which questions, insights, and problems can be handled, and sometimes even solved. It thus seems reasonable to view our "factual mode of thinking" as (generally) associated with the language mode, wherein it is understood that the function of the language mode is to *sum up or recap what was already thought through in the scenic mode*. To be sure, there is only a limited realm of themes that highly cerebralized primates living in groups need to be able to think through, namely: [1] real objects, their states, their uses (for example, tool use), and their experienced values for the individual, for the group, and in the framework of respective tradition; [2] real events in the present, past, and future, together with their values; and [3] other members of the group with their sensations, feelings, convictions, and practical intentions, concerning oneself or other group members. Though I leave it to the reader to find examples for the first two kinds of objects, I shall elucidate an example of the third.

At first glance, it seems difficult to imagine a scenic image of the *character* of a person and of his probable behavior towards me, especially within complex constellations with others who are involved in the action. Importantly, however, scenic phantasma offer a simple solution for this. For example, in remembering a brutal former classmate, I see his face looking at me with evil eyes, with clenched fists, and ready to give me a beating. But this "image" is not simply an image of him, it is, rather, a characteristic scene within which I am present, writhing with pain from his beating and in fear of further beatings from him. This scene presents central aspects both of his character and of his future behavior.

Of course, scenic presentation of the attitude and the behavior of a person need not be so one-dimensional, as in the case mentioned, since normally there are multiple facets of the character of other persons that we should be able to present. Thus, the question that arises is: How can I think a multitude of (changing) attitudes in a scenic mode? Think of a colleague with whom you work together successfully in most cases, but who occasionally gives off an air of high-nose arrogance. Both "faces," i.e., both aspects of his character, may come up in a scenic imagination, one after the other, or, even, as mixed in a changing way [*changierend*], which results in an uncertain base for your plan-making. Here, the character of possibility and uncertainty is thus present in the changing and merging face of your multi-attitudinal colleague, which you can also represent towards other persons and other situations, since you can easily extend the characteristic scenes in any way imaginatively possible.

In addition to the character of persons, the value and the use of objects can change, which is also reflected in the characteristic scene. For instance, if I own a car that usually breaks down and thus has to be towed off and repaired, the characteristic scene within which I am positively excited about my car is modified, and converted to one that is negative. The emotional aspects of this bad experience are especially mirrored in the characteristic scene: I no longer imagine the car with the joyful expectation of reliable use, but with the cheerless expectation of future harm, expense, and inconvenience. In this way, the two sorts of characteristic scenes – i.e., the characteristic scene that involves other subjects and the characteristic scene that involves objects or events – are analogous, insofar as both scenic presentations will change on the basis of the underlying scenic phantasma that give them their ground.

In the first part of this essay I demonstrated the possibility of thinking in primates by discussing alternative systems of representation that are working in primates as well as in humans. In the second part, I argued for the thesis that primates can engage in many mental performances that are similar to those of humans. In the third part of the paper, using concrete examples, I discussed a special system of representation, namely, scenic phantasma in daydreams, wherein I characterized this process as an "old mode of thinking" employed by humans and (probably) by primates as well. As a phenomenologist, I can not go further in my analyses. For the empirical proof that primates are really thinking in the mode of scenic phantasma must be done by other sciences, for example, by experimental psychology or by neuroscience. Nevertheless, a new and important task for phenomenological research is revealed, namely: to analyze the mode of alternative systems of representation in humans.

Notes

1. For Husserl's theory of meaning, see *Logical Investigations*, I and II. For the theory of categorial intuition, see Chapter 6 of *Logical Investigations,* VI, as well as D. Lohmar. "Husserl's Concept of Categorical Intuition," *Hundred Years of Phenomenology*. eds. D. Zahavi, F. Stjernfelt (Dordrecht: Springer, 2002), pp. 125–145.
2. See the contributions of P.C. Wason and J. St. B. T. Evans. "Dual Processes in Reasoning*?,"* *Cognition* 3 (1975), 141–154; Johnathan St. B. T. Evans. *The Psychology of Deductive Reasoning*. (London: Routledge & Kegan Paul, 1982), Chapter 12; Jonathan St. B. T. Evans. "In two minds: dual-process accounts of reasoning," *Trends in Cognitive Science*, Vol. 7 (2003), pp. 454–459. A good overview of the different dual-process theories is offered by Keith E. Stanovich and Richard F. West. "Individual Differences in Reasoning: Implications for the Rationality Debate?" *Behavioral and Brain Sciences*, Vol. 22 (2000), Issue 5, pp. 645–726 (Chapter 6: "Dual Process Theories and Alternative Task Construals").
3. This is also the case in dreams in sleep. On this, see, Symons, Donald. "The stuff that dreams aren't made of: Why the wake-state and dream-state sensory experiences differ," *Cognition 47* (1993), pp. 181–217.
4. Immanuel Kant. *Kritik der reinen Vernunft, in Gesammelte Schriften, Band 3*, (Berlin: hrsg. von der Königlich- Preussischen Akademie der Wissenschaften zu Berlin, 1902).
5. Scheler, Max. *Die Stellung des Menschen im Kosmos*, *Gesammelte Werke*, Vol. 5, ed. Maria Scheler. (Bonn: Bouvier Verlag, 2005). [original 1928]
6. Jean Piaget. *The Origins of Intelligence in Children*. (New York, 1952). See also the discussion in Marc D. Hauser. *Wild Minds. What Animals Really Think*. (New York: Henry Holt and Company, 2000). [German: *Wilde Intelligenz*. Beck: München, 2001), Chapter 2]..
7. For this, see Roger Fouts. Next of Kin. *What Chimpanzees Have Taught Me About Who We Are. (*NY: William Morrow, 1997) [German: *Unsere nächsten Verwandten. Von Schimpansen lernen, was es heißt, ein Mensch zu sein*. München 1998]. See also, Sue Savage-Rumbaugh / Roger Lewin. *Kanzi. The Ape at the Brink of the Human Mind*. (New York: Wiley, 1994). [German: *Kanzi - der sprechende Schimpanse. Was den tierischen vom menschlichen Verstand unterscheidet*. München 1998].
8. Richard Bryne / Andrew Whiten. "Tactical deception of familiar individuals in baboons," *Animal Behaviour* 33 (1985), pp. 669–673; R. Bryne / A. Whiten (eds.). *Machiavellian Intelligence*. (Oxford: Clarendon, 1988); R. Bryne / A. Whiten. "Tactical deception in primates: the 1990 database," *Primate Report* 27 (1990), pp. 1–101; and Volker Sommer. *Lob der Lüge*. (Beck, München 1992), pp. 72–96.
9. These categories are: concealment, distraction, attraction, creating an image, deflection, using a social tool, and counter-deception.
10. This is reported by Frans de Waal, in R. Bryne / A. Whiten "Tactical deception in primates: the 1990 database," *Primate Report* 27 (1990), pp. 1–101, Episode 238.
11. Frans de Waal. *Chimpanzee Politics. Power and Sex among Apes*. (London: Jonathan Cape Ltd., 1982. [German: *Unsere haarigen Vettern. Neueste Erfahrungen mit Schimpansen*. München 1983, S. 134].

12. M. Milinski / D. Pfluger / D. Külling / R. Kettler. "Do sticklebacks cooperate repeatedly in reciprocal pairs?" *Behavi. Ecol. Sociobiol.* 27 (1990), pp. 17–21.
13. See my interpretation, given in "Mirror Neurons and the Phenomenology of Intersubjectivity." Forthcoming: *Phenomenology and Cognitive Science* Vol. 4.2 (2004). [German*: Interdisziplinäre Phänomenologie* I, 2004, 241–254].
14. For a description of the faculties of the chimpanzees in the Tai national parks that are cracking palm nuts with the help of stones, and pass this ability also on to their children, see Boesch C. / Boesch H. "Mental map in wild chimpanzees. An analysis of hammer transports for nut cracking. In: *Primates* 25 (1984), 160–170; C. Boesch: *Teaching among wild chimpanzees*," *Animal Behaviour* 41 (1991), pp. 530–532; and T. Matsuzawa. "Field experiments on use of stone tools in the wild," in R.W. Wrangham / W. C. McGrew / F. B. M. de Waal / P. G. Heltne (eds.), *Chimpanzee Cultures*. (Cambridge: Harvard University Press, 1994), pp. 351–370.
15. I am thinking of collective methods of hunting in dolphins and in whales; the method of hunting swarms by using curtains of bubbles [Bläschenjagd] is particularly impressive. There are also methods of joint aid in whales, the so called "marguerite," within which a member of the group that is ill or seriously hurt is brought to the surface (to be able to breathe) by other members of the group. This social kind of joint aid has been well known for some time, which is evidenced by the fact that whale hunters take extensive advantage of this behavior in order to harpoon the whole group.
16. Frans de Waal. *Chimpanzee Politics. Power and Sex among Apes*. (London: Jonathan Cape Ltd., 1982). [German: Unsere haarigen Vettern. Neueste Erfahrungen mit Schimpansen. München 1983]; and *Peacemaking among Primates*. (Cambridge: Harvard University Press, 1989) [German: *Wilde Diplomaten. Versöhnung und Entspannungspolitik bei Affen und Menschen*. München 1991].
17. Frans de Waal: *Good Natured. The Origins of Right and Wrong in Humans and other Animals*. (Cambridge, Harvard University Press, 1996) [German: Der gute Affe. Der Ursprung von Recht und Unrecht bei Menschen und anderen Tieren. München 1997, Chapter 3].
18. Frans de Waal / Sarah Brosnan. "Monkeys reject unequal pay," *Nature* 425 (2003), pp. 297–299.
19. M. D. Hauser. "Costs of Deception: Cheaters are Punished in Rhesus Monkeys (Macaca mulatta*)*," *Proceedings of the National Academy of Sciences* Vol. 89 (1992), S. 12137–12139.
20. This example is given by Frans de Waal, who points our attention to the handicapped macaque Mozu:. Frans de Waal. *Good Natured. The Origins of Right and Wrong in Humans and other Animals*. (Cambridge: Harvard University Press, 1996) [German: *Der gute Affe. Der Ursprung von Recht und Unrecht bei Menschen und anderen Tieren*. München 1997, Chapter 1].
21. Kant writes: "Aber, obgleich es möglich ist, dass nach jener Maxime ein allgemeines Naturgesetz wohl bestehen könnte: so ist es doch unmöglich, zu WOLLEN, dass ein solches Prinzip als Naturgesetz allenthalben gelte. Denn ein Wille, der dieses beschlösse, würde sich selbst widerstreiten, indem der Fälle sich doch manche ereignen können, wo er anderer Liebe und Teilnehmung bedarf, und wo er durch ein solches aus seinem eigenen Willen entsprungenes Naturgesetz sich selbst alle Hoffnung des Beistandes, den er sich wünscht, rauben würde." (Immanuel Kant: *Kants Werke. Akademie - Textausgabe. Band IV*, Walter de Gruyter, Berlin, 1968, p. 423).
22. Michael Tomasello. *The Cultural Origins of Human Cognition*. (Cambridge: Harvard University Press, 1999). [German: *Die kulturelle Entwicklung des menschlichen Denkens*. Frankfurt a. M., 2002].
23. See my arguments on the phenomenon of phantasmatic self-affection in: "Zum Projekt einer Phänomenologie der Selbstaffektion. Über einige Methodenprobleme

und die Leistung der Selbstaffektion für die Analyse des Zeitbewußtseins," *Grenzen und Grenzüberschreitungen.* (Hrsg. W. Hogrebe, Bonn 2002, S. 1065–1075); in "Über phantasmatische Selbstaffektion in der typisierenden Apperzeption und im inneren Zeitbewußtsein. Beitrag zur Konferenz "Attualida della Phenomenologia," Mailand 2002, in: http://www.ledonline.it/leitmotiv/, S. 67–80. In English: "The function of weak phantasma in human and animal visual perception," *Image, Reason and Reasoning*, ed. by P. Grialou, G. Longo, M. Okada et. al. (Toyko: Keio University, 2005), pp. 165–181; "On the function of weak Phantasmata in Perception. Phenomenological and psychological clues for the transcendental function of weak phantasma in normal perception and in the Charles Bonnet Syndrome.," *Phenomenology and Cognitive Science* Vol. 4 (2005), pp. 155–167. Also, a book, entitled, *Phänomenologie der schwachen Phantasie. Beiträge der Psychologie, Neurologie und Phänomenologie zur Funktion der Phantasie in der Wahrnehmung*, is currently in preparation.

24. For Husserl's types in his genetic phenomenology, see: D. Lohmar. "*Husserl's Types and Kant's Schemata," The New Husserl: A Critical Reader*. ed. Donn Welton. (Indiana: Indiana University Press, 2003), pp. 93–124; and "*Über phantasmatische Selbstaffektion in der typisierenden Apperzeption und im inneren Zeitbewußtsein*" (also mentioned above), pp. 67–80.
25. Cf. here note no. 3.

6

Phenomenology and the Study of Animal Behavior

Erika RUONAKOSKI

Has the research on animal behavior anything to gain from phenomenology? And vice versa: has phenomenology something to learn from the different disciplines operating in this field, or is it a self-sufficing doctrine without any serious aspiration to look outside its immediate scope? After all, one might argue that it follows from the phenomenological reduction that the claims made by the empirical sciences are put aside in order to make room for lived experience. Using Merleau-Ponty's philosophy as my point of departure, I will show, however, that the experiental material collected by the empirical sciences can, nevertheless, be valuable to phenomenology, and moreover, that phenomenology can be helpful to the study of animal behavior, by elucidating the role of the scientist in her investigations.

Nowadays, animal behavior is studied from several perspectives, which partly overlap, including, comparative psychology, ethology, cognitive ethology[1], sociobiology, and social ecology. These approaches differ from each other in how much emphasis is given to general psychological theories, to the theory of evolution, and to physiology, and depending upon whether the research is performed predominantly in a laboratory or in field conditions. In this paper, I will focus my discussion on recent studies in two-way communication between humans and non-human animals, from the fields of comparative psychology and cognitive ethology. I will argue that phenomenological insights assist the study of animal communication, primarily by clarifying the relationship between the scientist and the research subject.

I. Merleau-Ponty on Studying Animals

In his early work, *The Structure of Behavior* (1942), as well as in his lectures on nature from the 1950's, Merleau-Ponty reviews a large body of psychological and ethological material on animal behavior.[2] Indeed, he studies numerous experiments on and descriptions of chimpanzees, hens, toads, etc., in great detail. What is his relationship to this material? What does a philosopher need it for?

First of all, for Merleau-Ponty the question of behavior is important philosophically, especially since it is in the living body of the other – the

C. Painter and C. Lotz (eds.), Phenomenology and the Non-Human Animal, 75–84.

body endowed with subjectivity, motivation, expressivity, and intentionality – that we encounter the other. From this perspective, it is not difficult to see how Merleau-Ponty comes to claim that already in animal behavior we encounter something that challenges the division of being into "being-in-itself" and "being-for-itself," which is to say, the division between pure being and pure consciousness. Second, one of Merleau-Ponty's aims is to criticize the philosophical inconsistencies in the psychological approaches, and as such, he works to give a new interpretation to the material. Accordingly, even though Merleau-Ponty finds psychological material helpful, he does not embrace the ontological presuppositions of psychology, whether they are those that belong to behaviorism or to Gestalt psychology. On the contrary, he is very critical of them. Third, Merleau-Ponty claims that animal studies can be used to challenge philosophers' own customary views, both about animal nature and about intersubjectivity. Consequently, it is hardly surprising that in *The Structure of Behavior*, Merleau-Ponty's views on human specificity draw heavily from the insights of psychiatrist Kurt Goldstein, as well as from the Gestalt psychologist Wolfgang Köhler's insights. Indeed, in his later lectures on nature, Merleau-Ponty focuses on detailed ethological data, on the basis of which he comes to modify his views, making them subtler and ultimately allowing room for the notion of "animal culture".[3]

Moreover, Merleau-Ponty questions the behaviorist way of interpreting the scientist's role, which demands that the scientist be detached from her subject of study and that she avoid using terms that might carry her own emotions along with them. In sharp contrast to this attitude, Merleau-Ponty suggests that when describing what she sees in the animal, the scientist should start from her own emotions and expressions, and their meanings. In the Gestalt psychologist Wolfgang Köhler's work, he claims to have found precisely this kind of approach.

Köhler was well-known for his findings on the problem-solving abilities of chimpanzees. In *The Mentality of the Apes* (1925/59; originally published in 1917), Köhler attributes emotions such as joy and excitement to chimpanzees, and he tries to specify the context within which the gestures and body positions associated with these emotions are displayed, and to see the possible differences between human and chimpanzee behavior.[4] In regard to Köhler's work, in his essay, "The Metaphysical in Man," Merleau-Ponty writes:

> K[ö]hler's work shows indisputably that, in addition to our own perceptual universe, we have to reconstitute the animal's universe in all its originality, with its "irrational" connections, its short-circuits, and its lacunae, and that any success we may have will come from taking our human experience as our starting point.[5]

According to Merleau-Ponty, the scientist's aim should be to describe the animal's behavior as it appears to us, i.e., to humans. What is more, the scientist should not be too afraid of using qualitative concepts that we link to our own behavior or experience, even though they may not exhaust the phenomena with which we are dealing. To be truly scientific, psychology should not reject altogether the human experience of the animal but should embrace it. Consequently, we should not exaggerate our fears of anthropomorphism, though this does not mean, of course, that we should allow dubious conclusions. Rather, we should acknowledge that *human experience is the only possible starting point for our investigations*, and we should grow increasingly sensitive to the possible differences and similarities between the human and the non-human.

In Merleau-Ponty's view, it is essential to see that knowledge is only possible through one's finite situation – i.e., through finitude – and that it is precisely this situation (of finitude) that provides one with a connection to other people and to their points of view. The awareness of one's own situation makes one interested in other people's situations and allows one to see one's own situation as a variation of these others.[6] According to Merleau-Ponty, the sciences of man make it evident that all knowledge within them means:

> the taking up by each, *as best he can*, the acts of others, reactivating from ambiguous signs an experience which is not his own, appropriating a structure (e.g., the *a priori* of the species, the sublinguistic schema or spirit of a civilization) of which he forms no distinct concept but which he puts together as an experienced pianist deciphers an unknown piece of music: without himself grasping the motives of each gesture or each operation, without being able to bring to the surface of consciousness all the sediment of knowledge which he is using at that moment.[7]

Here, the term "*a priori* of the species" refers, specifically, to non-human species. However, it is clear that we may approach these non-human others from our own human perspective, as we try to reactivate in ourselves this foreign experience to which we always-already have a connection.

On the other hand, to do this is a difficult task; for, just as we cannot live the experience of a poet of the 16th Century, neither can we capture the experience of a chimpanzee, a parrot, or a gorilla, without any mediations. We can, however, without abandoning the standards of scientific rigor, give ourselves over to the task and the project of interpretation, and in so doing, we can be open to non-human animal others. In this connection, Merleau-Ponty writes, "here we no longer have the positing of an *object*, but rather we have communication with a way of being."[8] Accordingly, on his view, if we are studying a dog, a chimpanzee, or a parrot, we do not treat it as an object but encounter it as a living body with which we can communicate. As Merleau-Ponty points out, we cannot really approach the animal from any other perspective than our own, the human one – if we assume or claim something else, we are deluding ourselves. On the other hand, it is entirely necessary to develop a sensitivity towards the nuances of the animal other's behavior, since without this our understanding remains vague and confused.

In this connection, Jane Goodall, who is well-known for her long-term study on chimpanzees living in the Gombe National Reserve in Tanzania, writes that when she started her work in 1960, it was not permissible to talk about an animal's mind or personality. Having no undergraduate education in science, however, she ended up freely using the forbidden, "anthropomorphic" terms.[9] Since then, the atmosphere has become more tolerant. Interestingly, Goodall points out that empathy and intuition are tremendous tools when attempting to "understand certain complex behavioral interactions, provided that the behavior, as it occurs, is recorded precisely and objectively."[10] In fact, she even states that it is difficult to empathize with emotions we have not experienced ourselves; for instance, after having an infant of her own, she reports that it became easier for her to understand the feelings of a chimpanzee mother protecting her child, and that after experiencing the numbing grief that followed the death of her husband, she could "begin to appreciate the despair and sense of loss that can cause young chimps to pine away and die when they lose their mothers."[11]

Goodall's description is in harmony with the phenomenological understanding of our relationships to others, or, more specifically, of empathy as something through which we can understand others. For, I am able to empathetically project myself into the living body of the other, and understand her gestures and facial expressions *through my own bodily experience*. In this vein, if the young chimpanzee looked joyful or did not display any change in its behavior after the death of his mother, and we claimed that it was grieving, then we would be falsely projecting our own feelings about the death of a close person to the chimpanzee. However, this would also mean that we were not truly empathetic towards him but that we overlooked his actual behavior, and instead made a false inference about his emotions. What is called for, then, is continuous sensitivity towards the other living body, since this makes correction of earlier interpretations possible.

With some gestures of non-human animals we can empathize with ease, while others remain more distant. But even if it may be difficult to understand the meaning of a dog's wagging tail as such, in Edith Stein's words, it is possible to "understand the tail wagging of a dog as an expression of joy if its appearance and its behavior otherwise disclose such feelings and its situation warrants them."[12] There is, here, a unity of meaning: something that has been unfamiliar to me so far, becomes intelligible, as it happens within a meaningful whole and in a situation, which includes a possibility to learn more about the other soul-body.[13]

II. The Situatedness of the Human Experience of Non-human Animals

In the beginning of our encounter with another species we may hesitate, or be too fearful or too trustful; for instance, if we are not familiar with dogs, we do not know what to expect from them in a given situation. This means that when we encounter a barking dog, we may not be able to tell whether she is aggressive or whether she is barking for some other reason. However, the experience of encountering another human being or a dog does not happen in a void. Rather, the situation will provide us with hints about the meaning of the other's behavior: does it seem likely that the dog feels threatened? Or is there a ball on the floor that the dog might expect me to throw for her to fetch?

Similarly, I might encounter a seagull while drinking tea on the terrace of a seaside café, and I might enter into a non-voluntary exchange with it. The situation may lead me to interpret the seagull's intentions in a certain way: perhaps it watches for an opportunity to snatch some of my cake. Later, as a result of a momentary lapse of attention, this anticipation may prove well-founded. Had I never been in a similar situation before, I might think that the gull is there to make friends, but again, the development of the situation would guide my interpretation. In this way, many of the scientists' claims that come in the form "it may *seem* to us humans that the animal is 'X'… but *in reality* it is…'Y' " do not stem from any detached observation of the animal, nor do they depend upon a higher level of objectivity, which escapes the layman's subjective way of viewing things. Instead, they draw precisely on an empathetic understanding of the other. With time, scientists will naturally make the interpretation increasingly nuanced, according to the particular features of the encounter and the environment; nevertheless, they still rely upon a non-detached, subjectively situated interpretation of the "object" of study.

Indeed, starting from the actual encounter with the non-human animal, it soon turns out that it is impossible to describe her behavior without referring to the common surrounding world. Surely, for instance, the dog's perception of the world is different from mine – this becomes evident when I perceive something that the dog cannot perceive with the same ease, and vice versa – but we nevertheless share the same space-time, against the background of which our behavior appears as meaningful and as goal-oriented. I can throw the ball over *there*, and the dog will bring it back *here*. Our gestures and movements take place in a particular space, they trace directions onto it, and the directedness of our bodies is to me – as a participant in the game – constitutive of the fundamental level of our *mutual understanding*. In the same way, my interactions with the seagull depend upon a bodily understanding of the directedness of the gull's body.

In this connection, in his article "Cognitive Ethology, Vigilance, Information Gathering, and Representation: Who Might Know What and Why?," Marc Bekoff maintains that claims "about minds and electrons are posited as hypothetical constructs because they make the most sense of the data that have been collected."[14] It is hard to believe, however, that the animal "mind" would be merely a *hypothesis*; for, indeed, the researcher has very likely already experienced the living bodies of the animals as manifesting a certain kind of intentionality, motivation, and subjectivity – and thus intelligibility – rather than as exhibiting a mere mechanical relationship with the environment.

Following this line of thought, intentionality, understood in the Merleau-Pontian way, does not (in its original form) consist in beliefs or thoughts but in motility, just as consciousness does not originally appear in the form of "I think" but in the form of "I can."[15] This helps us to understand why we experience animals' actions as intentional, even though we may not have a clear picture of what, exactly, goes on "in the animal's head." The actions of an animal, such as walking toward a goal or going round an obstacle, already manifest to us a directedness and motivation, which cannot be explained away by saying that we project our own intentions onto it; for, as Merleau-Ponty points out, "we could not project our feelings into the visible behavior of an animal if something in this behavior itself did not suggest such an inference to us."[16]

In any case, phenomenology does not posit "hypothetical constructs," as it aims to describe what appears in experience as truthfully as possible. And, as phenomenology makes clear, what appears, *appears to somebody*. As such, the problem of the other mind arises only if we cut ourselves out of the picture, i.e., if we presuppose that the existence of another mind should be *demonstrated* without any reference to our role as participants in the situation. Thus, in phenomenology embodied, situational subjectivity is not understood as a source of confusion, but as a necessary point of departure for knowledge. Consequently, when we interact with others, we experience a certain subjectivity manifesting itself, but we do not grasp this subjectivity in the same way as we grasp our own consciousness; neither, however, do we experience it as something non-bodily[17], or as something to which we only have inferential (formally epistemic) access. For this reason, from the point of view of the study of animal behavior, an approach dealing with the directedness of the body may prove more fruitful than leaping directly into speaking about the animals' "beliefs." On the other hand, the newest research on two-way communication between humans and non-human animals can prove enlightening to phenomenology itself.

III. Do Animals Mean What They "Say?"

While Köhler described in detail the various gestural ways in which the chimpanzees at the Anthropoid Station communicated both with each other and with humans, he remained skeptical of their actual language abilities.[18] Since Köhler's days, it has been established that the difficulties in teaching spoken human languages to anthropoids primarily stem from their physical inability to produce the sounds needed in human languages. Today, Washoe, the chimpanzee, and Koko, the gorilla, are well known for their abilities to communicate via ASL (American sign language), for which both received instruction since a very early age. Koko's current (2006) vocabulary, is reported to consist of over 1000 ASL signs, and she is said to understand about 2000 spoken English words.[19] In addition to this, Irene Pepperberg has developed a method for teaching parrots to speak English referentially. The best known of the parrots is named Alex, and according to Pepperberg, Alex has labeled "over 50 exemplars, 7 colors, 5 shapes, quantity to 6," and used the expressions "no," "come here," "wanna go X," and "want Y" referentially.[20]

These two-way communication projects are still in progress and are presently under evaluation. According to one of the critiques, animals in these projects are treated unfairly because they have to perform tasks for which they are not well-suited. Primatologist Frans de Waal, for instance, admits having mixed feelings about ape language research: on the one hand, it is "a thoroughly anthropocentric enterprise," while, on the other hand, it can be seen as an important "window on the ape mind."[21] To be sure, the apes and parrots in these studies are introduced to human culture and they can therefore be viewed, to some degree, as "humanized." However this may be, in acknowledging that this introduction to human culture is possible, and that communication between animals and humans is possible, the following question arises: What kind of relationship between these animals and the researchers makes this possible?

Both Koko and Washoe were taken care of in ways similar to the way in which human infants are (typically) cared for. Moreover, the attitude of Francine Patterson, Koko's instructor, could even be described as motherly.[22] As such, the attitude of the scientist is, in this case at least, from the beginning on, interactive rather than detached. It is important to note, here, that even a human child would not learn to communicate with others, if she were not treated as a potential interlocutor from the very beginning. Irene Pepperberg, for her part, uses what may be called a model-rival technique, within which the parrot can observe while the trainer pretends to be training a human assistant to recognize different objects, etc. Here, the assistant is both a model for the parrot's responses and a rival for the trainer's attention. Thus, what we are dealing with is a "social learning situation," which could be compared to the learning situation within a family with several children.[23] It is interesting to note, in this connection, that Kanzi, a bonobo with outstanding communication skills, started to learn lexigrams in a similar situation: spontaneously, after watching the less successful efforts of the researchers to train her mother.[24] I would claim that in these studies of two-way communication, the scientists make implicit use of the intercorporeity that exists between humans and non-human animals; for, indeed, if one did not see the gestural comprehensibility between humans and parrots as at least possible, there would hardly be any efforts to teach parrots using a method that presupposes an ability to learn in a simplified but still humanly defined social context.

In the kind of approach that has been discussed in the preceding pages, the nature of the animal's experience can be left open. As in Köhler's case, we can take the human experience as a point of departure, but not blindly, such that we would deny the possible differences between humans and animals. This approach could be described as a gradual awakening to the different mode of being of the non-human animal, and, it would imply a certain humility, as well as an attitude of wonder. As such, this approach to the human study of animal behavior would cease to cling to a set of presuppositions, and it would likewise stop encouraging the researcher to detach herself from her research subject, given that such a detachment is not only undesirable, but also, from a phenomenological perspective, impossible.

IV. Phenomenology and the Study of Animal Behavior

Let us return to my initial question: can there be any *dialogue* between phenomenology and the study of animal behavior in its many forms? As I have tried to demonstrate, phenomenology can help the study of animal behavior by clarifying the relationship between the scientist and the research subject. In this vein, it is possible to follow Merleau-Ponty's footsteps and take a closer look at the fundamental ontological assumptions of the researcher, the way that he did when dealing with Köhler's work, for instance, on the basis of which he showed that despite the success Köhler had in studying animal behavior, there still remained a conflict between his initial approach and his final reductionism to physical reality. Similarly, it would be illuminating to try to think in detail about whether the representational theory of mind that Pepperberg and Bekoff apply is the best way of dealing with animal behavior, or whether a phenomenological approach can further clarify things. On the other hand, if Pepperberg's description of the results of the model-rival technique is accurate, is this something that phenomenology can overlook? The answer should be "no," since we are dealing with well-recorded experiences that a philosopher cannot obtain from her armchair and that can in turn serve to challenge her customary views. As a case in point, contrary to Merleau-Ponty's presumption, non-human animals are – we now know – able to acquire skills in symbolic (human) language, so long as they are exposed to methods sensitive enough to their particular learning abilities. In this way, the boundary between humans and non-humans appears less clear-cut than was earlier thought, and it is scientific research that has helped us to learn this.[25]

Even if we did not want to modify our ways of viewing the human mode of being, we might have to be more careful about what we claim about non-human animal species. In any case, our views regarding human specificity will have to be reconsidered and modified, as we see that many skills, earlier considered specifically human, now turn out to be shared with other animal species. Instead of positing non-human species as "deficient" human beings or as less developed versions of humans, we might attempt to take on an attitude of wonder, on the basis of which we could try to see non-human animals absent our habitual presuppositions. Here, the studies of researchers such as Pepperberg can act as an inspiration, inasmuch as they reveal to us a well-recorded and surprisingly rich experience of non-human animals. From this perspective, a plurality of different modes of being is opened up, and in this way, we can acknowledge that we are not dealing with a minor, philosophically uninteresting "detail," but with a new opening to our very being-in-the-world.

To be sure, the dialogue that Merleau-Ponty established between the study of animal behavior and phenomenology should be carried further. Indeed, according to Merleau-Ponty, the relationship between science and philosophy is not one-way but *reciprocal*. For, as Merleau-Ponty argued:

> A science without philosophy would literally not know what it was talking about. A philosophy without methodical exploration of phenomena would end up with nothing but formal truths, which is to say, errors.[26]

In Merleau-Ponty's view, philosophy continually needs to "try to think through to the very end the same phenomena which science lays siege to, only restoring to them their original transcendence and strangeness."[27] As regards animal behavior, or more correctly, as regards our possible communication with non-human animal experience, this philosophical effort is only in its beginning stage.

Notes

1. Cognitive ethology is a comparatively new, interdisciplinary approach, which draws from both classical ethology and cognitive science. During its existence, cognitive ethology has been strongly informed by contemporary, analytic philosophy of mind.
2. See Merleau-Ponty, Maurice. *Structure du comportement* (Paris: Presses Universitaires de France 1942/90) and Merleau-Ponty, Maurice. *The Structure of Behavior*. Translation by Alden L. Fisher. (Pittsburgh: Duquesne University Press 1962/98).
3. See Merleau-Ponty, Maurice. *La Nature. Notes. Cours du Collège de France* (Paris: Seuil, 1995).
4. Köhler's research was not about chimpanzee emotions, however, but about intelligent behavior and insight.
5. Merleau-Ponty, Maurice. "The Metaphysical in Man" in *Sens and Non-Sens* (Evanston: Northwestern University Press, 1964), p. 84.
6. Merleau-Ponty, Maurice. "Le philosophe et la sociologie" in *Signes* (Paris: Gallimard, 1960), pp. 137–138.
7. Merleau-Ponty, 1964, p. 93.
8. Ibid, p. 93.
9. Goodall, Jane. *Through a Window. My Thirty Years with the Chimpanzees of Gombe* (Boston: Houghton Mifflin Company, 1990), p. 14.
10. Ibid., p. 17.
11. Ibid.
12. Stein, Edith. *On the Problem of Empathy. The Collected Works of Edith Stein*, Volume Three. (Washington, D.C.: ICS Publications, 1989). Translated by Waltraut Stein. (*Zum Problem der Einfühlung*. Halle, Buchdruckerei des Weisenhauses, 1917), p. 98.
13. For a more detailed analysis of the role that empathy plays in human access to animal others, which draws heavily upon the work of Edith Stein, see: Painter,

"Appropriating the Philosophies of Edmund Husserl and Edith Stein: Animal Psyche, Empathy, and Moral Subjectivity," which appears in this volume.

14. Bekoff, Marc. "Cognitive Ethology, Vigilance, Information Gathering, and Representation: Who Might Know What and Why?" *Behavioural Processes* 35 (1996), pp. 225–237.
15. Merleau-Ponty, Maurice. *Phénoménologie de la perception* (Paris: Gallimard, 1945/98), p. 123.
16. See Merleau-Ponty, Maurice, 1962/98.
17. Ibid., pp. 124–128.
18. See Köhler, Wolfgang. *The Mentality of Apes* (Vintage: New York, 1925/59), pp. 271–274.
19. This is the figure given by the webpages of "Koko.org" in January 2006.
20. See Pepperberg, Irene, "Lessons from Cognitive Ethology: Animal Models for Ethological Computing" *Proceedings from the 1st International Workshop on Epigenetic Robotics: Modeling Cognitive Development in Robotic Systems* (URL: http://www.lucs.lu.se/epigenetic-robotics/papers/Pepperberg.pdf., 2001) "Wanna go X" is here short for wanting to go somewhere, whereas "want Y" is short for wanting something.
21. Pepperberg, Irene. "Vocal Learning in Grey Parrots (Psittacus Erithacus): Effects of Social Interaction, Reference and Context." *The Auk* 111 (1994/2), p. 44.
22. See Patterson, Francine and Linden, Eugene. *The Education of Koko* (New York, Holt, Rinehart, and Winston, 1981).
23. See Pepperberg, 1994 and 2001.
24. Waal, Frans de. *Bonobo – The Forgotten Ape. Photographs Frans Lanting* (Berkeley: University of California Press, 1997), p. 44.
25. Of course, this does not mean that we should deny the differences between ourselves and non-human animals. After studying chimpanzees for several decades Jane Goodall writes (1990, 207): "[E]ven if we do not differ from the apes in kind, but only in degree, that degree is still overwhelmingly large. [...] Above all, we have developed intellectual abilities that dwarf those of even the most gifted chimpanzees." She also suggests certain reservations towards the language abilities in chimpanzees: "It is true that they can be *taught* to use signs or symbols of a human-type language. And they have cognitive skills to combine these signs into meaningful sentences. Mentally, at least, it would seem that chimpanzees stand at the threshold of language acquisition. But those forces that were at work when humans began to speak have obviously played no role in shaping chimpanzee intellect in this direction" (Goodall, 1990, 208).
26. Merleau-Ponty, 1964, p. 97.
27. Ibid.

7

The Intentionality and Animal Heritage of Moral Experience

What we can Learn from Dogs About Moral Theory

Charles S. BROWN

> I fully subscribe to the judgment of those writers who maintain that of all the differences between man and the lower animals, the moral sense or conscience is the most important
>
> (Charles Darwin, *The Descent of Man*)

> Besides love and sympathy, animals exhibit other qualities connected with the social instincts, which in us would be called moral; and I agree with Agassiz that dogs possess something like a conscience
>
> (Charles Darwin, *The Descent of Man*)

> In the agony of death a dog has been known to caress his master, and every one has heard of the dog suffering vivisection, who licked the hand of the operator; this man, unless he was fully justified by an increase of our knowledge, or unless he had a heart of stone, must have felt remorse to the last hour of his life
>
> (Charles Darwin, *The Descent of Man*)

> Dogs shew what may be fairly called a sense of humour, as distinct from mere play; if a bit of stick or other such object be thrown to one, he will often carry it away for a short distance; and then squatting down with it on the ground close before him, will wait until his master comes quite close to take it away. The dog will then seize it and rush away in triumph, repeating the same maneuver, and evidently enjoying the practical joke
>
> (Charles Darwin, *The Descent of Man*)

Animal welfare theorists and environmental philosophers have generally come to reject what they see as anthropocentric assumptions, which they claim limit the power and scope of traditional moral theory in its attempt to provide

C. Painter and C. Lotz (eds.), Phenomenology and the Non-Human Animal, 85–95.

an adequate understanding of moral phenomena and the moral life. Ecofeminists have expanded this critique to argue that traditional moral theory is not just structured by and biased in favor of anthropocentric assumptions, but structured by and biased in favor of a series of metaphysical and epistemological assumptions resulting from an interlocking and mutually supporting series of value hierarchical dualisms that privilege reason over emotion, objectivity over subjectivity, the universal over the particular, the human over the animal, and the masculine over the feminine. In this vein, Val Plumwood argues that the resulting approach to moral philosophy is inadequate, as it typically devalues "particular, emotional, and kinship-based attachments."[1] Feminist philosophers, animal welfare theorists, and environmental philosophers have each sought to pursue ethical theory in a manner that overcomes this incompleteness or inadequacy of traditional moral philosophy.

On Plumwood's analysis, traditional moral theory further assumes a conception of the self (human self) that is structured by these interlocking dualities in a way that renders this self excessively masculine, egoistic, as well as separate from and superior to non-human nature. Over and against this view of the self,[2] she considers Arne Naess's conception of an "ecological self" which, on her reading, defines the self as *indistinguishable from*, rather than *opposed to* nature. As an alternative to both of these conceptions, Plumwood proposes a conception of the self as "self-in-relationship." She argues that such a conception of human identity – indeed, a conception of human *moral subjectivity* – would provide an appropriate foundation for an ethic of connectedness and caring for others.

I contend that Plumwood is correct to see a correspondence between moral theory and a conception of the moral self, which is the self of moral experience. Her suggestion of a "relational self" is surely on the right track toward developing a more sophisticated, comprehensive, and adequate moral theory. With this in mind, in the following pages, I will develop the outlines of a philosophical anthropology that is capable of providing the sort of foundation for an ethic of connectedness and caring for others that Plumwood seeks. This will require a conception of human self-identity that is informed by a Darwinian conception of the animal heritage of moral experience and a phenomenological conception of the intrinsic rationality of moral experience. This framework for understanding moral phenomena allows us, as Plumwood suggests, to pay attention to the "rich, caring, relationships of kinship and friendship rather than to the increasing abstraction and detachment from relationship."[3] Additionally, this approach to moral philosophy allows us a way into Plumwood's project of "revaluing and reintegrating what rationalist culture has split apart, denied, and devalued."[4] The resulting conception of the self will allow for a framework within which we can find a place for emotion, subjectivity, particularity, and animality in moral philosophy.

One way to begin the project of revaluing and reintegrating what has been devalued and denied (by mainstream moral philosophy) lies in the possibilities of a naturalistically informed phenomenology of moral experience.

The perspective of moral phenomena – which necessarily includes moral subjectivity – explored here will be a "bottom-up approach," which begins with an exanimation of moral experience that will highlight the importance of animality, subjective feeling, and particularity to value experience. By describing the intentional structure that lies within the meaning and significance of value experience, we will see that ordinary value experience exhibits a *prima facie* form of rationality, which cannot be dismissed as "mere" sentiment. Attention to this sort of experience undermines the mutual exclusivity within the traditionally drawn dichotomy of reason and emotion. Furthermore, the value sentiments and feelings examined here are understood to have a long natural history, shaped by the process of natural selection. On this understanding, the root phenomena of moral experience lie directly in our animality and not in the uniquely human capacity of language and abstract calculation.

Phenomenology's distinctive method of describing the subjective realities of human experience has always been proceeded by a refusal to reduce subjectivity, and more importantly, meaning, to the bare facts of nature. This traditional methodological restraint will not be violated here. What will be violated is phenomenology's insistence that description of the subjective and the meaningful (i.e., the intentional) must be strictly independent of any natural sciences or natural facts. This methodological limitation, which is responsible for much of phenomenology's success for the last one hundred years, now stands as a barrier to a more comprehensive account of subjectivity and meaning. By placing the subjectivity and meaningful realities of human existence in a natural context (here, a Darwinian account of human nature), while not reducing them to the bare facts of nature, it may be possible to establish a pragmatic "middle ground" between moral objectivity and the subjectivity of "mere" sentiment. This will, in turn, allow us to consider a naturalistic-phenomenological alternative to, or perhaps version of, the feminist conception of a relational self. This inquiry is a first step in that direction.

In the *Descent of Man*, Charles Darwin attempts to show that humanity's "moral sense" follows from "the enduring and ever present nature of the social instincts." In this connection, Darwin writes that,

> Animals endowed with the social instincts take pleasure in one another's company, warn one another of danger, defend and aid one another in many ways... [Moreover], as they (social instincts) are highly beneficial to the species, they have in all probability been acquired through natural selection.[5]

A few natural scientists and philosophers are currently exploring the implications of Darwin's speculations on the origin of morality. Common to this general line of thought is the idea that the distinctly human "moral sense" is made possible by the combination of these social instincts with the faculty of reason or language. While the claim that morality is made possible by the linguistic conceptualization of inherited social feelings is on the right track, I believe, it overlooks an important phenomenological fact about moral experience, namely: moral experience and moral phenomena display an intentional structure not captured by the view of morality as "instinct plus language" (*logos*). Thus, what is missing from the received view concerning a Darwinian account of morality is a theory of intentionality.

Our basic dispositional ways of being open to the world, i.e., our basic possibilities are, no doubt, pre-figured in our genes and thus in our kinship with other animals. Consequently, while the fundamentals of our moral psychology may start off as gut instinct, these basic proto moral sentiments are not just reactions to outside stimuli but have the quality of being directed to something or being about something. Empathy, for instance, is always empathy about something. Altruism, similarly, is aimed at the other. Moral sentiments are experienced by humans not as "raw feels," or unstructured qualia, but as referring to the other in an attitude of empathy. These are psychological-somatological moments that exhibit a pre-discursive intelligibility and a *prima facie* rationality. These social instincts, as Darwin refers to them, i.e., compassion, sympathy, and feeling, are not simply Humean impressions (as Darwin seems to think) but display an intentional structure that provides or denies justification of the lived sense of that experience.[6] For instance, to experience life within a community of living beings as good, is to interpret and impose the sense of good upon life within a community of living beings, but it is also to expect to continue to find goodness in that life and to have such expectations met. It is precisely here, I submit, that we may begin to find a measure of rationality within our moral experiences.

Moral theory and moral philosophy may be a uniquely human activity, but humans are not alone in their basic capacity to respond to the world in an attitude of concern. Social mammals are very much like humans in this respect and thus they share with us, at least in some basic way, a moral or proto moral openness to the world. Dogs – as well as cats, horses, and some others – have been "taken out of the wild" and bred to fit into human community more smoothly, the result of which has been a human-canine symbiosis within which dogs and humans are emotionally in tune, inasmuch as our concerns often overlap, as we (humans and dogs) care about many of the same things. The following moral fable will focus on the emotionality and particularity of moral experience, while illustrating the moral openness to the world shared by humans and dogs. This, in turns, locates the roots of our moral nature in our animal nature.

Imagine that my canine companion, Lily,[7] and I are playing in my backyard, which is separated from my neighbor's back yard by a large privacy fence. Because of this fence, Lily and I cannot see into the neighbor's yard, where another dog lives. Further imagine that one day the dog in the adjacent yard is terribly injured and Lily and I hear the dog's screams and howls even though we cannot see him. Lily and I share a common response to the other dog's suffering. We hear and understand his pain and suffering in his howls. We both experience a considerable anxiety and an empathetic concern directed toward the injured dog. We both experience a sense of dread over what will happen next. We know something is wrong. We share the immediacy and urgency of the situation. She feels she needs to do something but she doesn't know what. She feels frustration on top of an anguished concern for the dog. I know Lily feels this, because I feel it as well. In fact, *we feel it together*. This is a *shared experience*; in this moment of intersubjectivity, my anxieties and concerns are reinforced by Lily's and hers by mine. I see her behave very nervously, running to the fence, pawing at it, running back and forth and around in circles; she looks at me and seems to be frightened, she whines and barks. I can hear the agitation and concern in Lily's sounds and she can hear it in mine. She and I are *co-witnesses* to vulnerability, tragedy, and suffering.

Skeptics will claim that my interpretations of Lily's experience are mere projections. Yet I believe that Lily and I share a feeling with a similar intentional structure, a similar cognitive directedness toward the injured dog with similar anticipations. One large difference is that I interpret my anguish at the dog's pain through numerous millennia of linguistic history and the metaphysical categories that dominate those worldviews. But the basic way of experiencing the suffering of the wounded dog is not so different between me and Lily. Neither of us has direct access to the dog's pain, but we seem to have something close to, if not identical to, direct access to the dog's suffering, just as we have with humans. Both of us experience a sense of urgency, that something is terribly wrong, and a sense that something must be done now, as well as the frustration of not knowing what, exactly, to do. This sense of urgency, experienced as a vague and diffused imperative to act, is intimately tied up with the immediacy and the particularity of the situation. I believe this kind of response is a part of human moral psychology that we share with many mammals and primates.

Both Lily and I share an attitude of concern and empathy toward the other's suffering. Indeed, we share an immediate intuition that something is wrong. This intuition is as much somatic as it is cognitive. We feel it, as Hume would say, in our "breast," as much as we project it toward the howling dog. My own human response to the howls of the hurt dog – which includes the somatic anxiety dreadfully directed to the suffering dog, a gut reaction that something is wrong, and a vague and diffuse feeling that something should be done (I think I share all this with Lily) – is integrated into my own linguistically based conceptual system and worldview. The pre-linguistic intentional comportment of my felt sentiment is conceptualized in ways that Lily's is not. I suspect that Lily's pre-linguistic intentional comportments, in this case, an empathetic openness to the suffering of others, come and go, and play themselves out quickly, whereas in my own case, the symbolic power of language extends these sentiments by binding them to longer term projects.

While I think that Lily and I begin at a similar place, from a mammalian response to suffering, my own intentional comportment toward the injured dog goes far beyond what I suspect Lily is capable of. Both Lily and I try to get past the fence to access more closely what is happening. The original experience of hearing those howls has been extended into a seeking out of more information: we both look to see what is wrong, we both anticipate and project. These anticipations and projections may be confirmed or disconfirmed in future experience. If we managed to come face to face with the injured dog and I see that the dog is caught in a non-humane wolf trap, I will search for a way to release the dog. My recognition of the trap as a human artifact opens my experience into new conceptual domains and worlds, which bleed into my understanding. In contrast, I do not think Lily would understand the wolf trap, as her projections are more immediate. However, if we got through the fence and saw that the dog was being eaten by a lion, Lily would, I think, understand this. For Lily, all this would unfold into projections of her immediate future. She would run from the lion, anticipating trouble if she stays put, but her power to extend her experience into the future or into other symbolic domains is cut short by her lack of language.

The structure and content of human cognition, moral or otherwise, is distinguished from other pre-linguistic animals by the temporal range and symbolic worlds that language gives to our immediate sentiments. As our moral instincts are folded into our conceptual systems they take on new meanings. I can imagine, for example, that if I came through the fence and found the dog in an old and carelessly discarded wolf trap, my empathetic anxiety of shared suffering would begin to take on an air of moral disapproval, as the trapped animal opens up the world of animal trapping, which in turn, opens up the world of human domination of nature. To be sure, this sense of disapproval is largely cultural and conceptual, but it is made possible and sustained over time by the gut feeling, the moral instinct, that something is wrong. Lily and I can both hear that in the howls; we share this experience in common.

Because value experiences are intentional, they bring with them their own procedure for confirmation, which is grounded in the temporal structure of anticipation and either the satisfaction or the frustration of such anticipation. Value experiences are structured by an intrinsic temporality (a reference to the future) that provides or denies a justification for the lived sense of that experience. If I experience friendship or marriage to be good for me, it is not simply that I *enjoy* friendship and marriage, it is because I have a sense, even if unarticulated, of how and why they are *good*. Even if we cannot express it, we know that friendship and marriage extend our sphere of concern, while comforting us in ways that provide our lives with meaning. To experience friendship and marriage as good is to interpret and impose a *sense of good* on these relations, but it also implies an expectation of continuing to find these relations good and to have such expectations fulfilled. The very experience of positive values, like marriage and friendship, is bound up with an implicit understanding of the meaning of marriage and friendship. Our experience of these *as good* is also subject to the possibility of a breakdown or a rejection, as the "final test" of value is the test of time.

Lily would not understand marriage, as it is subject to complex social rules, but friendship is a different story. Whether we wish to call it "friendship" is, perhaps, debatable, but Lily does experience an emotional connection to her human family that provides her life with some kind of meaning. Experiences of positive value that we call good involve knowing what to expect. It is this anticipatory structure that provides an ongoing validation of our experiences of the good. If we initially find friendship and marriage to be bad and fraud to be good, openness to further experience will almost always correct this. Finding value in friendship and disvalue in fraud is not arbitrary. Rarely do these things disappoint us. Our experience continues to establish these as goods in an ever evolving process of being open to the good.

The approach to moral philosophy sketched here differs considerably from the traditional and mainstream approach to moral theory critiqued by Plumwood. The Darwinian assumptions concerning the animal heritage of humanity's social instincts and moral sentiments disrupt the anthropocentricism of traditional moral theory, while the phenomenological description of the intentionality inherent in these sentiments disrupts the primacy of the objectivity, universality, and rationality that is characteristic of traditional moral theory. Traditional moral theory is a top-down and monistic affair, which typically begins by assuming that moral phenomena can be reduced to some single essential criterion; for Kant, it is a good will, for Bentham, consequences, for the Egoist, self-interest, and for the contract theorist, shared agreements. Once these essential insights are in place, moral philosophy becomes a matter of unpacking the implications inherent in the first principles or master rules based on those essential insights. Each of the historically influential modern moral theories admirably makes the case for the moral relevancy of the feature (or features) it picks out as the essential mark(s) of moral phenomena. Each theory claims to do a better job than its rivals at explaining its carefully chosen set of core examples, but each does a poor job of making philosophical sense out of others. While these theories provide us with deep and rich insights into moral phenomena, they fail to provide the single and universal set of criteria for all moral phenomena, as they claim. Instead, they highlight certain aspects of moral phenomena at the expense of others.

The approach to moral philosophy that begins with the description of *lived moral experience* assumes an attitude of respect for pre-theorectical experience and is open to a kind of moral pluralism within which a duty to tell the truth may be grounded, in one case, in utility, and in another case, in respect for persons. In any case, a phenomenological approach to moral philosophy does not rule out, in an a priori manner, the moral relevance of subjectivity, emotion, animality, or particularity, but instead finds a place for these elements of moral experience that have been dismissed by the excessive rationalism of traditional moral theory. By taking a phenomenological approach and returning to the moral "things themselves," i.e., our actual experiences, we are in a position to rethink the dualities structuring and silently colonizing traditional moral thinking. Here, we, like Plumwood, find the human-animal or reason-emotion distinctions to be inadequately characterized by that tradition. The *prima facie* from of rationality found within moral experience is not separate or discontinuous from subjectivity, emotion, animality, or particularity.

Traditional moral theory is monistic in another way that differs from a phenomenological approach in that it assumes a monistic criterion for whom or what matters morally. To the extent that traditional moral philosophy is anthropocentric, it typically assumes that moral considerability results from either being made in the image of God, or being rational, or simply being human. The relevant criterion for moral considerability is objective, determinately specifiable, and independent of particular beliefs or sentiments. Traditional attempts to establish a single criterion of moral essence and moral considerability, once again, run counter to ordinary experience. In everyday experience we intuitively find that both the consequences of our actions and respect for the subjective integrity of the other are morally relevant; we also regularly find both humans and nonhumans as being worthy of moral regard.

When metaphysical theories, such as anthropocentricism (rooted in value-hierarchical dualities and structured by a logic of domination), are at odds with ordinary experience, it is often the meaning or significance of the direct experiences that gets played down or even dismissed in order to protect the theory. Darwin's story of the dog suffering vivisection reminds us of the power of worldviews to guide and interpret experience. Darwin seems to assume that if the vivesector "was fully justified" by an increase in knowledge, he could, quite properly, dismiss his feelings, stirred by the dog's behavior, as mere sentiment. Is it really possible that scientists, under the sway of Cartesian dualism, could perform vivisection on animals while interpreting their screams and howls, not as genuine expressions of suffering and distress, but as mere unmeaning mechanical responses? Lily would never make this kind of "mistake," although it seems that humans often do. On the other hand, Darwin's story hints at how difficult this dismissal can be. His story hints at the power of sentiments. Surely, if we look at and listen to such screams and howls, not through the distorting lenses of an anthropocentric metaphysics, we are immediately confronted not with mechanically produced sound and motion, but with the immediate and natural expression of pain and suffering.

In the aftermath of the attacks on the World Trade Center, a news report covered the funeral of a working dog killed in those attacks. This was a massive public tribute given by the New York K-9 community. The national media reported the dog's trainer and companion as saying, "To many people he was a dog, but to me he was a friend." We all understand such an expression, even if we dismiss it as "mere sentiment." We dismiss such experience when we do not claim it as our own. We let such experiences float freely as mere "epiphenomena." We enjoy the content of such experiences, but let it go before the import and implication of such experience makes its way to the center of our lives and experience. This kind of dismissed experience never gains the authenticity needed to serve as a ground of a more generalized non-anthropocentric thinking. The sharp boundaries imposed by anthropocentricism keep this from happening. Although our companion animals are regularly experienced as having their own good, the significance of this sort of experience is frequently denied or dismissed in moments of bad faith, as we systematically overlook the import of such moments and interpret these experiences as mere subjective sentiment.

When thinking is dominated by metaphysical assumptions inherent in the dualities structuring our thought, such as the idea that only humans possess intrinsic value, our natural and spontaneous openness to non-anthropocentric goods and values is often dismissed or even falsified. And yet, the basic tenor and feel of much of our everyday moral experience is decidedly not anthropocentric. Dogs lie in our laps and cats rub against our ankles. Their flesh, their vulnerability, and their mortality concern us. We feed them when they are hungry and comfort them when distressed. We recognize the dignity and integrity of their lives as we take up their good as our own.[8] Many humans are deeply and empathetically intertwined with the lives of our companion animals. These relationships, not only support the idea or the feeling that these non-human animals are worthy of our moral regard, they demand it. And yet, we dismiss and disrespect these experiences as mere sentiment, even while they help to structure and bring meaning into our lives.

In the preceding pages, I have tried to sketch an approach to moral philosophy and moral theory that allows us to revalue and reintegrate "what rationalist culture has split apart, denied, and devalued."[9] This approach begins to make the case that emotion, animality, and particularity are important features of moral experience, and that in order to understand the complexities of moral life it is necessary to find a place for these aspects of moral experience in our moral philosophy. This approach also results in a philosophical anthropology that is capable of supporting a sophisticated model of the "ecological self," which is discussed both by feminist and by environmental philosophers. This philosophical anthropology provides a foundation for an approach to moral philosophy that is rooted in caring and connectedness, and provides a theorectical platform from which we can reconceptualize the mutually exclusive value hierarchical dualities structuring our thought and silently colonizing traditional moral theory.

I shall conclude this essay with two quick examples of how this Darwinian and phenomenological (i.e., empirical and experiential) approach to moral theory would further differ from traditional moral theory. On the conception of moral phenomena articulated and defended here, moral experience and the moral life are made possible not only by our personal and privately felt responses to the world, but by the empathetic intersubjectivity with others that these responses engender. On this view, moral subjectivity is not the subjectivity of an isolated ego but the subjectivity of shared feelings and responses; it emerges from a "being-with-others." This empathetic, shared, being-with-others has a deep causal history in our kinship with all living beings and is accessible, in part, to phenomenological description. The shared feelings and concerns between Lily and myself show that the community of egos or selves that constitute the community of moral subjects is not entirely human. Non-human animals are co-witnesses to the world; their responses to the brute materiality of the world, e.g., shared responses to blizzards, droughts, and hunger reinforce our experiences of those same things. A similar thing is true in our moral lives: non-human animals are co-witnesses to tragedy, suffering, and vulnerability, and thus they have the power to reinforce our own moral experiences just as other humans do. Even if it is true that humans are at the center of moral life, non-human animals are certainly present in the margins and are, in many cases, active participants in shared and co-constituted value experiences. This approach has clearly moved away from the traditional anthropocentric interpretation of moral phenomena, both in terms of the nature of the subjectivity open to moral concerns and in terms of the nature of the things in the world worthy of moral concern.

In rejecting the traditional approach, which emphasizes the objectivity and universality of who or what is worthy of moral concern, we must also reject the traditional understanding of the notion of "intrinsic value." The idea that we should extend the notion of intrinsic value, not only to animals, but to all living things, and perhaps to eco-systems, has been at the heart of many admirable attempts to develop a non-anthropocentric moral theory. To the extent that the notion of intrinsic value is part of a binary involving extrinsic value, the notion of intrinsic value is a part of the conceptual apparatus of rule-based moral monism and as such it gives rise to the instrumental reasoning inherent in that model.

The analysis of moral phenomena given here offers an experiential and epistemic understanding of the rationality inherent in value experience rather than a metaphysical interpretation of value as an objective and atemporal property inherent in things. On the analysis given here, the goods we appreciate for ourselves and for others are never given as absolute but always as provisional, and as subject to the satisfaction or frustration of future experiences. This approach to moral phenomena and the moral life is characterized by its intrinsic revisability in the face of an always open future. Moral experience is always directed toward a future that is yet to come. Thus, the "final" categories of moral understanding are forever postponed. By tracing our capacity for moral experience to the temporality and becoming of natural selection, to our direct face to face relations to others, and to the conceptual historicity of our world views, we can learn to interpret our various intuitions and experiences of value as a *prima facie* understanding of goodness to be born out in the future. This notion of goodness and value is a naturalistic and pragmatic understanding, which is informed by a deep falliblism within which our experiences of value and our understandings of the good are subject to continual assessment in light of subsequent experience.

Notes

1. Val Plumwood. "Nature, Self, and Gender: Feminism, Environmental Philosophy, and the Critique of Rationalism" in *Hypathia* Vol. 6 no. 1 (spring 1991), pp. 3–27. Reprinted in *The Environmental Ethics & Policy Book*, ed. Donald VanDeveer and Christine Pierce. (Wadsworth Publishing Company, 1998), p. 249.
2. See Christian Diehm's "The Self of Stars and Stone: Ecofeminism, Deep Ecology, and the Ecological Self," in *The Trumpeter*, Vol. 19, no. 3 (2003). In this essay, Diehm articulates Plumwood's reading of Naess' concept of the ecological self and discusses some comments by Naess made in a recent interview, which can be read as his response to this problem.
3. Plumwood, p. 240.
4. Ibid., p. 249.
5. Charles Darwin. *The Descent of Man*. (NY: New York, The Heritage Press, 1972), p. 319.
6. Charles S. Brown. "The Intrinsic Rationality of Moral Experience," in *Skepsis* XV/i-2004, pp. 477–494.
7. Lily is a small black dog, mostly Pug, but with an unusual snout and face. She is approximately ten years old. My wife, Dianne, and I took her in about eight years ago, after she was found lost on the edge of town.
8. See Robert Sokolowski's *Moral Action: A Phenomenological Study* (Bloomington: Indiana University Press, 1985). My understanding of the categorical structure of moral experience is influenced by Sokolowski's work.
9. Plumwood, p. 249.

8

Appropriating the Philosophies of Edmund Husserl and Edith Stein

Animal Psyche, Empathy, and Moral Subjectivity

Corinne M. PAINTER

> "Boundless compassion for all living creatures is the firmest and surest guarantee of pure moral conduct"
> (Schopenhauer).[1]

In this paper, [1] I shall employ Edmund Husserl's account of animal consciousness as he presents it in *Ideas II*, in order to present a compelling description of animality that emphasizes the phenomenological basis for acknowledging the psychic qualities that human and non-human animals share. Then [2] I shall complement Husserl's account of animal consciousness with an elucidation of Edith Stein's phenomenological account of empathy (*Einfühlung*) as it is laid out in her seminal philosophical work, *On the Problem of Empathy*. On this basis [3] I will attempt to establish that empathy makes human access to the psychic life of the animal other possible, and that as such, it characterizes one of the most fundamental intersubjective relations not only between humans but also between human and non-human animals. In so doing, in contrast to their own respective understandings of animal consciousness and empathy, which neither thinker (explicitly) characterizes as moral,[2] I shall try to argue that insofar as both accounts rely upon a notion of a psycho-physical individual's relation to nature (or to the world), to objects in nature, and to other subjects in nature that is possessed by non-human and by human animals alike and is characterized by care and concern, moral subjectivity is located in the animal psyche rather than in the human psyche. Finally, [4] I will conclude by arguing that because moral subjectivity (in its most basic form) is located in the animal psyche rather than in the human psyche, empathy provides an appropriate foundation for an ethic of care that crosses species boundaries.

C. Painter and C. Lotz (eds.), Phenomenology and the Non-Human Animal, 97–115.

I. Edmund Husserl: Animal Consciousness and the Personalistic Attitude

In section 12 of *Ideas II*,[3] Husserl makes an important distinction between two kinds of nature, to which I shall (critically) appeal as a basis for my claim that human and non-human animals share an important fundamental feature, namely, their "what it is to be a natural being," which is the condition for personal relationships, and thus, as I will argue, the basis of moral subjectivity. Elucidating two distinct kinds of nature, Husserl writes that there is a distinction between "nature in a more strict sense, the lowest and first sense, i.e., *material nature* (*materielle Natur*) and nature in a second, broadened sense, i.e., things that have a soul, in the genuine sense of 'living,' *animal nature" (animalische Natur)* (30, italics his). Moreover, continuing his explication, he maintains that

> everything that we take as existing in the ordinary sense, including, therefore, sensations, representations, feelings, and psychic acts and states of every kind, belongs to living nature; these are "real" acts or states, ontologically characterized precisely in that they are activities or states of *animals or humans...* (35-35, italics mine).

Although Husserl was not interested in developing what he refers to as the "second, broadened" sense of nature in the way that I propose to develop it, he nonetheless continues with his explication of psychic reality, emphasizing what is common to animal nature as such. In this vein, Husserl goes on to claim that

> taken in their full concretion, animal realities, characterized as Bodies with a soul... are founded realities, which presuppose in themselves, as their lower stratum material realities, so-called material Bodies... [and also], besides their specifically material determinations, still new systems of properties, namely, psychic ones... (*Ideas II*, 35–36).

Moreover, on Husserl's view, "according to what is specifically human and animal, that is, according to what is psychic,... men and animals cannot be fragmented" (ibid., 36). This is because, taken as a totality – i.e., as unified, natural, living beings – both animals and humans are constituted by a stream of consciousness that hangs together in such a way as to identify the animal and the human as the self-same psycho-physical entity that it is. That human and non-human animals share this feature of psychic unity is important, because it seems to provide the foundation for ascribing to beings the capacity for experiencing oneself and one's world in a certain way, and, moreover, for enjoying personal relationships. In the remainder of this section of the essay,

I shall briefly elucidate Husserl's claims in this regard, with the intention of returning to this point later in my consideration.

In connection with the question of the way in which animal beings experience themselves and their world, in section 49 of *Ideas II*, where Husserl is concerned with distinguishing between naturalistic and personalistic worlds and attitudes, he describes the experience of seeing a playing cat (*spielende Katze*). The playing cat, Husserl claims, is not perceived as a mere, inanimate material substance, but, rather, as a

> sensing and animated Body,... precisely as a cat... In its own way, the cat is seen, and in the seeing, its existence as this animal, cat, is experienced, and... has the... fundamental character of the experience of animals, namely, the cat is there as present in the flesh – specifically as a physical thing with sensing surfaces, sense organs, etc. The stratus of sensation is not there as something beside the physical thing, however; what is there is a Body, a Body which has physical and aesthesiological qualities *as a unity. In this way, the body is experienced as Body of a soul...* (185, italics mine).

Of course, Husserl does not have in mind a religious notion of the soul, but a classical-philosophical notion, which conceives of the soul as the condition for organic life, for self-movement, for awareness, for lived experience (*Erlebnis*).[4] And although Husserl is not interested in examining whether the animal – in this case the cat – is a being who makes specific ethical or moral demands, it is nonetheless important to underscore that his phenomenological description of the cat lays bare not only how we (humans) experience the cat, but how, in our experience of the cat, we perceive and understand the cat as a unity of body and soul, indeed, as an organic, somatically unified being that experiences and senses herself. In this connection, he writes that the cat

> is something physical and moves physically just like other things, except that beyond the merely physical qualities it constantly has aesthesiological and psychic qualities. The excess of reality beyond the mere physical thing is not something that can be separated off by itself, not something juxtaposed, but something in the psychical thing; thus it moves along with the thing and acquires its spatial determination by its being in something which is itself spatial (*Ideas II*, 186).

To be sure, the way in which we, in our experience of a psyche other than our own – whether it be the psyche of a cat or of another human – have access to its experience of itself, has been the topic of much philosophical debate, both within and outside of the phenomenological tradition.[5] Moreover, one can distinguish (at least) two questions here: first, one can raise the question of how we can have "general" knowledge of an other, foreign consciousness (*Fremdbewußtsein*), and second, one can raise the question of how we can have "specific" knowledge of or access to the contents of an other's psyche. Some philosophers tend to merge these questions together, while others (particularly those working within the phenomenological tradition) attempt to keep them separate, as we will see shortly. Many philosophers (both those who tend to merge the two forms of knowledge and those who try to distinguish them) have argued that our access to (i.e., our knowledge of) other psyches is inferential-analogical. As Dan Zahavi[6] puts it, according to this account, in order to access another psyche,

> [I start] from my own mind and link it to the way in which my body is given to me, [after which] I then pass to the other's body and by noticing the analogy that exists between this body and my own body, I *infer* that the foreign body is probably also linked in a similar manner to a foreign psyche... And although this inference does not provide me with indubitable knowledge about others, and although it doesn't allow me to actually experience other psyches, at least it gives me more reason to believe in their existence than to deny it (Zahavi, 151, italics mine).

However, again, both within (e.g., Scheler, Husserl, Stein) and outside (e.g., Wittgenstein) the phenomenological tradition, such accounts have been widely criticized on various grounds, and while these criticisms are too numerous to recount fully here, for our purposes we would do well to acknowledge that many emphasize the sense in which *even in our experience of ourselves*, as in our experience of foreign consciousness, it is not that we make *inferences* between our psychic (so-called "interior") life and our bodily (so-called "exterior") behaviour; rather – from the beginning on – in our experience both of ourselves and of others

> we are neither confronted with a mere body, nor with a hidden psyche, but with a unified whole... [such that] in some sense, experiences are not internal, they are not hidden in the head, but rather *expressed in* boldly gestures and actions... Moreover *bodily behaviour is itself meaningful*, it is intentional, and as such it is neither internal nor external, but beyond this artificial distinction (*Zahavi*, 153, italics mine).

Consequently, we should, according to Zahavi, "realize that the body of the other differs radically from inanimate objects and that our perception of this body is quite unlike our ordinary perception of objects" (ibid.). Of course, as Zahavi correctly points out, while this accounts for our "general" knowledge of foreign consciousness,[7] "it does not imply that I can experience the other in the same way as she herself does, nor that the other's consciousness is accessible to me in the same way as my own is" (ibid.). However, this does not therefore imply that I must either *infer epistemically* or *remain totally excluded from* the other's psychic life. As we will soon see (in the next section), we can know and have access to the other's psychic life through empathy.[8]

However, before we turn to an explication of empathy and of the fundamental role that empathy plays in terms of characterizing intersubjective relationships, including (as I will argue) cross-species relationships, we shall first consider Husserl's account of the distinction between the personalistic and the naturalistic attitude, since this will prepare the way for our consideration of empathy. Although Husserl (ultimately) seems to grant personhood only to humans and not to animals,[9] in his discussion of the personalistic attitude that he offers in section 49 of *Ideas II*, we find a description of animal nature – of animal consciousness – that allows us[10] to conceive of non-human animals as beings who (at the very least) possess a *personalistic attitude* in a rudimentary, wholly non-reflective way. For, certainly, animals cannot live in a *naturalistic attitude*, since they seem to be incapable of engaging in the reflective, objectifying thinking about objects that is characteristic of this attitude, which describes a specific attitude of humans.[11] Thus, given (a) that animal beings can experience themselves and their worlds either "naturalistically" or "personalistically,"[12] and (b) that non-human animals are unable to experience themselves or their worlds "naturalistically," the attitude shared in common by humans and non-human animals is the personalistic one, which is precisely the attitude that captures, according to Husserl, the way in which "we live with one another,... or are related to one another in love and aversion, in disposition and action,..." (192), and not the way in which we reflect upon ourselves and our relations to and within the world. For Husserl, as is well-known, the naturalistic attitude – which for him is not "natural" at all – is actually founded on, or presupposes, the personalistic attitude, which is the more fundamental, basic, and, thus, *genuinely natural (i.e., originary) attitude*. In this connection, Husserl writes:

> it should appear that there are not here two attitudes with equal rights and of the same order,... but that the *naturalistic attitude is in fact subordinated to the personalistic*, and that the former only acquires by means of an abstraction or, rather, by means of a kind of self-forgetfulness of the personal Ego, a certain autonomy – whereby it proceeds *illegitimately*... (193, italics mine).

Here, the central point seems to be that the basic attitude, i.e., the basic way in which beings experience their environments, that gives rise to and makes possible other, founded and abstract attitudes (such as the naturalistic attitude) is a personal attitude, wherein intersubjective relationships characterized by various non-theoretical modes of concern and care, for example, love, hate, aversion, attraction, etc., operate as the basis for meaning, indeed providing the context and point of departure for any and all abstract, theoretically motivated reflections.

One way to further distinguish these two, very different attitudes – i.e., the personalistic and the naturalistic – is to highlight the way in which the naturalistic attitude requires one to relate to objects of concern as "mere things" (*reine Dinge*) as opposed to beings who demand what may be referred to as moral attention. In this connection, in section 51 of *Ideas II*, Husserl claims (in this regard) that "to treat humans and animals 'as mere things' has… various senses, [including] a juridical and moral sense, and, on the other hand, a scientific sense" (200), but that both senses have something in common: namely, from a moral-practical standpoint, one treats a being[13] as "a mere thing" when one does not take her "as a being related to the moral, as a member of a moral association of beings within which the work of morality is constituted" (ibid.). And while (once again) Husserl is not here concerned with arguing that we *should* take one another – other humans, and perhaps also non-human animals – as moral subjects, what his description nevertheless permits us to surmise – even if Husserl himself would not follow us – is that a more fundamental – and, thus, natural – way of understanding ourselves and our way of relating to one another is not as "mere things" but as "personal subjects" who experience themselves in a particular, non-objectifying, non-theoretical way. Indeed, according to Husserl, in order to take another being as the sort of being that is not a mere thing, we must understand that being as a "personal subject and thereby as related to objectivities to which we, too, are related: the earth and sky, the fields and the woods, the place in which we dwell communally" (ibid., 201). And while it is (probably) true that (most) non-human animals do not reflectively conceive of various objects in their environments as "objectivities" to which they are related, one would be hard-pressed to establish that the objects to which they are related are not meaningful to them and that they do not relate to them on the basis of care and concern.

I submit that it is our animal nature (*animalische Natur*), which is *not* specifically human, that supplies the proper personal foundation upon which moral subjectivity is grounded. In this vein, according to Husserl, such beings who relate to each other personally, relate to each other from within or on the basis of a personalistic attitude wherein they view one another as " '*companions*', not as *opposed objects but as counter-subjects who live 'with' one another,…* and are related to one another, actually or potentially, in acts of love and counter-love, of hate and counter-hate, of confidence and reciprocated confidence, etc." (*Ideas II*, 204, italics his). Moreover, these acts of mutual relation that occur only from within the personalistic attitude are, Husserl says, "especially pre-eminent in the acts of one-sided empathetic understanding of the life of the other" (ibid.), wherein lies the possibility for mutual relationships between beings who co-inhabit the personalistic world, even while their capacities for understanding one another are not necessarily identical. However, because, in agreement with Dermot Moran[14] (and presumably others), it is my contention that Husserl's various "meditations on empathy,[15]... while illuminating are not entirely satisfactory" (Moran, 290), and that his reflections on the connection between "empathy and intersubjectivity... while possessing a certain consistency in approach, call to mind some kind of Humean 'contiguity and resemblance' account" (ibid.), I shall turn my attention to Edith Stein's account of empathy.[16] For, in my view, Stein's fuller, more thoughtful understanding of empathy,[17] will pave the way for my claim that when construed in a particular way, empathy characterizes one of the most basic ways in which human and non-human animals share a world and personal relationships with one another, which, in turn – as I earlier mentioned and will later attempt to establish – provides a foundation for forming an ethic of care that applies not only to humans but extends to animals as well.

II. Edith Stein: Empathy as Access to Foreign Consciousness

Although I can not do justice to Edith Stein's (in my view) impressive account of empathy (*Einfühlung*) as she advances it in *On the Problem of Empathy*,[18] in what follows I shall offer an overview of her description of empathy, within which (some of) its central features are emphasized and on the basis of which I shall argue[19] that it constitutes a fundamental mode of intersubjective, cross-species relation. First, however, in order to develop an appreciation for the complicated nature of the project of attempting to adequately describe empathy, consider the following interesting observations, (humorously) presented by Ernest McCullough:[20]

> The large *Oxford English Dictionary* [21] does not even have an entry for empathy in its general contents, while the fourth edition of the *Oxford Paperback Edition* defines empathy as 'the ability to identify oneself mentally with a person or things and so understand him or her feelings or its meaning'.[22] [Interestingly] this definition seems to accord best with Husserl's definitions. The *Oxford Universal Dictionary* of 1955, however, provides what seems to be an idealist conception in defining empathy as 'the power of projecting one's personality into and so fully understanding the object of the contemplation',[23] while still a recent *Webster's Dictionary* (1997) provides both the first sense of identification and the second sense of imaginative projection[24] (McCullough, 129).

In addition, many scholars have struggled in their attempts to properly distinguish empathy (*Einfühlung*) from sympathy (*Sympathie*). According to one such scholar, Irene Switankowsky,[25] while " 'sympathy' and 'empathy' refer to two distinct and complex psychological capacities that have quite distinct meanings, philosophers and psychologists, nevertheless, have had tremendous difficulty keeping the two concepts distinct" (Switankowsky, 86). Indeed, she writes, "since the classic works by Max Scheler on sympathy and Edith Stein on empathy, theorists have been trying to define the terms by supposing empathy is merely a type of sympathy" (ibid.).

Stein (like Husserl and others before her) was not unaware of the difficulty of properly defining empathy, and appreciated the difficulty of keeping empathy distinct from sympathy. Indeed, whereas for Max Scheler, who, in *The Nature of Sympathy*,[26] was (obviously) focally interested in offering a description of sympathy, and for whom there was a tendency to associate sympathy and empathy,[27] as Switankowsky notes, Edith Stein not only "finds a clear distinction between sympathy and empathy, but she takes the position that empathy is categorically distinct and different from sympathy" (Switankowsky, 87). Although some scholars question whether in the end Stein successfully distinguished empathy from sympathy, (at the very least) one marker of her attempt to distinguish the two phenomena can be gleaned from her acknowledgement that empathy is an "act which is primordial as present experience, though non-primordial in its content" (Stein, 10), by which she seems to mean that in an act of empathy, one experiences another subject – i.e., another consciousness, another psyche – as the peculiar object of her empathic experience, within which an "other living subjectivity is announced… to one's consciousness" (Moran, 302) but does not become coincident (*übereinstimmend*) with it.

On this account, the way in which foreign subjectivity is announced is decisively different from the manner in which an other subjectivity is announced in sympathy, given that the latter seems to refer to (something like) a "passive sense of emotional identification" with the feelings or psychic states of another (Switankowski, 91), wherein one (in a sense) becomes coincident with the other. As will (hopefully) become more transparent in what follows, empathy, in contrast to sympathy, refers, for Stein, to "the whole range of phenomena in which the other living subjectivity is… revealed to my consciousness..." (Moran, 302). Here, what is shared in common by the phenomena in question is the sense in which empathic experiences ultimately "force me to feel, as it were, led by a primordial [experience] not experienced by me but still there, manifesting itself in my non-primordial experience as a primordial experience issuing from an other 'I' " (Stein, 11). Accordingly, Stein defines empathy as "the experience of foreign consciousness in general, *irrespective of the kind of the experiencing subject or of the subject whose consciousness is experienced*" (ibid., italics mine), furthermore claiming, importantly, that this is indeed "how beings comprehend the psychic life of their fellows" (ibid.).[28]

As many scholars have noted, Stein's account of empathy distinguishes itself from other accounts (for instance, from Lipps' account) in that it preserves the sense of non-primordiality or foreignness that is characteristic of empathy.[29] For, indeed, Stein rejects the notion that empathic experience has a tendency to fulfill itself, which is to say, she rejects that the empathizing subject becomes *coincident* with foreign consciousness through empathy, i.e., that the non-primordiality that characterizes empathy undergoes a conversion and becomes primordial (Stein, 12–14). In addition, Stein rejects the supposition that empathy should be defined as "fellow feeling" (*Das Mitgefühl*) (14–15) or as a "feeling of oneness" (*Eins-fühlung*) (16–18), which, according to Stein herself, serves to further differentiate empathy from sympathy, given that the latter is often associated with these notions, particularly with the first notion of fellow feeling: "we can designate the *primordial* act of [for instance] joy-with-him... as fellow feeling, or as sympathy" (14, italics mine), while we cannot designate acts of empathy in this way, since they are *not primordial* (ibid., italics mine). Interestingly, Stein does not claim that fellow feeling or the feeling of oneness with a foreign consciousness is impossible, or that it should be avoided; rather – and this will be important for our purposes – she is simply critical of the idea that in empathy we eliminate the felt awareness of our own non-identification, our difference, our non-coincidence with the being to whom we relate empathically. She claims, in this connection, that if the empathic experience is "ideal" (not clouded by deception or by some other obstacle that threatens its fulfillment), the experience will be *identical in content* to a primordial, immanently comprehended experience, such that the experience "has the same content even though it has a different mode of givenness" (15). Furthermore, regarding the connection between empathy and oneness, she claims that it is "not through the feeling of oneness, but through empathizing that we experience others. The feeling of oneness and the enrichment of our own experience become possible through empathy" (18). This is extremely important, since it underscores both (a) that the feeling of oneness and empathy are not to be identified with one another, and (b) that *empathy actually makes possible such a feeling* and not that such a feeling makes empathy possible, the latter of which is often the way it is mistakenly formulated in studies of empathy.

Finally, then, in the context of criticizing Scheler's theory of how foreign consciousness is accessed, which he claims is accomplished through inner perception (*innere Wahrnehmung*),[30] Stein makes even more transparent the nature of empathy as she understands it, writing,

> if I experience a feeling as that of another, I have it given twice: once primordially and my own and once non-primordially in empathy as originally foreign. And precisely this non-primordiality of empathized experience causes me to reject 'inner perception' for the comprehension of our own and foreign experience (34).[31]

We may put this in still another way, namely, as Moran (paraphrasing Stein) puts it:

> *Einfühlung* is distinct from *Eins-fühlung* ("feeling-one-with" or "identification"), [since in the former experience] it is not the case that I am one with [the other], rather I am "with" him. There is a fictional I distinct from the actual I, even though my actual I has its attention fixed on the fictional I (Moran, 307, emphasis his).

Earlier, I mentioned that it is through empathy, according to Stein, that "beings comprehend the psychic life of their fellows" (Stein, 11), and just a moment ago I acknowledged that empathy makes possible something like fellow feeling or oneness with a foreign consciousness (18) (and not the other way around). According to McCullough, with whom I agree,[32] empathy does more than this for Stein, insofar as "empathy becomes the foundation for all intersubjective experience" (McCullough, 130), while the precondition for empathy is the perception of a physical, animated body (Stein, 87, 99; Moran, 309). According to Moran,

> there is a possibility of "sensing in" (*Einempfindung*) to the other living body. [And while] the kind of fulfillment (*Erfüllung*) possible in my empathizing with another is not adequate, a certain degree of projection or "introjection" (*Hineinversetzen*) is possible, which is warranted by the fusion of my inner and outer sense and by my ability to make an imaginative transposition. [For instance], my hand is not given in so fixed a type that I cannot understand a child's hand, or a woman's hand, or a "hand" of whatever kind, including a dog's paw, or a cat's paw. I can indeed project myself into the dog's – or the cat's – paw (309).

In this way, I experience the other, through empathy, as "having another 'zero point of orientation' (*Null-Punkt der Orientierung*).[33] I retain my own zero-point while recognizing the other in a non-originary consciousness. I also experience the other subject, not just as sensing but as carrying out acts" (ibid., 310).

In the next section of the paper (which directly follows), drawing both on Husserl's explication of animal nature and of the non-reflective personalistic attitude that characterizes animal relations in the world, as well as on Stein's denial "that empathy involves a fusion or identification with the other, and that the essence of empathy involves recognition of the other as both individual personal subject and as other inhabitant of a co-occurring separate psychic stream" (Moran, 312), I shall try to trace out the sense in which empathy characterizes one of the most fundamental intersubjective relations between humans and animals, allowing the former access to the latter as a psychic being who relates to the world through *care and concern* . Then, in the concluding section of the paper, I will argue that because moral subjectivity is located in the animal psyche rather than in the human psyche, an ethic of care provides an appropriate basis for building moral relationships between humans and animals.

III. Empathy, Human Access to the Animal Other, and Moral Subjectivity

Admittedly, as was noted earlier, the project of properly describing empathy and of distinguishing it from sympathy has a long and complicated history, and it is not clear whether this project has met its successful completion. For instance, in her essay, "Attention to Suffering: A Feminist Caring Ethic for the Treatment of Animals,"[34] in the context of attempting to establish that sympathy, compassion, and caring provide a proper ground for developing a moral theory that considers animals as members of the moral community Josephine Donovan traces the critical discourse regarding the distinction between sympathy and empathy, further highlighting its complexity. In this connection, in elucidating and referring to Schopenhauer's criticism of Kantian morality, she writes:

> compassion, he [Schopenhauer] maintains, requires a kind of empathetic identification so that one can understand the other's situation. "I suffer directly with him, I feel his woe just as I ordinarily feel only my own... but this requires that I am in some way *identified with him*, in other words that this *difference* between me and everyone else, which is the very basis of my egoism, is eliminated"[35] (88, italics hers).

Donovan goes on to note that "later sympathy theorists, such as Scheler, criticized Shopenhauer... for relying on empathy rather than sympathy, and thus sanctioning a loss of self in the identificatory process" (Donovan, 88). I here refer to this "disagreement," in order not only to draw attention to the complexity of the matter (which was already duly noted) but also to draw attention to the sense in which when considered in conjunction with Edith Stein's account of empathy – which is the account that guides the present consideration – empathy is actually understood by some thinkers as a form of sympathy, while sympathy is understood as a form of empathy. This should be clear, insofar as, for Stein, the phenomenal mark that distinguishes empathy from sympathy is precisely the preservation of the foreignness of the other, indeed *the inability of the empathizing subject to become one, coincident, or identified with the foreign consciousness to which she relates empathically*, which provides the basis for her related claim that empathy should not be conceived as a feeling of oneness or as fellow feeling, as thinkers such as Scheler proposed. Taking Stein's understanding of empathy, as well as Husserl's articulation of animal consciousness, as my point of departure, in what follows I shall appeal to certain claims about empathy, which are often cited,[36] mistakenly (though understandably) as claims about sympathy, in order to establish that empathy characterizes a fundamental mode of human access to animal consciousness.[37]

One could argue that although Husserl himself was not advancing morally normative claims in *Ideas II*, Scheler's argument, which claims that humans would do well, as Donovan formulates it, "to develop (or redevelop) their sympathetic intellectual capacities in order to decode the symbolic language of nature, and that humans need to learn to read this language in order to truly understand natural life, including the life of animals…" (Donovan, 84), since this would allow us, for instance, to appreciate that "when a dog expresses its joy by barking and wagging its tail… we have here… a universal grammar valid for all languages of expression" (ibid.), is compatible with how Husserl seems to understand the legitimacy and "natural" character of the personalistic attitude. For given that this attitude characterizes the attitude of humans as they relate to objects of concern not as theoretical objects, i.e., not as "mere things," but instead – if I may state it boldly – as moral subjects, i.e., by which I mean beings of personal concern, one could argue that it is within this attitude and world that one can enjoy genuinely intersubjective, personal relations with beings who command moral attention, even if these beings are different from oneself by virtue of belonging to a different species. Such relations occur between beings who are themselves, as Husserl claims "related to the moral, and conceived as a member of a moral association of beings within which the work of morality is constituted" (*Ideas II*, 200). Since, according to Husserl, in order for another being to be constituted as the sort of being that is not a mere thing, that being must simply be a "personal subject and thereby related to objectivities to which we, too, are related: e.g., the earth and sky, the fields and the woods, the place in which we dwell communally" (ibid., 201), *where the relation is not in the first place a theoretical or reflective relation but a lived one*, animals may not (in my view) be denied personal subjectivity, nor thus, should they be excluded from the moral community. For indeed, according to Husserl, in experiencing animals as unified psycho-physical beings who relate to their worlds "personalistically" and not mechanically, we must already conceive of animals as entities with whom we enjoy intersubjective relations, and as such it is precisely here, that is, *in the animal psyche*, that we find moral subjectivity.

Further interpreting Husserl's understanding of animal nature and the personalistic attitude (discussed in §I of the essay) and Stein's understanding of empathy (discussed in §II of the essay), we might say that Husserl, Stein, and Scheler seem to agree that there is a way of understanding our worldly, personal, intersubjective relationships that is characterized by empathy (or sympathy, depending upon how these phenomena are understood), which allows one "to see organic, psychic life as it is, and not as translated into manipulable objects for human use" (Donovan, 85). In this way, none of these thinkers conceive of empathy (sympathy) "as a whimsical, erratic, and irrational response, but rather, as a systematic investigatory tool, as a form of knowledge" (ibid.), namely, knowledge of foreign consciousness. Importantly, given that both Husserl and Stein acknowledge animal consciousness, i.e., given that they admit that animals have a psychic life, and given that neither Husserl nor Stein explicitly deny that empathy can explain intersubjective access between humans and animals and indeed both seem to allow this, we are permitted to conclude that knowledge of the other *as other*, as, indeed, *foreign,* is an access or knowledge of others that extends to non-human animal others. For, as Stein herself writes, "empathy is the experience of foreign consciousness in general, *irrespective of the kind [species] of the experiencing subject or of the subject whose consciousness is experienced*" (Stein, 11, italics mine).

Additionally, "this [empathy] is how beings comprehend the psychic life of their fellows" (Stein, 11), according to Stein, where "fellows" is meant to refer to all beings that enjoy a psychic life, and not to a particular species of psychic life. It should be clear that both Husserl and Stein consider animals as psychic beings, i.e., as the sorts of beings that have a psychic life and therefore that they experience the world in a personal, meaningful way, even if they (the animals) are not themselves reflectively aware of this. It should also be clear that empathy, for them – but especially for Stein – identifies a mode not only of *perceiving* animals as certain sorts of beings capable of experience, but of (in some sense) *comprehending, intuiting and feeling*, non-primordially, their psychic life, not as identical to our own psychic life, but as different from, non-coincident with, and other than our own, even while it is in content "like ours." Indeed, that empathy does not require coincidence, identification, or (even) fellow-feeling with foreign consciousness, is one of the most original aspects of Stein's understanding of empathic experience, which not only serves to distinguish her account from other accounts, but creates the necessary space for allowing humans to access the psychic life of animals; insofar as coincidence (identification) is not necessary for empathic experience, and moreover, insofar as a feeling of oneness or fellow-feeling is *not the precondition for*, but a possible *consequence of,* empathy, the possibility for relating to animals empathically becomes more than just a remote possibility: it becomes, rather, an actuality. For on this account, it is not that one must become coincident with the animal, or that one must "feel" primordially what the animals feels, which is precisely what many critics object to when responding to the claim that humans and animals relate to each other through empathy; in contrast, it is because empathy grants us access to the psychic life of animals and allows us to acknowledge that they are lead by their own separate psychic stream of consciousness, even if they themselves are not reflectively aware of this, that we are able to "imaginatively transpose" and "interject" ourselves into the psychic life of an animal other, while "retaining our own zero-points" and "experiencing the other – [in this case animal] – subject, not just as sensing but as carrying out her own acts" (Moran, 310). It is this felt recognition that I would contend provides the proper basis for establishing an ethic of care and concern that extends beyond humans so as to cross species boundaries. I shall conclude this paper by arguing for why such an ethic of care is justified.

IV. Animal Consciousness and Moral Subjectivity: A Cross-Species Ethic of Care

In agreement with other empathy (sympathy) theorists that have come before me, I submit that empathy precedes justice, such that empathy determines which beings get to be "included under the umbrella of justice" (Donovan, 89). I also take it to be fairly obvious (though possibly debatable) that genuine empathy can only characterize a relationship between creatures who can feel, i.e., between creatures who have the capacity for suffering and enjoyment, which is simply to say, beings who have a psychic life, to use phenomenological terminology. While we may – and probably should – certainly distinguish between "empathic agency" and "empathic patiency," such that we understand the conditions for being granted empathic *agency* to be more rigorous than the conditions for being granted empathic *patiency*,[38] I am here interested in claiming that the *empathizing agent* must be aware that the other to whom she relates "has feelings, or is a subject of feelings" (ibid.), which involves an awareness that is based in our non-inferential intuition that "our experience of the body of the other differs radically from inanimate objects and that our perception of this body is quite unlike our ordinary perception of objects" (Zahavi, 153.), given that it involves our experience of an other subject who senses and carries out her own acts (Moran, 310) in some sort of intentional, meaningful, concerned (non-random) way. Following the formulation of Kathleen Haney,[39] who emphasizes the bodily gestures that we interpret through empathy, we might put this in the following way: "empathy has as its field the sensuous, meaningful experiences of the other's expressions and gestures,... [and lets me] understand the Other's lived body, [thereby] rendering his meanings into my own lived life,..." (Haney, 59). Indeed, she claims, the "empathic grasp of the other's physically presented meanings is an everyday experience... which provides the guiding clue" (ibid.) of the other as a psycho-physical, experiencing being, which in turn serves to "open up the moral dimension of empathy" (ibid.). According to Haney, moreover,

> empathy suggests one of the paramount motivations behind holding empathy to be a moral *obligation*,... since one cannot serve the community of others if she lacks other perspectives on the world, nor can one help an other without empathizing with his meanings (ibid., italics mine).

Here, it is obvious that serving one's community and aiding others is taken as morally obligatory. Accordingly, I will not attempt to establish this thesis here, as I think most moral theories (with the exception of moral egoism) acknowledge these as moral duties in the *general sense*, though whether *specific duties* can be generated from these general duties is debatable. Importantly, as Haney recognizes, "acts of empathy do not necessarily imply reciprocity, since in empathy one turns oneself towards the other in expressive communication… including via body language,… and… need not seek an empathetic response in return for its acts" (Haney., 60). While what Haney refers to as "mutual empathy" is possible when empathy is *reciprocally manifest* between the empathic agent and the empathic patient such that both members of the "empathic pair" are at one and the same time agent and patient (ibid.), since it is unclear whether mutual empathy is possible in the case of the human-animal pair,[40] in what follows I want to focus my attention on non-reciprocal empathetic acts between human agents and animal patients, where the ultimate goal is to establish that this relation requires an ethics of care and concern that is not restricted to human beings.

At this juncture, it is important to underscore that it has already been established that (at least according to Husserl and especially Stein) empathy makes human access to foreign psychic life, including animal psychic life, possible. It has also been established that to experience the other as other in this way, through empathy, presupposes that the empathizing agent perceives, grasps, takes, feels, and relates to this other not just as a sensing being but as a being who carries out her own acts (Moran, 310), from her own "zero-point of orientation" (ibid.), in a world that is shared and experienced as personally meaningful. Moreover, as Moran reminds us, in empathy, "it is not the case that I am one with [the other], rather I am 'with' him" (ibid., 307). Importantly, to be genuinely "with" the other, one must not only recognize this other as other, and in so doing refuse psychic or bodily identification with this other, one must also "respect the other's uniqueness and the universal claim that *every other makes upon one another*" (Haney, 63, italics mine). This in turn means, I submit, that as empathizing agents, we are no longer permitted to treat these others as mere things or objects (Donovan 89), since this constitutes an inappropriate manner of relating to an other psychic being, with interests of her own, which she relates to and tries to satisfy in various ways. Indeed, in *actually seeing* an other's reality – that is, in actually experiencing empathy for an other – we must constitute him or her as a subject with felt needs and desires that may be different from our own, which, according to Donovan, makes it difficult to treat that other as a mere thing (ibid., 96), given that "mere things" do not have needs or desires that call out for recognition. The possession of needs and desires, having one's own zero-point of orientation, sensing, and carrying out one's own acts (Moran, 310), are characteristic marks of the experience of *all* psychic beings, including animal psyches, and as such, animals are *empathic patients* and thereby subjects of moral concern. In this way, moral subjectivity lies in animal consciousness, indeed in *empathic patiency*, and not in human consciousness or in *empathic agency*.

To be sure, while the fact that as an empathizing agent I may not appropriately take an other psychic being, with whom I enjoy an empathic relationship (as agent to patient) as a mere thing, answers the question of why I should be motivated to conceive of that other as a being who makes moral demands upon me – *indeed, it presupposes that I already comprehend and relate to this other in exactly this way, even if I fail to admit this explicitly* – it does not answer the question of why I should be motivated to respect *specific moral demands*, such as "you must take my interests as equal in worth to your own," or "you cannot eat me." And, as answering this question is beyond the scope of this essay, I will not attempt to answer it here. However, I do hope to have shown that because non-human animals can be and are the subjects of human empathizing, they are not mere things or objects, but subjectivities with whom we share a world of concern, and to whom we are therefore connected in very personal and morally significant ways. This then means, finally, that an ethic of care that appreciates what might be referred to as a "moral kinship" between humans and animals provides an appropriate phenomenological basis for a morality that crosses species boundaries. In closing, then:

> Genuine morality is outraged by the proposition… that… animals are things and therefore should be treated merely as means… this constitutes a failure to realize the essence that exists in every animal, and shines forth with inscrutable significance from all eyes. *(Schopenhauer)*[41]

Notes

1. Schopenhauer, Arthur. *On the Basis of Morality,* trans. E.F.J Payne. (Indianapolis: Bobbs-Merrill, 1965): p. 172. [German Text: *Über die Grundlage der Moral.* (1840)]. All citations of this text refer to the English translation cited here, and will be cited by the author's last name, followed by the appropriate English pagination.
2. Although empathy may be thought to be necessarily – per definition – associated with the moral or the ethical, it need not be, and in Stein's initial analysis of empathy, she does not focus on ethical empathy, insofar as her emphasis seems to be on describing a "general" access beings have to foreign consciousness.
3. Husserl, Edmund. *Ideas Pertaining to a Pure Phenomenology and to a Phenomenological Philosophy*, Second Book, trans. Richard Rojcewicz and André Schuwer (Boston: Kluwer Academic Publishers, 1993). [German Text: *Ideen zu einer reinen Phänomenologie und phänomenologischen Philosophie.* Zweites Buch: Phänomenologische Untersuchungen zur Konstitution. Edited by Marly Biemel. The Hague: Martinus Nijhoff, 1952 (Husserliana IV)]. All citations of this text refer to the English translation cited here, and will be cited as *Ideas II*, followed by the appropriate English pagination.
4. This conception of the soul can be traced back to Antiquity. (References to Ancient thinkers are too numerous to recount fully here, but see, for instance, Aristotle's *De Anima*).
5. Here and throughout this paper, I am presupposing that we are confronted with (i.e., that we experience) objects – which may turn out to be subjects – and thus

I do not address the problem of solipsism, which is to say that I do not try to give an answer to the epistemological question of how I can know or be sure that anything exists outside my mind (psyche). Indeed, I take seriously the claim that from a phenomenological standpoint, this question is senseless (or at least uninteresting). In this vein, I acknowledge that things are given to us, i.e., that they are announced to awareness, as distinct from us and that we experience them as such. Thus, my point of departure takes this for granted and is here focally concerned with accounting for how it is possible that another psyche – i.e., a foreign consciousness – is given as an other subjectivity and not as, for example, a mere object or thing.

6. Zahavi, Dan. "Beyond Empathy: Phenomenological Approaches to Intersubjectivity," *Journal of Consciousness Studies*, 8, no. 5–7 (2001): 151–167. All further references to this author have this text as their source and will be cited by author's last name, followed by the appropriate page number(s).
7. In other words, it gives an answer to the first (general) question regarding how we can know or have access to a foreign consciousness.
8. This would constitute an answer to the second (specific) question regarding our access to the contents of a foreign consciousness. In this paper, although I think that it might be the case, I do not intend to argue that empathy is the *only* manner in which we can know a foreign consciousness in this way; rather, I want to argue that it is *one of the most fundamental ways* in which we have access to others, i.e., to foreign consciousness. And ultimately, I want to argue that one of the most fundamental relationships between human and non-human animals is characterized by empathy. Interestingly, Zahavi rejects empathy as the proper way in which to describe intersubjectivity at its most fundamental level, a claim that I will not take up here.
9. For this, see Husserl's three volumes on intersubjectivity: *Hua XIII*, *Hua XIV*, and *Hua XV* (Den Haag: M. Nijhoff, 1973).
10. Even if Husserl would disagree (though I think his own position requires him to admit this point).
11. See *Ideas II*, p. 192ff.
12. And perhaps there are other attitudes; however, it is probably the case that these additional attitudes might be subsumed under or be variations of these main attitudes, which may (reasonably) be conceived of as *overarching attitudes*, or as *fundamental ways of dealing with one's world.*
13. I here substitute "being" for "human being" (and elsewhere for "person"), since, according to Husserl himself (in these sections of *Ideas II*), he refers to human beings as standing in for animals in general: "the human man may suffice for us as a representative of animality in general" (190).
14. Moran, Dermot. "The Problem of Empathy: Lipps, Scheler, Husserl and Stein." *Amor amicitiae: On the Love that is Freindship. Essays in Medieval Thought and Beyond in Honor of the Rev. Professor James McEvoy*, ed. Thomas Kelly and Philipp Roseman. (Belgium: Peeters, 2004): pp. 269–312. All further references to this author have this text as their source and will be cited by author's last name, followed by appropriate page number(s).
15. Husserl's reflections on and various discussions of empathy, as Dermot Moran lays out, span a period of over thirty years, and are located in several different texts, including not only *Ideas II* (which I have focused upon here) but also *Cartesian Meditations*, (particularly *Meditation V*), as well as his three volumes on *Intersubjectivity* (*Hua*, *XIII*, *XIV*, and *XV*, respectively).
16. Indeed, as is well known, Stein was Husserl's assistant, and as such she not only worked very closely with him, but she also edited *Volume II of Ideas*, which deals to a large extent with the same problems as her own work on empathy.
17. Particularly, the way in which it accounts for its distinction from other – or from "mere" – perceptual experiences, which will be discussed shortly.

18. Stein, Edith. *On the Problem of Empathy*, trans. Waltraut Stein (Washington D.C.: ICS Publications, 1989). [German text: *Zum Problem der Einfühlung* (Halle: Buchdruckerie des Wasenhauses, 1917)]. All citations of this text refer to the English translation cited here and will be cited by author's last name, followed by the appropriate English pagination.
19. Admittedly, this is to go beyond what Stein (and most other phenomenological thinkers) argue.
20. McCullough, Ernest. "Edith Stein and Intersubjectivity." *Husserl and Stein*, ed. Richard Feist and William Sweet. (Washington, D.C.: The Council for Research in Values and Philosophy, 2003). All further references to this author will have this text as their source and will be cited by author's last name, followed by the appropriate page number(s).
21. *Oxford English Dictionary* (New York: Oxford University Press, 1972).
22. *The Oxford Paperback Dictionary 2000* (New York: Oxford University Press, 2000).
23. *The Oxford Universal Dictionary, 3rd edition* (New York: Oxford University Press, 1955).
24. *Webster's Universal College Dictionary* (New York: Gramercy Books, 1997).
25. Switankowsky, Irene. "Sympathy and Empathy." *Philosophy Today*, Vol. 44, no. 1 (Spring 2000): pp. 86–92. All further references to this author will have this text as their source and will be cited by author's last name, followed by the appropriate page number(s).
26. Scheler, Max. *The Nature of Sympathy* (London: Routledge & Kegan Paul, 1954). [German text: *Wesen und Formen der Sympathie* (Munich: Francke, 1973)]. All further citations of this text refer to the English translation cited here, and will be cited by author's last name, followed by the appropriate English pagination.
27. While Scheler distinguishes between four distinct senses of "sympathy," namely: (1) an immediate community of feeling; (2) a fellow-feeling about something or other; (3) an emotional infection; and (4) an emotional identification with the feelings or states of another (Scheler, 12), according to Switankowsky, he seems to believe that these four senses, taken together, "adequately capture the central meaning of empathy,... and that he does not find a specific need to distinguish between sympathy and empathy" (86).
28. I will come back to these points in the next section of the paper.
29. Husserl also preserved this foreignness, though he did so differently.
30. See Stein, pp. 27–34.
31. Stein is careful to note, however, that if one were interested in highlighting what the two experiences – i.e., the primordial and the non-primordial – have in common, something like "inner intuition" might be appropriate (34).
32. However, I will not argue for this here.
33. See Stein, p. 61, 68.
34. Donovan, Josephine. "Attention to Suffering: A Feminist Caring Ethics for the Treatment of Animals." *Journal of Social Philosophy*, Vol. 27, Issue 1 (1996): pp. 81–102. All further references to this author will have this text as their source and will be cited by author's last name, followed by the appropriate page number(s).
35. Schopenhauer, 144.
36. For instance, by Scheler and Donovan (but, presumably by others as well).
37. It might be the case that empathy also characterizes a fundamental mode of *animal access to human psychic life*, though I will not attempt to establish this admittedly challenging thesis here.
38. For instance, we might claim that in order to be an *empathic agent*, a being must be able to comprehend the psychic life of a foreign consciousness in such a manner as to be able to make cognitive claims about that psychic life, and/or in such a manner as to be able to place oneself, imaginatively, into the situation of this other. If this is the case, then it is likely that many non-human animals

will not be granted empathic agency; it is interesting to note, in this connection, that in addition to excluding many (or most) non-human animals from possessing empathic agency, this understanding of the phenomenon would also exclude some humans from it as well.

39. Haney, Kathleen. "Empathy and Ethics." *Southwest Philosophy Review*, Vol. 10, Issue 1 (1994): pp. 57–65. All further references to this author will have this text as their source and will be cited by author's last name, followed by the appropriate page number(s).
40. As mentioned in note 38 (though in a slightly different context), I will not try to argue for this here, though I do think mutual empathy between animals and humans is possible. For a discussion of this possibility, see Brown, "The Intentionality and Animal Heritage of Moral Experience: What We Can learn from Dogs about Moral Theory," which appears in this volume.
41. Schopenhauer, 95–96.

9

The Human as Just an Other Animal

Madness, Disability, and Foucault's Bestiary

Licia CARLSON

> "What is so perilous, then, in the fact that people speak, and that their speech proliferates? Where is the danger in that?"[1]
>
> "Killing animals, and allowing them to die, are morally far more serious matters than we have supposed. But allowing severely retarded human beings to die, and perhaps even killing them, are correspondingly less serious matters than we have believed."[2]

There is a complex story to be told about the presence and treatment of two kinds of beings on the philosophical stage: the non-human animal, and the mentally disabled.[3] There are many parallels in the ways that these groups have been treated philosophically: they have occupied a place in a long list of beings against which "rational man" has been defined in the history of philosophy; they have been relegated to a space beyond the scope of moral consideration in many ethical theories; and they have also provided the positive content for many ethical, political, and epistemological claims regarding the binaries that they inhabit (e.g., human-non-human, rational-mentally disabled). Yet there is an even more fascinating story to be told about the intersections *between* these two groups, intersections that are historical and contemporary, conceptual and concrete, ethical and political. In the last few decades, philosophers have begun to pay more attention both to non-human animals and to the "cognitively disabled," and this theoretical work coincides with, and in many cases has been informed by, the burgeoning animal rights and disability rights movements.

History bears witness to a whole bestiary of human *others*, human beings that have been defined as "subhuman" and animal-like. Examples can be drawn from a wide variety of groups and contexts, including women, individuals who belong to a particular race, ethnicity or nationality, criminals and other "deviant" individuals, and the physically and mentally disabled. One reason, then, to pay attention to the "discourse of animality" is in order to make sense of these connections. In his introduction to *Zoontologies*, Carey Wolfe writes,

C. Painter and C. Lotz (eds.), Phenomenology and the Non-Human Animal, 117–133.

> One might well observe that it is crucial to pay critical attention to the discourse of animality quite irrespective of the issue of how nonhuman animals are treated. This is so because the discourse of animality has historically served as a critical strategy in the oppression of *humans* by other humans – a strategy whose legitimacy and force depend, however, on the prior taking for granted of the traditional ontological distinction, and consequent ethical divide, between human and nonhuman animals.[4]

In fact, this particular strategy of dehumanization has been challenged on numerous fronts, and as a result references to certain animalized *others* have all but disappeared. Though the discourse of animality has been disavowed as a strategy to define (and thereby oppress) many human kinds, it has nevertheless not disappeared entirely. And while in many communities and contexts (e.g., legal, psychological, educational, political, sociological) there are efforts to assert the personhood and humanity of persons with severe cognitive disabilities, connections with non-human animals still abound in philosophical discourse. The existence and persistence of these associations raise a number of questions, including: Does the discourse of animality used in the context of disability contribute to concrete forms of oppression and dehumanization? What is it about this group of human beings that justifies the continued associations between them and non-human animals? Put bluntly, why don't the descriptions and comparisons of persons with cognitive disabilities in relation to non-human animals provoke the same response as speaking about other groups in terms of their "animal nature"?

It is in response to these questions and in the context of broader challenges to the able-bodied world's perception of disability that one finds what I will call the "disability critique" of the associations between non-human animals and persons with disabilities.[5] This position takes on an interesting hue, however, when it is considered in the context of another, far more visible set of challenges, namely, the critical discourse on non-human animals.[6] It is against the backdrop of these two concurrent critiques, then, that I would like to focus on an apparent tension that emerges between them. They have both been formulated in critical and positive terms: on the one hand, the disability critique challenges associations between the "cognitively disabled" and non-human animals, and calls for us to humanize our view of disability; on the other hand, the critical discourse on non-human animals calls in to question the ontological and ethical privileging of the human over the non-human animal, and calls for us to "reassert our human animality,"[7] i.e., to recognize our own animal nature. The problem emerges when one considers the implications that each of these positions has for the other. When considered in tandem, the following questions arise: How does challenging the associations between the cognitively disabled and non-human animals obscure or deny our *animal* nature and perpetuate negative views about non-human animals?[8] Conversely, does blurring the line between the human and non-human in an effort to challenge the domination of the human over the non-human world further entrench the oppressive practices and beliefs about the "cognitively disabled?"

There are numerous ways to respond to this apparent tension. One response is to say that this tension creates a false dilemma: one does not have to privilege one group over the other and view "the cognitively disabled" and non-human animals as having competing interests. For example, Cora Diamond and Eva Kittay argue that the juxtaposition of non-human animals and persons with cognitive disabilities in critiques of speciesism is both unnecessary and problematic. Diamond argues that challenging the connections between non-human animals and the disabled does not entail a speciesist position, and that it is possible to assert the "importance of being human" without diminishing the moral status of animals.[9] Kittay, in her extended critique of Jeff McMahan's contention that we must rethink our mistreatment of non-human animals in the context of our misguided solicitude toward the cognitively disabled, argues that it is, in fact, possible to hold the position that "we should treat the CSMJ [congenitally severely mentally retarded] as we treat other persons, and also that we should treat animals better than we do now."[10]

Another response to the tension maintains that defining certain human beings in relation to their animal nature may, in fact, highlight what is powerful and positive in both groups. Consider the following example, which is related to gender, not disability. In addressing the ways that Nietzsche has defined woman in terms of her animality, Jennifer Ham argues that this is not, as many have contended, evidence of his blatant misogyny. When Nietzsche asks in *Human, All Too Human:* "Truth as Circe- Error has transformed animals into men; is truth perhaps capable of changing man back into an animal?"[11] Ham sees empowerment, rather than dehumanization:

> In this final rhetorical association of femininity and animality, in the image of the fearful sorceress of antiquity who indeed had the power to transform the companions of Odysseus into swine, Nietzsche states again one of the major projects of his philosophy: to reveal and restore the animal nature of human beings.[12]

Alisdair MacIntyre echoes this idea in the context of disability, and maintains that to acknowledge our human animality, in all of its vulnerability and dependence, can lead to greater respect both for persons with disabilities and for non-human animals.[13]

While I am sympathetic to these approaches (and of course these are by no means the only responses to the tension that I have outlined), I would like to consider the implications of these simultaneous calls to challenge the dehumanization of *human others* and the devaluation of *animal others* from a very different perspective. To do so I will turn to an unlikely source: the work of Michel Foucault. This may seem an odd choice in a volume devoted to phenomenology and the non-human animal, as Foucault was neither a phenomenologist nor did he devote much attention to non-human animals. However, Foucault's work is of interest in this connection for a number of reasons. First, a Foucauldian approach to this tension can further illuminate what is problematic about the associations between the "cognitively disabled" and non-human beings in contemporary philosophical discourse. Second, a close consideration of *Madness and Civilization*, the text where Foucault talks most explicitly about the non-human animal, provides the occasion to consider Foucault's own view of the human-non-human divide. Finally, in exposing some of the limitations of a Foucauldian approach to these questions, new spaces emerge wherein disability, animality, and the relationship between them can be phenomenologically explored.

I. Madness and the Mask of the Beast

"Madness borrowed its face from the mask of the beast."[14]

In *Madness and Civilization*, Foucault discusses the ways in which madness emerged as an object of knowledge within the course of a few centuries. In this rich and vivid account, Foucault also highlights the relationship between madness and animality, and the ways in which this connection shifted with certain changes in the definitions and treatment of madness. This is no incidental association, however, for upon closer examination it becomes clear that animality was integral to the Classical conception of madness in three interrelated ways: it defined madness as a *category;* it allowed the madman-animal to emerge as a distinct *individual;* and it provided the justification for the *treatment* of this group of human others.

Insofar as Foucault's history of madness traces the conditions for the possibility of madness emerging as a distinct category, it also illuminates how the relationship between human and non-human has been central to this evolution. It is not merely through analogy that madness is related to the non-human animal; rather, animality lies at the heart of madness itself:

> For classicism, madness in its ultimate form is man in immediate relation to his animality....It is not on this horizon of *nature* that the seventeenth and eighteenth centuries recognized madness, but against a background of *Unreason*; madness did not disclose a mechanism, but revealed a liberty raging in the monstrous forms of animality.[15]

The category that develops over the course of the seventeenth and eighteenth centuries and the fear that it generates is based upon a particular vision of the non-human animal, which completely dissociates animality from the laws and order of nature. According to this view, the animality that is revealed in madness represents a kind of "anti-nature":

> From the start, Western culture has not considered it evident that animals participate in the plenitude of nature, in its wisdom and its order....In fact, upon close examination it becomes evident that the animal belongs rather to an anti-nature, to a negativity that threatens order and by its frenzy endangers the positive wisdom of nature. It is this frenzy that defined madness in the 17th and 18th centuries: the animality that lends its face to madness in no way stipulates a determinist nature for its phenomena. On the contrary, it locates madness in *an area of unforeseeable freedom* where frenzy is unchained.[16]

Madness, then, is not viewed as dangerous because it represents the untamed forces of nature; rather, in its associations with animality it, too, is perceived as in opposition to what is natural. In addition to its importance for our understanding of madness, Foucault's formulation here is particularly interesting, insofar as it challenges the idea that animality and nature have always been viewed as opposed to reason. While many challenges to the dominant view of non-human animals have placed them on the "nature" side of the reason-nature dichotomy, Foucault's history betrays a deeper schism between the madman-animal and Nature itself.[17]

This belief that madness, in its animality, was in opposition to the natural order, ultimately dictated the forms of treatment that would eventually be rejected by the "liberators" of madness in the nineteenth century. Just as Foucault argues in *Discipline and Punish*, that the delinquent and the penitentiary techniques were, "in a sense, twin brothers,"[18] so the madman as a distinct kind of individual and the techniques for taming and brutalizing this animalized *other* emerge together. Here we see that animality not only provides the soil within which the meaning of madness could be nourished, it also offers a face to the madman and a shape to the institutional structures that would attempt to "cure" him. Foucault explains that by the seventeenth century, with the opening of the "Hôpital General" that was to house all kinds of individuals who symbolized "unreason" (e.g., the poor, the criminal, the insane), the perception of madness changed: "Madness had become a thing to look at: no longer a monster inside oneself, but an animal with strange mechanisms, a bestiality from which man had long since been suppressed."[19] Thus, the "theme of the animal-madman was effectively realized in the eighteenth century,"[20] and with it came a series of techniques and practices that attempted to tame the "anti-natural violence of animality."[21]

Since "unchained animality could be mastered only by discipline and brutalizing,"[22] it was necessary to treat these human animals in a way befitting of beasts. Because the madman was so closely aligned with the animal, it was believed that he shared the same physiological responses and was thus able to be treated as such:

> Animality, in fact, protected the lunatic from whatever might be fragile, precarious, or sickly in man. The animal solidity of madness, and that

> density it borrows from the blind world of beasts, inured the madman to hunger, heat, cold and pain….There was no need to protect them, they had no need to be covered or warm.[23]

For example, in one case madmen are literally transformed into "beasts of burden" in farm settings, a moment that seals the total dehumanization of the madman, while ensuring that the truth of madness resides in its animality: "In the reduction to animality, madness finds both its truth and its cure; when the madman has become a beast, this presence of the animal in man, a presence which constituted the scandal of madness, is eliminated: not that the animal is silenced, but man himself is abolished."[24] For the Classical age, then, the human face of madness is covered by the mask of the beast, and thus it follows that only that which allows for the madman's "true" animal nature to flourish can serve as a response.

The human face of madness does not disappear for long, however. With the birth of the asylum the overt connections between animality and madness recede; as madness becomes enclosed in a moral and medical space, and *homo medicus* takes over the management and rehabilitation of this sickness, the madman's human face emerges, thanks to the "humanitarian" reforms of the nineteenth century.[25] However, just as madness is adopting a human face, appeals to animality nonetheless continue to define "unreason," and serve to organize knowledge about another category of *otherness* that emerges, namely, idiocy; for if read alongside Foucault's work on madness, the history of "idiocy" can be viewed as another variation of the same complex, ever-changing relationship between the human and non-human.

II. A New Face Behind the Mask

Foucault highlights a long historical legacy of defining human beings relegated to the realm of "unreason" as animal-like. Just as the definition of madness and the madman relied upon concepts of animality in all its freedom and frenzy, in distinct opposition to the wisdom and order of "nature," so we find the mask of the beast shaping late nineteenth and early twentieth century conceptions of "idiocy" and "feeblemindedness," replacing the madman-animal, as madness leaves the stage to become defined in terms of a distinctly human pathology in need of moral therapeutics.[26]

From its inception, the category of "idiocy" relied heavily upon defining these individuals in terms of their animal nature.[27] This can be seen in the language used by Dr. Issac Kerlin, superintendent of the Pennsylvania Training School for the Feebleminded, to describe two of his students: "Two children have attached themselves to all of us, on account of their infancy and beauty, and are justly entitled to the appellation of 'pets' in our household."[28] In like fashion, Samuel Gridley Howe, one of the early pioneers of schools for the "feebleminded," characterizes "idiots" in relation to their animal-like qualities. In exclaiming his dismay at the discovery of idiocy in his homeland, Howe writes, "But alas!...[one] finds, even in our fair commonwealth, breathing masses of flesh, fashioned in the shape of men, but shorn of all other human attributes....Idiots of the lowest class are mere organisms, masses of flesh and bone in human shape...."[29] In a description of one case, he even says, "he is, in form and outline, like a human being but in nothing else."[30] However, even the outward shape or form could be inhuman, and betray signs of animality. Howe speaks of the "peculiar look so common with idiots, and which may be better expressed by the word *monkeyish* than any other."[31] In some extreme cases, the individual is below the animal kingdom: "Very few cases (we were inclined to think none could) can be found in which a being in human shape is so much below even insects, and so little above a sensitive plant."[32] Years later, in his famous hereditary study of feeblemindedness, *The Kallikak Family*, H. H. Goddard said of Deborah Kallikak's mother,

> [h]er philosophy of life is the philosophy of the animal. There is no complaining, no irritation at the inequalities of fate. Sickness, pain, childbirth, death – she accepts them all with the same equanimity as she accepts the opportunity of putting a new dress and a gay ribbon on herself.[33]

In addition to invoking the non-human animal in describing the "feebleminded," the same arguments that were used to justify the treatment of madness based on its animal nature during the Classical period can be found centuries later in the "schools" and "hospitals" for the "feebleminded." Foucault points to "the belief that madmen, like animals, were able to endure 'the worst inclemencies,' and it was this obsession with animality that created the imagery responsible for all the practices of confinement and the strangest aspects of its savagery."[34] Foucault further explains that "those chained to the cell walls were no longer men whose minds had wandered, but beasts preyed upon by a natural frenzy....This model of animality prevailed in the asylums and gave them their cage like aspect."[35] Similarly, the institutional structures for the "feebleminded" that survived well into the 1970's, in various guises, reiterated this model. It is not difficult to find instances of the "feebleminded" and "mentally deficient" being treated as animals, in earlier cases becoming "beasts of burden" in the farm colonies constructed for the "feebleminded" in the early twentieth century, and in later instances being kept naked, lying in feces in virtual cages, in the wards of Willowbrook, as recently as in the 1970's.[36]

While contemporary practices may no longer be based on the assumption that the "cognitively disabled" are more like non-human animals than humans, the face of the beast still haunts the rational world's perception of unreason. And nowhere is this more apparent than in philosophy. The associations between the "cognitively disabled" and "non-human animals" in philosophical discourse take a number of forms: they provide a means of comparison; they provide a basis for defining the nature of severe cognitive disability; and they question whether a line can even be drawn between the cognitively disabled and non-human animals, when it comes to moral status.[37] These connections can be found in animal rights literature and in arguments that are intended to address the moral status of non-human animals (e.g., in Peter Singer's refutation of speciesism),[38] and in work explicitly devoted to ethical issues regarding mental retardation.[39] There are also instances whereby these two groups are juxtaposed in order to highlight a particular moral argument that has implications for them both. For example, Jeff McMahan's recent book provides one example of how the "cognitively disabled" and non-human animals work together to shape a moral argument about the ethics of killing:

> [k]illing animals, and allowing them to die, are morally far more serious matters than we have supposed. But allowing severely retarded human beings to die, and perhaps even killing them, are correspondingly less serious matters than we have believed....Certain commonsense beliefs, both about animals and about the severely retarded, have to be revised. Our vague, intuitive commitment to a fundamental moral equality among all human beings – all members of the species *Homo sapiens* – has to be abandoned.[40]

How might one explain the prevalence of such examples and articulate why they are so troubling? One answer (which time does not permit me to fully explore here) may be found, broadly speaking, in the differences between philosophical traditions. The approach embodied in the above examples is based upon defining a set of criteria for the purpose of determining the moral status of these marginal *others*. What is disappointingly left out of such accounts is a fuller conception of the individual as a relational being, an articulation of the horizon upon which these relations emerge and are nourished, and a deeper investigation of the means through which these *others* are constituted as marginal. A shift in philosophical orientation, then, may begin to reveal why these associations between non-human animals and the "severely cognitively disabled" should, at the very least, give us pause.

Beyond mapping historical resonances between the animal-madman and the animal-idiot, how can Foucault's work on the relationship between the human and non-human animal allow us to critically rethink these contemporary philosophical examples? [41] First, Foucault's work on madness emphasizes the historical and epistemological importance of tracing the roots of our present classifications, and the necessity of viewing them as contingent incarnations rather than as atemporal, ahistorical self-evident categories. The "severely retarded" and the "madman" are not unproblematic human kinds about which certain ethical and political questions can be posed.[42] In this connection, Foucault's efforts to trace "the archaeology of the silence" that resulted in the split between "reason" and "unreason," for instance, prompts philosophers interested in cognitive disability to consider the silences and dichotomies that underlie contemporary definitions and perceptions of cognitive disability. Foucault's work also leads us to consider the possible continuities and discontinuities between the historical and contemporary discourses that bring certain human *others* and non-human animals into close proximity.

This question of continuity opens the possibility that the persistence of such associations may perpetuate the dehumanization of people with cognitive disabilities. Though Foucault is famously resistant to being prescriptive in his texts and rarely provides his readers with any explicit normative claims, I read his texts as *sites of resistance* in themselves and thus view *Madness and Civilization* as a polemic against the effects and justifications of dehumanization. In this regard, we ought to be suspicious of certain institutional and discursive practices that perpetuate forms of domination and oppression. In considering the reasons to critically examine the discourse of animality, Wolfe writes, in this connection, that

> [e]ven though the *discourse* of animality and species difference may theoretically be applied to an other of whatever type, the consequences of that discourse, in *institutional* terms, fall overwhelmingly on nonhuman animals, in our taken-for-granted practices of using and exploiting them.[43]

However, the one glaring human exception may be the case of cognitively disabled individuals whose institutional history betrays horrific forms of mistreatment and abuse, and whose very lives are imperiled through the often "taken-for-granted" arguments that justify infanticide and euthanasia in these "marginal cases."

In drawing out the complexity and dynamism of the connection between the human and non-human, in exposing the "savagery" that accompanied the treatment of the madman through the Classical period, and in calling into question the "truth" about the liberatory intentions of the new methods employed in the asylums, Foucault reveals the complex processes by which a *human other becomes animal*. His work, then, leaves us to consider whether philosophical discourse is able to maintain a gap between the "cognitively disabled" and the non-human animal, which is wide enough to ward against further forms of dehumanization.[44]

III. A Foucauldian Bestiary?

Insofar as Foucault challenges us to consider our historical and moral distance from the conceptions and practices of the past, and to problematize the underpinnings of contemporary (so-called) "liberatory" and "humanitarian" efforts, his work is as important to cognitive disability as it is to madness. Yet, while it is clear that Foucault's work is consonant with a critique of the animalized disabled other, what might he have to say about the other side of the tension occasioned by these reflections? Is there any sense in which Foucault simultaneously calls upon us to reassert (or at the very least recognize) our animal nature? While his work on madness exposes the dehumanization of the madman that resulted from madness finding its "truth" in animality, Foucault does not explicitly argue that we must sever ties with our animal nature altogether. In studying the mask of the beast worn by the madman, does Foucault unmask some dimension of *our animal nature* as human beings?

One trace of the animal might be found in the treatment of the madman. While the animal-madman becomes animal as a "beast of burden," the "savagery" of these acts and treatments may betray a second animality, wherein the efforts to tame and brutalize *themselves* become another incarnation of the animal in human form. Jami Weinstein suggests that Foucault's model of animality is "...the practice of superimposing the animal onto certain human bodies, [which] follows from his treatment of bio-power and its relation to the production of the subject."[45] Yet another incarnation of the human animal may be evident in the techniques of power and in the cages of reason itself. Though the explicit language that ties *madness* to animality ends with the birth of the asylum, does a different beast emerge by unmasking the *hegemony of Reason*? Interestingly, Foucault effects a reversal whereby another face of madness appears as the *other of Unreason*. Borrowing the words of Pascal in his introduction: "Men are so necessarily mad, that not to be mad would amount to another form of madness,"[46] Foucault suggests that this "other form" refers to the sovereignty of reason "which relegates Reason and Madness to one side or the other of its action."[47] If the Reason that silences and excludes madness is *itself* a new form of madness, does this darker side of Reason betray another face of the beast?

Though readers may be thinking that I am seeing beasts where there are none in Foucault's text, I think that Nietzsche's appearance as philosopher, artist, and madman at the end of the book does, at the very least, leave us to wonder to what extent the madness and savagery of reason reveals another incarnation of the beast within the human. Insofar as his work problematizes the dichotomies between Reason-Unreason and Nature-Anti-nature, and raises suspicions about appeals to the "humanism" that sustains them, Foucault is certainly an heir of Nietzsche and might also be read in the company of ecofeminists and other environmental philosophers who challenge the practices and ideologies that justify human sovereignty over the non-human world.[48] In leaving us with the image of Goya's *Idiot,* who "shrieks and twists his shoulder to escape from the nothingness that imprisons him," in pointing to a madness that amplifies "those barely audible voices of Unreason" to "shrieks and frenzy...restoring their primitive savagery," does Foucault himself animalize the human? Does the beast that haunts Goya's Monk, with "its paws on his shoulders and its mouth panting at his ear," lurk behind *rational man* in Reason's attempt to dissociate itself from the madman?[49]

To suggest that in dehumanizing human others we are exposing an animality in ourselves, however, does not translate into a *positive* philosophy of the non-human animal; in fact, some could argue that it simply perpetuates the negative associations between animality and violence, brutality and savagery.[50] Foucault certainly does not seem to *celebrate* or revel in the human *as animal* in the way that Nietzsche's work does.[51] Thus, beyond his explorations of how certain human beings have become the *animal other* and beyond his Nietzschean critiques of "reason's monologue," we are left to wonder what a Foucauldian approach to the human-non-human animal divide would look like.[52] Perhaps we can detect glimpses here, as Foucault intimates that there may be other configurations of the human-non-human relationship to be explored:

> Why should the fact that Western man has lived for two thousand years on his definition as a rational animal necessarily mean that he has recognized the possibility of an order common to reason and animality?...Independently of what Aristotle really meant, may we not assume that for the West this 'rational animal' has long been the measure of the way in which reason's freedom functioned in the locus of unreason, diverging from it until it constituted its opposite term? From the moment philosophy became anthropology, and man sought to recognize himself in a natural plentitude, the animal lost its power of negativity, in order to become, between the determinism of nature and the reason of man, the positive form of an evolution. The formula of the "rational animal" has utterly changed its meaning: the unreason it suggested as the origin of all possible reason has entirely disappeared. Henceforth madness must obey the determinism of man perceived as a natural being in his very animality.[53]

What Foucault ultimately means by an "order common to reason and animality," and what the implications are of this "determinism," wherein human beings are perecieved as natural beings in their "very animality," are questions that must be left for another time. Even in the absence of a clear "Foucauldian bestiary," however, Foucault's work on madness teaches us to look for traces of the human face and masks of the beast on *both* sides of the divide between Reason and Unreason. In doing so, we find new possibilities for interrogating the convergence of two contemporary discourses: one which asks us to humanize our view of the "cognitively disabled" and the other which demands that as humans we embrace our animality and rethink our relationship to the *animal other*. Rather than offering a resolution to the apparent tension between them, a Foucauldian approach asks us to consider what it is that makes these two positions simultaneously possible at all: "To one set of difficulties, several responses can be made....But what has to be understood is…the point in which their simultaneity is rooted; it is the soil that can nourish them in all their diversity and sometimes in spite of their contradictions."[54]

IV. A Phenomenological Coda: Unmasking the Face of the Other

The distance between Foucault and phenomenology has been noted by many, and Foucault himself addressed his reasons for rejecting the phenomenological method.[55] In what ways, then, do the preceding Foucauldian reflections leave open a space for a phenomenological exploration of the relationship between disability and animality? The two discourses that I have addressed can be found within the boundaries of contemporary phenomenology; indeed, the essays in this volume reflect many ways that the distance between the human and non-human can be cast in phenomenological terms, and there is a growing body of work looking at disability (primarily physical disability) from a phenomenological perspective.[56] When considered together, we can ask whether a similar tension is produced between these efforts to address the dehumanization of disabled *others* and calls to rethink our relationship to non-human animals.[57] In the spirit of initiating a dialogue in response to this question, this brief coda is a gesture toward the possibility both of moving beyond Foucault and of returning to him in the context of phenomenology.

While Foucault's text on madness provides a unique window into the intricacies of the human-non-human relationship, and suggests new ways to conceive of this in the context of disability, there are many remaining questions that may require a move away from the Foucauldian text. The cases of madness in the Classical age and of cognitive disability in contemporary philosophical discourse provide two examples of how a particular human kind can become defined in terms of its animal *otherness*. The emphasis in both Foucault's and my own analyses, however, has been upon discursive and institutional practices within which these *others* have been constituted in terms of their animality. While this paints a rich and complex historical and philosophical portrait of the animalization of those individuals at the margins of reason, a fuller account is needed to explain exactly *why* this happens. It is here that a phenomenological approach may lead to new questions, and, thus, to new answers. What are the conditions for the possibility of being able to perceive these human *others* as so radically other? And moreover, in formulating the question in this way, in assuming that seeing the face of the beast in another human being *is* in fact viewing them as *radically other*, what distance is assumed between the human and non-human animal? How can one probe the nature of embodied subjectivity and the experience of the lived body for individuals with *cognitive* disabilities specifically, (and more generally, for beings for whom language is not readily available as a means of expression)? And how can one begin to explain the gulf that separates the rational self and the cognitively disabled *other*, a space that mirrors the gap traditionally found between the human and non-human, and which simultaneously challenges it and perhaps exceeds it?[58]

These methodological questions give way to ethical questions where, again, Foucault's work may leave us at sea. His work on madness illustrates the ways in which madmen were enclosed in a moral space in the asylum, and he suggests that the "humanitarian" reforms were not, in fact, the liberatory practices they purported to be. Yet though his text unmasks the animal face of the dehumanized madman, the problem of ethical responsibility in the face of a human or non-human *Other*, whose capacity to reason and to speak is diminished or non-existent, is left unanswered.[59] While there is a growing body of literature in analytic ethics that brings together ethical considerations about non-human animals and cognitive disability,[60] there may be new ways to bring these two *others* together in a different discursive space. Consider Levinas and his dog, for example.

In "The Name of a Dog, or Natural Rights," Levinas recounts his encounter with Bobby, a "wandering dog" who appeared in the prison camp and who Levinas characterizes as "the last Kantian in Nazi Germany." Levinas highlights the dehumanizing effects of the camp, writing, "We were subhuman, a gang of apes…How can we deliver a message about our humanity which, from behind the bars of quotation marks, will come across as anything other than monkey talk?"[61] Bobby was unlike the "other men, called free," who "stripped us of our human skin," because for him "there was no doubt that we were men."[62] This story raises the question of what to make of Levinas' view of non-human animals, and "whether, in Levinas' sense of the word, the animal has a face."[63] The claim that this dog was "without the brain needed to universalize maxims and drives" certainly suggests that he would not be part of the Kantian moral universe. However, we are left to wonder what "his friendly growling" and "his animal faith" ultimately say about Bobby's ability to *humanize* these men who, "despite all their vocabulary," were also "beings without language."[64] And just as we can ask whether Bobby inhabits Levinas' realm of moral obligations, this story also leaves us to wonder about those human *others* who, as beings without language, *do* have a human face: namely, the severely cognitively disabled.[65]

While this glimpse at Levinas's work is far too brief, it speaks to the possibility of renegotiating our relationship to an *other* for whom language is not available. Perhaps in recognizing the particularity of these faces and the richness of our encounters with them, the tension we have been exploring – a tension that suggests that we cannot simultaneously and justly encompass these two very distinct beings within the same moral universe – may begin to dissipate. In its wake, however, a new philosophical tension – between a Foucauldian and a phenomenological approach – seems to emerge, one that raises the problem of how best to accomplish this task.

Foucault was at his most phenomenological in his early work on *Mental Illness and Psychology,* and while he moved on to define archaeology and genealogy as his methods, some hear echoes of these earlier days in his later work. For instance, Todd May suggests that a continuity can be found in the question "Who are we?", a question that can be traced throughout Foucault's work.[66] Certainly, this question speaks to the issue at hand, as we consider the nature, limits, and dangers of defining oneself in relation to an *other* who is either "animal" by definition, or has become "animalized" by virtue of her profound otherness. This critical project demands work at multiple levels, and perhaps the celebration of difference that is implied herein can extend to the reaches of distinct philosophies of the human and non-human animal, and bring Foucault into a new and unexpected dialogue with phenomenology.

There is a danger of repeating the very errors that one is trying to correct,[67] and thus I must consider whether, in bringing the "cognitively disabled" and non-human animals under the same roof, so to speak, I am somehow repeating the same philosophical move that I have sought to challenge. It is far too facile to simply reject all associations between these two groups outright, and the vast differences in *how* these connections can be made in philosophical discourse speak to the complexities of this area of inquiry. However, let the voices of Foucualt and Levinas serve as reminders that the contexts, reasons, and justifications for bringing these two *others* face-to-face cannot be ignored, and that only by continuing to ask who is speaking, who is unmasking, who is silent, and who is revealed, will the rational world begin to bring its monologue to an end.

Notes

1. Michel Foucault. "The Discourse on Language," *The Archaeology of Knowledge,* trans. Alan Sheridan. (New York: Pantheon Books, 1972), p. 216.
2. Jeff McMahan. *The Ethics of Killing: Problems at the Margins of Life.* (New York: Oxford University Press, 2002), p. 230.
3. Here I include both the mentally ill and the cognitively disabled.
4. Carey Wolfe. *Zoontologies: The Question of the Animal.* (Minneapolis: University of Minnesota Press, 2003), p. xx.
5. See: Licia Carlson. "Rethinking Normalcy, Normalization and Cognitive Disability" in eds. Harding and Figueroa, *Sceince and Other Cultures: Issues in Philosophies of Science and Technology* (New York: Routledge, 2003), pp. 63–64; and Chapter 5 of "Mindful Subjects: Classification and Cognitive Disability," Ph.D. Diss., University of Toronto, 1998. See also: Eva Feder Kittay. "At the Margins of Moral Personhood" *Ethics 116* (October 2005), pp. 100–131; Paula Boddington and Tessa Popadec. "Who are the Mentally Handicapped?" *Journal of Applied Philosophy* 8 (2), pp. 177–190; Paul Spicker. "Mental Handicap and Citizenship." *Journal of Applied Philosophy* 7, (2) 1990, pp. 139–151.
6. By this phrase I mean the wide variety of theoretical and political work that includes, but is not limited to, the animal rights movement.
7. I borrow this phrase from Alisdair MacIntyre.

8. As one philosopher pointedly asked me at a conference in response to my articulation of the disability critique: "In challenging the connections drawn between cognitive disability and animality, aren't you guilty of speciesism?"
9. Cora Diamond. "The Importance of Being Human," in ed. D. Cockburn, *Human Beings* (Cambridge: Cambridge University Press, 1991), pp. 35–62.
10. Kittay, 125.
11. Jennifer Hamm. "Circe's Truth: On the Way to Animals and Women" in eds. Accampora and Accampora, *A Nietzschean Beastiary* (Lanham: Rowman & Littlefield, 2004), p 193.
12. Ibid., p. 208.
13. Alisdair MacIntyre. *Dependent Rational Animals: Why Human Beings Need the Virtues* (Chicago: Open Court, 1999), p. 5.
14. Michel Foucault, *Madness and Civilization* (New York: Vintage Books, 1988), p. 72.
15. *Madness and Civilization*, 74, 83.
16. Ibid., 77.
17. This interpretation of madness and animality as "anti-nature" calls for further attention, in Foucault's own text and beyond, though space does not permit it here.
18. Michel Foucault, *Discipline and Punish* (New York: Vintage Books, 1979), p. 255.
19. *Madness and Civilization*, p. 70.
20. Ibid., 75.
21. Ibid., 78.
22. Ibid., 75.
23. Ibid., 74.
24. Ibid., 76.
25. It is Foucault's intention to call this "liberation" into question in the remainder of the book.
26. The question of whether the connections between animality and madness do, in fact, wane, in the nineteenth and twentieth centuries, would require further exploration. Thus, I do not mean to suggest a simple or straightforward replacement of the "madman" by the "idiot" when it comes to associations with non-human animals; I have no doubt that there is a more complex story to be told.
27. See Carlson, "Mindful Subjects," Chapter 2.
28. Issaac Kerlin. "Our Household Pets" eds. Marvin Rosen, Gerald Clark, and Marvin Kivitz. *The History of Mental Retardation: Collected Papers, Volume I*, (Baltimore: University Park Press, 1975), pp. 283–291.
29. Samuel Gridley Howe. "On the Causes of Idiocy." *History of Mental Retardation: Collected Papers, Volume I*, (1848): pp. 31–60, p. 37.
30. Ibid., 38.
31. Ibid., 39.
32. Ibid., 37.
33. Henry Herbert Goddard. *The Kallikak Family: A Study in the Heredity of Feeble-Mindedness* (New York: The Macmillan Company, 1939), p. 66.
34. Foucault, 74, 77.
35. Ibid., 72.
36. See: James W. Trent. *Inventing the Feeble Mind: A History of Mental Retardation in the United States* (Berkeley: University of California Press, 1995); Wolf Wolfensberger. *The Principle of Normalization* (Toronto: National Institute on Mental Retardation, 1972); Burton Blatt, *Christmas in Purgatory* (Syracuse: Human Policy Press, 1974).
37. For specific examples, see Carlson, "Rethinking Normalcy" pp. 63–64; and Carlson, "Mindful Subjects," Chapter 5.
38. For example, in explicitly discussing the similarities between non-human animals and the "severely retarded" Singer writes, "As long as we remember that we

should give the same respect to the lives of animals as we give the lives of humans at a similar mental level, we shall not go far wrong." *Animal Liberation* (London: Pimlico, 1995), p. 21.

39. Numerous examples may be found in many of the contributions in eds. Loretta Kopelman and John C. Moskop. *Ethics and Mental Retardation* (Dordrecht, Holland: D. Reidel Publishing Company, 1984).
40. McMahan, *The Ethics of Killing*, 230, 233.
41. I realize that what follows here fails to attend to the specificity of each example, and unfortunately space does not permit me to go into greater depth with particular examples. Rather, I hope to raise questions here that can then be brought to bear upon these associations in a variety of contexts and arguments.
42. For a more extended discussion of this, see Carlson, "Docile Minds, Docile Bodies" in ed. Shelley Tremain. *Foucault and the Government of Disability* (Ann Arbor: University of Michigan Press, 2005), 133–152.
43. Wolfe, xx.
44. In order to fully trace these connections, one would have to consider the production of philosophical discourse from within a particular institutional set of practices, and consider their relation to other forms of institutional practices and discourses that bear more directly upon persons with disabilities.
45. Jami Weinstein. "Traces of the Beast: Becoming Nietzsche, Becoming Animal, and Faces of the Transhuman" in *A Nietzschean Bestiary*, p. 311.
46. Here Foucault quotes Pascal. *Madness and Civilization*, p. ix.
47. Ibid.
48. See, for example, Ladelle McWhorter. "Foucault and Ecofeminism" in *Philosophy Today,* Vol. 40 *(SPEP Supplement: Directions and Directives, Vol. 30, 2005*), pp. 110–115.
49. *Madness and Civilization,* pp. 280–281.
50. Clare Palmer suggests that ultimately Foucault does not overcome the reason-animal-madness binary. See: "Madness and Animality in Michel Foucault's *Madness and Civilization*" in eds. Peter Atterton and Matthew Calarco, *Animal Philosophy: Essential Readings in Continental Thought* (London: Continuum, 2005), pp. 72–84, esp. pp. 81–84.
51. For many wonderful illustrations of this see, *A Nietzschean Bestiary*.
52. Clare Palmer suggests that his conception of power might be useful in theorizing the human-non-human relation and in exposing patterns of domination and resistance. See "Taming the Wild Profusion of Existing Things: A study of Foucault, Power, and Human/Animal Relationships." *Environmental Ethics,* Vol. 23, (Winter 2001), pp. 339–358. Also, Jami Weinstein proposes that Foucault be read as one of the philosophers whose work opens up the possibility of "becoming-animal," and that in his examination of dehumanization we find a new form of the "trans-human". See: "Traces of the Beast: Becoming Nietzsche, Becoming Animal, and Faces of the Transhuman" in *Nietzschean Beastiary,* p. 315.
53. *Madness and Civilization*, 77.
54. Michel Foucault. "Polemics, Politics, Problematizations" in ed. Paul Rabinow. *The Essential Works of Michel Foucault, 1954–1984,* Vol. 1, (New York: New Press, 1997), p. 118.
55. For a few examples, see *The Order of Things* (New York: Vintage Press, 1973) 322–328; "Truth and Power," in ed. Paul Rabinow, *The Foucault Reader* (Pantheon, 1984), 59; "An Historian of Culture" in Michel Foucault, *Foucault Live*: *Interviews (1966–84)*, New York: Semiotext(e), 1989, 73–88.
56. For example, see Bill Hughes. "What Can a Foucauldian Analysis Contribute to Disability Theory?" *Foucault and the Government of Disability,* pp. 78–92; Miho Iwakuma, "The Body as Embodiment: An Investigation of the Body by Merleau-Ponty" in eds. Mairian Corker and Tom Shakespeare, *Postmodernity/Disability: Embodying Disability Theory* (London: Continuum, 2002), pp. 76–87.
57. It is possible that the tension I have identified is only a problem for a particular approach to defining moral status and personhood, and that when the questions

of disability and the non-human animal are addressed in a phenomenological context, the tension becomes less acute.

58. The "excess" is found in the fact that the question of the non-human animal has been given far more attention in philosophy than the question of the "cognitively disabled."
59. Paul Patton suggests that Foucault's work can, in fact, be instructive in considering our ethical obligations to non-human others in his article on horse training. See Paul Patton, "Language, Power and the Training of Horses" in Wolfe, p. 95.
60. An example where both of these concerns are addressed is found in Martha Nussbaum's latest book, *Frontiers of Justice: Disability, Nationality and Species Membership* (Cambridge: Belknap Press, 2006).
61. Emmanuel Levinas, "The Name of a Dog, or Natural Rights" in *Difficult Freedom: Essays on Judaism* (Johns Hopkins University Press, 1990), p. 153.
62. Ibid, 153.
63. John Llewelyn, "Am I Obsessed By Bobby? (Humanism of the Other Animal)," in eds. Robert Bernasconi and Simon Critchley. *Re-reading Levinas (*Bloomington: Indiana University Press, 1991), p. 240.
64. Levinas, 153.
65. I do not mean to suggest that *all* individuals with severe cognitive disabilities are without language or other means of expression; certainly, there are many complex epistemological questions in this context that deserve close philosophical consideration.
66. Todd May, "Foucault's Relation to Phenomenology." *The Cambridge Companion to Foucault*. Ed. Gary Gutting. (Cambridge University Press, 2005).
67. I am here reminded of Derrida's critique of Foucault's attempt to "speak *for madness*," using the very language that he was attempting to critique.

10

The Intertwining of Incommensurables

Yann Martel's Life of Pi

James MENSCH

In the "Author's Note" that introduces the *Life of Pi*, Yann Martel claims that he first heard of Pi in a coffee shop in India. A chance acquaintance tells him, "I have a story that will make you believe in God" (*LP*, vii).[1] The story concerns the life of an Indian boy who grows up surrounded by the animals of his father's zoo. When Pi is sixteen, his family decides to emigrate. His father sells off the animals to an American zoo and the family travels with them across the Pacific. The steamer sinks during a storm and Pi finds himself on a lifeboat with a hyena, a wounded zebra, an orangutan, and a Bengal tiger. The hyena attacks the zebra and then the orangutan, devouring both. He, in turn, is killed and eaten by the tiger. Pi stays alive by acting as the tiger's zookeeper. Feeding it with the fish he catches and giving it water from the solar stills that he finds on the lifeboat, he survives until the boat, carried by the equatorial current, reaches the shores of Mexico.

How is this improbable tale supposed to bring belief? What has this story of animals, first in the zoo, and then on the raft, to do with God? The mystery deepens when at the end of the book Pi relates a second story, one where humans rather than animals are the agents. In this account, related after the first provokes incredulity, the ship's French cook becomes the hyena, a wounded sailor the zebra, Pi's mother the orangutan, and Pi himself plays the role of the Bengal tiger. On this telling, the tale becomes one of cannibalism and human savagery. A Japanese official, who hears these stories while interviewing Pi, remarks "What a horrible story" (*LP*, 345) and admits: "The story with the animals is the better story," to which Pi responds, "And so it goes with God" (*LP*, 352). Again the question recurs: What have the animals to do with God? How can the first account, where animals take the place of human agents, lead to God?

Martel's tale is an account of alterity—the alterity both of animals and God. Like Pi, we tend to define our humanity by drawing a line between it and our animality, where the human is defined by a boundary excluding the animal. Yet animality is not just other than us; it is also within us. In Levinas' phrase, our relation to it is a "difference that is not indifference."[2] The same holds for our relation to the divine. This is also other and yet within

C. Painter and C. Lotz (eds.), Phenomenology and the Non-Human Animal, 135–147.

us. How do we draw the line between our humanity and divinity, defining our humanity in terms of it? In the story, Pi confronts these two forms of alterity, at times accepting, at times rejecting their presence within him. His passage across the Pacific is, in fact, a journey into the depths of these questions, the hidden reaches where our relations to our animality and divinity are deeply entangled. The entanglement is such that we cannot understand our humanity without including both forms of alterity. Indeed, Martel's tale shows how our humanity is defined by the boundaries we draw and the ways we are forced to trespass them.

I.

The first part of the *Life of Pi* contains a defense of the well run zoo and the lives animals lead in its enclosures. We should not think of the animals as imprisoned and yearning to be free. For the animal housed in a good zoo, his enclosure is his home. "A house," Martel writes, "is a compressed territory where our basic needs can be fulfilled close by and safely. A sound zoo enclosure is the equivalent for an animal" (*LP*, 19). The inhabitant finds within it "all the places it needs—a lookout, a place for resting, for eating and drinking, for bathing, for grooming, etc" (ibid.). Miraculously, without the need of hunting, food appears (*LP*, 19). By contrast, "animals in the wild live lives of compulsion and necessity" (*LP*, 17). They face "an environment where the supply of fear is high and the food low and where territory must constantly be defended and parasites forever endured. What is the meaning of freedom in such a context?" (ibid.). In fact, offering freedom to an animal comfortably settled in its enclosure is, Martel asserts, as "if you went to a home, kicked down the front door, chased the people who lived there out into the street and said, 'Go! You are free! Free as a bird! Go! Go!' " (*LP*, 18). Neither humans nor animals would appreciate the gesture. What we have in the well run zoo is, in fact, an artificial Garden of Eden, one where "all animals are content" (*LP*, 20). Martel concludes his defense of zoos with the words: "I know zoos are no longer in people's good graces. Religion faces the same problem. Certain illusions about freedom plague them both" (*LP*, 21). He does not specify what the illusion of freedom is that plagues religion. To learn this, we have to consider existence outside of this Eden-like state.

In his first days in the life boat, this existence assumes the form of a savage struggle. The zebra, whose leg has been broken by its jump into the life boat is the first to be attacked by the hyena. He bites and pulls the skin of his victim, which "came off the zebra's belly like gift-wrap paper comes off a gift…." (*LP*, 138). As Pi describes what follows:

> The zebra's attempts at self-preservation only whipped the hyena into a frenzy of snarling and biting. It made a gaping wound in the zebra's side…. It started pulling out coils of intestines and other viscera. There

> was no order to what it was doing. It bit here, swallowed there, seemingly overwhelmed by the riches before it.... the zebra was being eaten alive from the inside (ibid.).

The female orangutan meets a similar fate. At the end of their battle, she "lay ... next to the dead zebra. Her arms were spread wide open ... she looked like a simian Christ on the Cross. Except for her head. She was beheaded. The neck wound was still bleeding" (*LP*, 145-46). Pi is so outraged, he decides to throw himself on the hyena, but then he notices the tiger crouching beneath the tarpaulin covering the rear of the life boat. The tiger springs on the hyena, who surrenders to its superior force almost without a struggle. In Pi's description, the tiger's "jaws closed on the side of the hyena's neck. Its glazed eyes widened. There was a noise of organic crunching as windpipe and spinal cord were crunched. The hyena shook. Its eyes went dull. It was over" (*LP*, 166-67).

This account is interspersed with contrasting descriptions of the animals' lives in the zoo. The tiger, who by dint of a clerical error received the name of his captor, "Richard Parker," came to the zoo as a cub. He had never killed before. The orangutan, named "Orange Juice" because of her tendency to drool, was another long-time resident of the zoo (*LP*, 123). The "mother of two fine boys," she would enfold the young Pi with her arms. The zebra in the zoo would gently pull the carrots proffered it. Pi's religious mentor exclaimed on seeing it, "What a wondrous creature," while his science teacher called it "the Rolls-Royce of equids" (*LP*, 93). The Eden-like, religiously-tinged description of their encounter is in stark opposition to Pi's account of the zebra's helplessness on being eaten alive: "Once or twice it reared its head straight up, as if appealing to heaven—the abomination of the moment was perfectly expressed" (*LP*, 139). Only the hyena, "an animal to pain the eye and chill the heart" fails to receive some commendation, though Pi admits, "a hyena's catholicity of taste is so indiscriminate it nearly forces admiration.... Hyenas snack on the excrement of herbivores with clucks of pleasure.... They eat their own kind ... once they are dead" (*LP*, 129). These, however, are descriptions of hyenas in the wild, not in the zoo.

The contrasting descriptions of the other animals raise the question of the status of our humanity. They make us wonder whether our humanity is itself the result of the provision of zoo-like conditions—houses, supermarkets, police, the stable routines of work, etc.—without which we would also revert to a similar savagery. Would we, so deprived, cross what we take to be the line between the human and the animal? Pi faces this question in the most immediate way. A self-described "puny feeble, vegetarian life form" (*LP*, 203), he must kill to survive. The transformation he undergoes can be described in his reaction to such killing. He first kills a flying fish that lands in his boat. Pi relates: "I wept heartily over this poor little deceased soul. It was the first sentient being I had ever killed. I was now a killer ... now I had blood on my hands. It's a terrible burden to carry. All sentient life is sacred" (ibid.). But, then, using this fish as bait, he catches a dorado and takes the hatchet "in both hands and vigorously beats the fish on the head with the hammer head" (*LP*, 205). He comments: "You may be astonished that in such a short period of time I could go from weeping over the muffled killing of a flying fish to gleefully bludgeoning to death a dorado…. The explanation … is simple and brutal: a person can get used to anything, even to killing" (ibid.). As the journey progresses, his clothes rot away: "For months I lived stark naked except for the whistle that dangled from my neck by a string" (*LP*, 213). He now subdues fish like an animal: "A fish jumping out of water was confronted by a famished boy…. I stuck fingers into eyes, jammed hands into gills, crushed soft stomachs with knees, bit tails with my teeth…. With time and experience I became a better hunter. I grew bolder and more agile. I developed an instinct, a feel, for what to do" (*LP*, 216).

In fact, as he admits, "I descended to a level of savagery I never imagined possible" (*LP*, 218). Describing this descent, he remarks: "By degrees the range of my appetite increased. Whereas at first I gutted fish and peeled their skin fastidiously, soon I no more than rinsed off their slimy slipperiness before biting into them, delighted to have such a treat between my teeth" (*LP*, 235). Having noted that animals' cages must be kept clean, since, "animals being gluttons for anything that remotely resembles food," they will even eat feces (*LP*, 233), he admits, "I could put anything in my mouth, chew it and swallow it—delicious, foul, or plain … I tried once to eat Richard Parker's feces" (*LP*, 236-7). He only gives up when, having tried it, he finds "there is nothing to be had here" (*LP*, 238). Not taste, but lack of substance turns him away. In this, he is no different from Richard Parker. In fact, as he remarks: "It came as an unmistakable indication to me of how low I had sunk the day I noticed with a pinching of the heart, that I ate like an animal, that the noisy, frantic, unchewing, wolfing-down of mine was exactly the way Richard Parker ate" (*LP*, 249-50).

How then does Pi draw the line between the animal and the human? In Martel's descriptions, there is, first of all, his relation to the divine. He prays many times a day. In the list of activities he compiles to describe an average day, the first thing he does upon waking is "prayers." Prayers also mark the periods of mid-morning and late afternoon. He also prays at sunset and at night during his fitful sleeping (*LP*, 210–211). The sense of the divine that moves him to pray is illustrated in his reaction to lightning during a thunder storm. It is the opposite of Richard Parker's:

> I turned to Richard Parker and said, 'Look, Richard Parker, a bolt of lightning.' I saw how he felt about it. He was flat on the floor of the boat, limbs splayed and visibly trembling. The effect on me was completely the opposite. It was something to pull me out of my limited moral ways and thrust me into a state of exalted wonder (*LP*, 258).

After a particularly brilliant flash, Pi relates: "I was dazed, thunderstruck—nearly in the true sense of the word. But not afraid. 'Praise be to Allah, Lord of All Worlds, the Compassionate, the Merciful, Ruler of Judgment Day!' I muttered. To Richard Parker I shouted, 'Stop your trembling! This is a miracle. This is an outbreak of divinity' " (*LP*, 259).

The second way of drawing the line is in his relation to Richard Parker. Upon discovering the provisions in the life boat and constructing a raft on which he sits a safe distance from the boat, Pi considers his various options with regard to the tiger. He could attempt a direct assault on the animal in various ways—plans one through five—or he could follow "Plan Number Six: Wage a War of Attrition" (*LP*, 175). In Pi's first thoughts, "Waiting for him to waste away and die would require no effort on my part. I had supplies for months to come" (ibid.). But then he realizes that the narrow stretch of water that separates the raft from the boat is no obstacle to an animal "crazed with thirst and hunger.... He will swim as far as he has to, to catch the drifting raft and the food upon it" (*LP*, 178). Direct assault would be suicidal, while a war of attrition would almost certainly be lost. Only one option is left: "I had to tame him. It was at that moment that I realized this necessity. It was not a question of him or me, but of him *and* me" (*LP*, 181). Pi's method of taming Richard Parker was to stand on the prow, rock the boat and blow the lifeboat's whistle. Because the tiger associated the resulting sea-sickness with the sound of the whistle, Pi gradually gained command of him. Using the whistle, he even trained the tiger to jump through hoops.

How are we to understand these actions of Pi? What is the symbolic import? One clue is provided by Pi's matching second story, where the actions of the animals are ascribed to humans. Another clue is present in the clerical error that results in a human name, "Richard Parker" having been given to an animal. It is accompanied by a corresponding error that results in an animal's name being given to the hunter that found it. The hunter's family name is listed as "None Given," and his first name as "Thirsty"(LP, 148). The reversals of agency and names both point to a corresponding reversal where the animal actually names a property of the human, a property that we project on to the animal. If we accept this, then we can see Pi's assertion that both he and Richard Parker needed to survive—that it was not a question of one or the other—as a concealed acceptance of his own animality. The training of Richard Parker, so necessary if both are to survive, is actually a training of Pi's own animal nature. Drawing the line in this case means, not so much the exclusion of the animal, as its education. One humanizes the animal. If we take the word "educate" in its etymological sense of drawing or leading out, one can say that the habits inculcated by training *educate* the animal.[3] They do so by *drawing out* the human from the animal. The same claim can be made with regard to Pi's relation to the divine. The religious awe inspired by the lightning is educated by being placed within the framework of "Allah, Lord of All Worlds." The lightning is not seen as something to tremble at, but rather as an "outbreak of divinity." The training that accomplishes this education occurs during the times set aside for prayer. Its basis was formed by the religious education that Pi had gained from his religious mentors. To acknowledge the necessity of this training is to accept the necessities that confront us, not just with regard to our own animality, but also with regard to the divinity that also lays claim to us. It is, in fact, to begin to undo the "illusions of freedom" that plague religion.

II.

In psychoanalytic theory, the suppression of an experience or aspect of the self does not cause it to vanish entirely. Rather, it reappears in symbolic forms. Such forms substitute a "possible" or an "acceptable" representation for an unacceptable and, therefore, "impossible" representation. The *Life of Pi* contains a number of examples of such substitution. One of the most striking occurs when first Richard Parker and then Pi go blind. Pi admits that he has "failed as a zookeeper" and prepares to die (*LP*, 268). He says: "And now I leave matters in the hands of God, who is love and whom I love" (*LP*, 269). But just then he hears a voice asking, "Is someone there?" Pi replies, "Of course someone's there. There is always some *one* there. Who would be asking the question otherwise?" The voice replies, "I was hoping that there would be someone *else*" (ibid.). They also discuss food. While Pi concentrates on vegetarian dishes, his interlocutor is a meat eater. In fact, there is no flesh that he won't eat: boiled beef tongue, tripe, pancreas, a calf's brain in brown butter sauce, bleeding raw beef, marinated rabbit, frog's legs, etc.—all form parts of his diet. The only thing he abhors is vegetables. In his semi-conscious state, Pi concludes that he is talking to Richard Parker—"the carnivorous rascal." Forgetting that the tiger was brought to the zoo as a cub, he asks, "have you ever killed a man?" (*LP*, 273). The voice admits to killing and eating first a man and then a woman. When asked if he has any regrets, the voice replies, "It was them or me.... It was the doing of the moment. It was circumstance.... I didn't think about it." Pi replies by saying, "The very definition of an animal. That's all you are," and in response, the voice asks: "And what are you?" Pi replies: "A human being, I'll have you know." The voice then says: "What boastful pride," and Pi replies: "It's the plain truth" (*LP*, 274).

If, as the second story at the end of the book suggests, Pi is actually Richard Parker, what we have here is the exposure of the projections that Pi makes onto the tiger. Pi is not, in fact, "a puny vegetarian life-form," but actually a killer. Richard Parker here represents the animality that he cannot accept. The impossible representation of himself as capable of cannibalism is covered over by a possible one, namely, that there is a tiger on board that engages in the acts that he cannot own. The assertion that he is a human being conceals from him the truth that his humanity includes the animality of the tiger.

This point is driven home when he notices that the voice has a French accent. The voice now becomes that of someone like Pi, stranded on a lifeboat, who has also gone blind. Again, food is discussed and again the voice indicates that it will eat anything. Neither, however, actually has any food. Drawing their lifeboats together, Pi invites the stranger on board with the words, "Come my brother, let us be together and feast on each other's company" (*LP*, 282). The stranger falls on him and to Pi's remark, "My heart is with you," replies, "You're damn right your heart is with me! ... And your liver and your flesh" (ibid.). The blind stranger is a cannibal. But before he has time to act, Richard Parker appears and attacks him. Pi relates: "I heard the merest clicking of claws against the bottom of the boat ... and the next moment my dear brother shrieked in my face like I've never heard a man shriek before. He let go of me" (*LP*, 283). Pi now regains his sight and sees the stranger's carcass. He gaffs an arm to use as bait. He then confesses: "I ate some of his flesh. I mean small pieces, little strips that I meant for the gaff's hook .... They slipped into my mouth nearly unnoticed" (*LP*, 284). Again, the symbolism is clear. The stranger with the French accent also represents an aspect of Pi that he will not acknowledge. This is the part of him that will do anything to survive, even become a cannibal. The blindness of Pi and his double represents Pi's blindness to the censored chapters of his own history. What he cannot accept about himself, he projects onto the other. Here, however, the other is not just Richard Parker. It is also the chef of the second story. Just as the hyena kills the zebra and the orangutan, in the second story, the chef kills the wounded sailor and Pi's mother. He, like Pi, also eats part of the flesh he was supposed to use as bait. For Pi to call him "my dear brother" is, thus, to admit implicitly that the animality within him is *both tiger and hyena*. It includes the revolting, omnivorous habits of the hyena as well as the predatory power of the tiger.

Perhaps the strangest example of projection occurs in Pi's encounter with a mysterious floating island. Lacking any soil, the island's base is made up of "an intricate, tightly webbed mass of tubed-shape seaweed, in diameter a little thicker than two fingers" (*LP*, 286). Out of this dense web of vegetation, trees grow. The island appears to satisfy both Pi's and Richard Parker's every need. Pi, the vegetarian, finds the algae forming the base of the island "wet with fresh water" (*LP*, 287). Its consistency is that of water chestnuts; it has a "light sweetness" he finds delicious, and eating it gradually restores him to health. Richard Parker's needs are met by the island's innumerable meerkats. He had no need to hunt them since "these meerkats had gone for so many generations without predators that any notion of flight distances, of flight, of plain fear, had been genetically weeded out of them" (*LP*, 298). Soon, he too, is sleek and fit again. Finding all his needs met, Pi relates, "Nothing, I thought, could ever push me to return to the lifeboat and the suffering and deprivation I had endured on it—nothing! What reason could I have to leave the island?" (LP, 310).

What changes his mind is the discovery that the island's vegetation is actually carnivorous. Noticing a tree with fruit, he climbs it to investigate. He finds that the dull green fruit are densely packed masses of leaves. Pulling them off one by one, at its center he discovers "an unspeakable pearl at the heart of a green oyster: a human tooth" (*LP*, 311). When he peels the other fruit, he finds "Thirty two teeth. A complete human set. Not one tooth was missing. Understanding dawned on me.... The island was carnivorous" (ibid.). At night the algae turned acidic, digesting everything that did not, like the meerkats, shelter in the trees. A person, however, who died in a tree would also be digested. Although in no immediate danger, Pi cannot bear the thought of what the fruit concealed: "Nothing but teeth left! TEETH!" He makes a grim decision ... "I preferred to set off and perish in search of my own kind than to live a lonely half-life of physical comfort and spiritual death on this murderous island" (*LP*, 313).

Despite the satisfaction of his physical needs, Pi flees the revelation the island offers. What appears to be a Garden of Eden turns out to have teeth in the heart of what may be symbolically regarded as its "forbidden fruit."[4] Concealed within the vegetarian paradise is the action of a carnivore. Thus the symbol of the island points to repression and its breakdown. The truth of the island and, indeed, Pi's truth—that both are carnivores—are impossible representations. They must be fled from, in spite of the physical hardship such fleeing involves.

III.

Pi's journey ends when his boat runs aground on the shore of southern Mexico. Richard Parker leaps over him to reach the land. He runs towards the jungle, never looking back. In Pi's words: "Then Richard Parker, companion of my torment, awful, fierce thing that kept me alive moved forward and disappeared forever from my life" (*LP*, 316). The disappearance of Richard Parker marks Pi's reentrance into human society. Pi is discovered, bathed, clothed, and taken to the hospital. Sometime later, he is interviewed in the hospital by officials from the Maritime Department of the Japanese Ministry of Transport.

He begins by telling them his story with the animals, which they refuse to believe. In particular, the tiger provokes disbelief: "Not a trace of it has been found" (*LP*, 329). Pi attempts an elaborate defense of its existence, asserting improbably: "There is no doubt in my mind that feral giraffes and feral hippos have been living in Tokyo for generations without being seen by a soul.... And you expect to find a tiger in a Mexican jungle! It's laughable, just plain laughable" (*LP*, 330). The stress on the undiscoverability of the tiger indicates that Pi no longer needs the qualities he projected as those of the tiger. For once the "zoo" conditions of society—its stable boundaries and protections—have been reestablished, wildness is not required.

The disbelief that Pi's first story provokes makes him attempt a second story, "a story without animals." In this story, the cruelty of the animals is ascribed to the human survivors of the life boat. Thus, where in the first story, the hyena is introduced as snapping at flies, in the second story, Pi describes the cook "swinging his arms and catching flies and eating them greedily" (*LP*, 337). The cook also shares the hyena's omnivorous habits: "He was a disgusting man. His mouth had the discrimination of a garbage heap. He also ate the rat. He cut it up and dried it in the sun. I—I'll be honest—I had a small piece, very small, behind mother's back. I was so hungry" (ibid.). As for the wounded zebra, this becomes a young "beautiful" sailor who broke his leg jumping from the ship. When his foot became "black and bloated," the cook persuades Pi and his mother to help him amputate the sailor's leg. The sailor suffers horribly: "His screams were all the worst for being unintelligible" (*LP*, 338). When Pi wants to throw the sailor's leg overboard, the cook prevents him, saying he will use it as bait. This, as he admits to Pi's mother, was his motive in forcing the amputation (*LP*, 339). When the sailor dies, the cook butchers him: "He cut up everything, including the sailor's skin and every inch of his intestines. He even prepared his genitals" (*LP*, 341). And not just for bait. When Pi's mother catches him eating the sailor, she shouts, "You animal! How could you? He's *human*!" (*LP*, 342). When the cook later strikes Pi and his mother rushes to defend him, she pushes Pi into the water and is herself killed: "He caught her by the wrist and twisted it. She shrieked and fell. He moved over her. The knife appeared. He raised it in the air. It came down" (*LP*, 343). This scene is reminiscent of the orangutan's struggle with the hyena: "The hyena … jumped on the bench and caught Orange Juice on the wrist before she could strike" (*LP*, 144). Just as the hyena beheads the orangutan, the cook beheads Pi's mother, but goes even further in his savagery by tossing the head to Pi in the water (*LP*, 344). When Pi comes to kill the cook, again there is a parallelism of the details. In both cases, the victim yields without a real struggle (ibid.). In both cases, he is eaten. In Pi's description: "I stabbed him repeatedly. His blood soothed my chapped hands. His heart was a struggle—all those tubes that constructed it. I managed to get it out. It tasted delicious, far better than turtle. I ate his liver. I cut off great pieces of his flesh" (*LP*, 345).

The parallels between the two accounts are obvious. As the Japanese interviewers note: "Both the zebra and the Taiwanese sailor broke a leg … And the hyena bit off the zebra's leg just as the cook cut off the sailor's … The blind Frenchman they met in the other lifeboat—didn't he admit to killing a man and a woman? … The cook killed the sailor and his mother…." (*LP*, 346). Since "his stories match," the interviewers draw the obvious conclusion: "the Taiwanese sailor is the zebra, his mother is the orangutan, the cook is … the hyena—which mean's he's the tiger! … The tiger killed the hyena—and the blind Frenchman—just as he killed the cook" (ibid.). The questions that arise for the Japanese concern the truth of these matching stories. Is one of them true, are both true, or, is neither the truth? Pi remarks:

> In both stories the ship sinks, my entire family dies, and I suffer…. So tell me, since it makes no factual difference to you and you can't prove

> the question either way, which story do you prefer? Which is the better story, the story with the animals or the story without animals? (*LP*, 352).

The interviewers agree that "the story with the animals is the better story." Pi then replies "And so it goes with God" (ibid.).

The implication here is that the question of the better story is also a theological question. To understand the sense of "God" involved, we have to see what is implied in the projections that Pi makes. We can begin with his projection of his qualities onto the animals. The novel suggests that such projections go on all the time. In this connection, Martel relates that Pi's father had painted on the wall beyond the zoo's ticket booth the question: "Do you know which is the most dangerous animal in the zoo?" (*LP*, 34). An arrow pointed to a curtain to be pulled, behind which was a mirror (ibid.). Is man the most dangerous animal? Pi learns from his father that there is an "animal even more dangerous than us … the animal as seen through human eyes." The animal that is " 'cute,' 'friendly,' 'loving,' 'devoted' " is like the " 'bloodthirsty,' 'depraved' animals that inflame the ire" of those who are cruel to them in the zoo. "In both cases we look at an animal and see a mirror" (ibid.). The narrator adds: "The obsession with putting ourselves at the center of everything is the bane not only of theologians but also of zoologists" (ibid.). The two answers to the question of the most dangerous animal are, then, the same answer. Looking for the most dangerous animal in the mirror, we see ourselves. When we regard the animals themselves, we see only the traits that we have projected onto them—traits that point back to us. How is it that we do not see this—that we remain by and large unconscious of our projections?

The French psychologist, Jacques Lacan, writes: "The unconscious is that chapter of my history that is marked by a blank or occupied by a falsehood: it is the censored chapter."[5] The censored material reappears in "the distortions necessitated by the linking of the adulterated chapter to the chapters surrounding it."[6] It appears in symptomatic language—i.e., language that points back to what has been censored. For Lacan, what has ultimately been censored is "the other." In his words, "... the unconscious of the subject is the discourse of the other."[7] The patient's symptoms point to the repression of the other's role in the patient's self-recognition.[8] Not willing to admit the traits that he and the other share, the person cannot recognize himself. He cannot, for example, see his own animality, which remains a "censored chapter." The result is the projections that Pi's father deplores. If we accept this, then we have to say that neither story is true. Pi is not the "puny vegetarian life form" he calls himself in the first chapter. But he is also not just the tiger, Richard Parker, as the Japanese conclude. He is actually *all* the animals: the "loving" orangutan, the "beautiful" wounded zebra, the "magnificent" predatory tiger, and the "revolting" omnivorous hyena. All, however, are now buried in his unconscious. As a Japanese interviewer admits, the truth of Pi's story is concealed, since we are "not inside this boy's head" (*LP*, 346).

The fact that both the "story with the animals" and "God" are taken to be "better" stories makes us ask whether God is also a projection of the human. Is God also one of our censored chapters? To assume so is to see not just animality but also divinity within us. Yann Martel gives a number of indications that this is the case for Pi. For instance, Pi gives his name as "I am who I am" to a pizza delivery service in Montreal.[9] In listing the contents of the life boat, he includes the item "1 God" (*LP*, 162). He also attempts to keep his faith by touching the turban he made with remnants of his shirt and saying aloud "THIS IS GOD'S HAT!" Similarly, he points to his pants, saying aloud "THIS IS GOD'S ATIRE!" and to Richard Parker, saying aloud "THIS IS GOD'S CAT!," and still to the boat, saying aloud, "THIS IS GOD'S ARK!" and so on (*LP*, 231–232). There are also more subtle hints of the divinity within us. One of the most interesting concerns Mr. Kumar, a baker, who is a Sufi Muslim mystic. Mr. Kumar introduces Pi to Islam. As Pi describes their relationship, "I sometimes came out of that bakery feeling heavy with glory" (*LP*, 68). Yet, in spite of the closeness of their relation, he cannot recognize him. As Pi says to himself while waiting for Mr. Kumar at the zoo,

> Have you forgotten how plain he looks? You will never recognize him.... I *had* to recognize him.... But I had noticed before that it was when I tried my hardest to recognize him that I was least able to pick him out. The very effort seemed to blind me (*LP*, 89).

This suggests that the divinity within cannot be seen without. For, like our animality, it escapes us.

The presence of such divinity is, however, recognizable through its projections. Yann Martel gives a comical example of this when Pi's imam, pandit, and priest converge on him during a walk with his family. His parents have no idea that he is "a practicing Hindu, Christian, and Muslim" (*LP*, 71), and they listen amazed as he is successively praised for being a good Christian, Muslim, and Hindu boy. The three religious figures then begin to quarrel. The imam tells Pi, "Hindus and Christians are idolaters. They have many gods." The pandit responds, "And Muslims have many wives," while the priest asserts: "there is salvation only in Jesus." Soon insults are being traded: Christians are called the "flunkies of a foreign god," the pandit is referred to as "the slave driver of the caste system," while the priest calls their beliefs "myths from a cartoon strip" (*LP*, 75). This sorry display of intolerance is only brought to a halt when Pi explains, "Bapu Gandhi said, 'All religions are true.' I just want to love God" (*LP*, 76). This, however, does not ultimately satisfy his hearers, who depart with grudging smiles. Pi himself later reflects, "There are always those who take it on themselves to defend God, as if Ultimate Reality, as if the sustaining frame of existence, were something weak and helpless.... The degree of their indignation is astonishing. Their resolve is frightening" (*LP*, 78). These sentiments imply that no one of the religions has the ultimate truth about God. The fact that these religious figures act as if their God were "weak and helpless" points to a truth that they at one and the same time both accept and conceal from themselves. Each of their religions is, in its narrowness, a projection.

Granting this, how can we say that Yann Martel's story leads us to God? Isn't God, like the animals on the boat, a projection of what is only within us? For the author, however, the fact that it is a projection does not disqualify its reality. Our animality remains, even though it forms a censored chapter of our conscious life. So does our divinity. In both cases, we face an unspeakable alterity. Like Richard Parker, our animality vanishes in the confines of civilized life. We can only relate its story by projecting its qualities onto the animals about us. The same, Martel suggests, holds with regard to our divinity. The original experience of the divine, which Pi, for example, has when he leaves the baker "feeling heavy with glory," can only appear within the confines of ordinary life in distinct religious forms—Hindu, Muslim, Christian, etc. The improbability of the animals in the first story is matched by that of the aspects of each religion that the other religions criticize. In both cases, we have to deal with the distortions of symbolic substitutes, of possible representations substituting for impossible ones. One can put this in terms of Lacan's assertion that "the unconscious of the subject is the discourse of the other."[10] The discourse of the unspeakable alterity of our animal and divine natures is that of the unconscious—i.e., of the symbolic substitutes within which it necessarily clothes itself.

One way to express this is in terms of Pi's name. Pi's actual name is Picine, which he shortens to "Pi" in order to avoid being teased as "Pissing." As a mathematical symbol, "Pi" is an irrational number. It expresses the inability to find a common measure—an exact ratio—between the circumference and the diameter of a circle. It is a number that goes on forever. This suggests that there is the same irrationality in man: there is no common measure—no ratio—linking him either to his animality or to his divinity. He is in his being made up of incommensurables. Pi himself says "in that elusive, irrational number with which scientists try to understand the universe, I found refuge" (*LP*, 27).

How are we to understand this? It seems that to reach the animal and the divine, we have to go beyond the things for which we have common measures. The animal and the divine show themselves in "the madness that moves life in strange but saving ways" (*LP*, 95), the very madness without which "no species would survive" (*LP*, 45). This measure beyond measure is the unconscious understood as an alterity that, in remaining other, must always show itself in a series of symbolic substitutes. Martel's tale invites us to think of this unconscious in theological terms - that is, not just to position it, like the Freudian id, as below reason, but also as *above* reason.

This insight is expressed by Pi when he gazes out from his raft at the stars shining with "such fierce, contained brilliance" (*LP*, 196). Seeing them, he "felt like the sage Markandeya, who fell out of Vishnu's mouth while

Vishnu was sleeping and so beheld the entire universe, everything that there is" (ibid.). Before the sage could die of fright, Vishnu awoke and "took him back into his mouth" (ibid.). As this last line suggests, such a vision is not one we could bear. As Pi continues,

> For the first time I saw my suffering for what it was, finite and insignificant, and I was still. My suffering did not fit anywhere, I realized. And I could accept this. It was alright. (It was daylight that brought my protest: 'No! No! No! My suffering does matter. I want to live. I can't help but mix my life with that of the universe. Life is a peephole, a single tiny entry onto a vastness. This peephole is all I've got!') I mumbled words of Muslim prayer and went back to sleep (ibid.).

To live in this peephole is to live with the saving madness that allows Pi to pray and to care for Richard Parker. To recognize the necessity involved here is, Martel suggests, to avoid the "illusions about freedom" that plague both religions and zoos.

Notes

1. Yann Martel. *Life of Pi* (Canada: Random House of Canada, 2001). Hereafter, this novel will be cited as *LP,* followed by appropriate page number(s).
2. Emmanuel Levinas. "La Mort et le Temps" in *Dieu, La Mort et le Temps*, ed. Jacques Rolland. (Paris: Bernard Grasset, 1993), p. 127.
3. "Education" in Latin is *educatio*. It comes from *educo*, the verb signifying "to lead forth" or "to draw out." See Lewis and Short. *A Latin Dictionary*. (Oxford: Clarendon Press, 1966), p. 627.
4. What "forbids" them is Pi's resistance to the truth that they reveal. One can, of course, make a parallel claim about forbidden fruit in *Genesis's* account of the "Garden of Eden."
5. Jacques Lacan. "Function and field of speech and language." *Écrits, A Selection*. (New York, W. W. Norton and Company, 2002), p. 50.
6. Ibid.
7. Ibid., p. 55.
8. Ibid., p. 55.
9. When the pizzas arrive they are marked for "Ian Hoolihan" (LP, 22).
10. Lacan, p. 55.

Notes on Contributors

Charles Brown, Professor of Philosophy at Emporia State University in Emporia, Kansas, is co-editor of *Eco-Phenomenology: Back to the Earth Itself* as well as of *Nature's Edge: Boundary Explorations in Ecological Theory and Practice.* His interests include the convergence of phenomenological and environmental thought, as well as issues of environmental and global justice.

Licia Carlson currently teaches philosophy in the Expository Writing Program at Harvard University. She has broad philosophical interests in Continental philosophy, feminism, ethics and epistemology. Her publications include articles on philosophy and disability, Michel Foucault, feminist philosophy, and bioethics. She is currently completing a book that critically examines philosophical approaches to cognitive disability, and further explores the intersections between animal rights discourse and disability discourse.

Gerard Kuperus holds a Ph.D. in Philosophy from DePaul University with a dissertation on Hegel. He is currently a Visiting Assistant Professor at the University of San Francisco, and his areas of interest include Phenomenology, German Idealism, and Ancient Philosophy.

Dieter Lohmar, Professor of Philosophy at the University of Cologne, has a wide array of philosophical interests, including in phenomenology, transcendental philosophy, philosophy of the formal sciences, inter-cultural philosophy, empiricism, anthropology, and interdisciplinary approaches to phenomenology. His publications include the following books: *Phänomenologie der Mathematik* (1989); *Erfahrung und kategoriales Denken* (1998); *Edmund Husserl's 'Formale und Transzendentale Logik': A Commentary* (2000); and *Phänomenologie der schwachen Phantasie* (2007). In addition, he has edited several volumes and published numerous articles.

Christian Lotz is an Assistant Professor of Philosophy at Michigan State University. His interests are in Post-Kantian European philosophy. He has published *From Affectivity to Subjectivity: Husserl's Phenomenology Revisited* (Palgrave, 2007); and *Vom Leib zum Selbst. Kritische Untersuchungen zu Husserl und Heidegger* (Alber, 2005). In addition, he is co-editor of *Erinnerung. Philosophische Positionen, Perspektiven und Probleme* (Fink, 2004); *Subjektivität – Verantwortung – Wahrheit.*

Neue Aspekte der Phänomenologie Edmund Husserls (Lang, 2002); and *Philosophie als Denkwerkzeug. Zur Aktualität transzendentalphilosophischer Argumentation* (Konigshausen & Neumann, 2000).

Marjolein Oele is an Assistant Professor of Philosophy at the University of San Francisco. She obtained her Masters Degree in Philosophy from the University of Amsterdam, and holds a Ph.D. in Philosophy from Loyola University Chicago. Her primary research interests are in Ancient Greek Philosophy and in 20th Century Continental Philosophy.

James Mensch is Professor of Philosophy at Saint Francis Xavier University in Nova Scotia, Canada. His main areas of research are phenomenology and its contemporary applications. He has lectured widely both in America and in Europe, and serves on a number of editorial and research boards. Mensch is the author of eight books, six of which focus on phenomenology and its applications: *Hiddenness and Alterity* (Duquesne Univ. Press, 2005); *Ethics and Selfhood* (SUNY Press 2003); *Postfoundational Phenomenology* (Penn State Press, 2001); *After Modernity* (SUNY Press, 1996); *Intersubjectivity and Transcendental Idealism* (SUNY Press, 1980); and *The Question of Being in Husserl's Logical Investigations* (Martinus Nijhoff, 1981). He has also published *Knowing and Being* (Penn State Press, 1996), which is a work on the relation of epistemology to ontology, and *The Beginning of the Gospel of St. John* (Peter Lang 1992), which is a study in the hermeneutics of religion.

Corinne Painter, Assistant Professor of Philosophy at Washtenaw Community College in Ann Arbor, Michigan, received her Ph.D. from Loyola University in Chicago (2004). Her primary research interests include Ancient Philosophy, Phenomenology, and Animal Ethics. Her publications include articles in each of these areas, and she is currently working on two books, one of which offers a commentary on Plato's *Sophist*, the other of which presents an examination of the role that empathy plays in providing the proper foundation for a cross-species ethic of care.

Erika Ruonakoski is a researcher and a lecturer in philosophy at the Lahti University of Applied Sciences. Her doctoral dissertation, *Man and Animal in Phenomenology of the Body,* which she is preparing for the University of Helsinki, deals with human perception of non-human animals. Her primary research interests include Merleau-Ponty's philosophy of perception as well as feminist philosophy. Ruonakoski is the translator of Beauvoir's *Onko Sade poltettava? ja muita esseitä*; translation: *Must We Burn Sade? And Other Essays* (Helsinki, WSOY 2007).

Ted Toadvine, Assistant Professor of Philosophy and Environmental Studies at the University of Oregon, specializes in contemporary Continental philosophy and in environmental philosophy. He is the translator of Renaud Barbaras's *The Being of the Phenomenon* and the editor of five volumes, most recently *The Merleau-Ponty Reader* (Northwestern) and *Nature's Edge: Boundary Explorations in Ecological Theory and Practice* (SUNY Press). He is currently completing two monographs: *Merleau-Ponty's Philosophy of Nature* and *The Sense of Nature: Essays in Ecophenomenology*. Toadvine is managing editor of the journal *Environmental Philosophy* and director of the *Series in Continental Thought* at Ohio University Press.

Index

Contributions to Phenomenology

IN COOPERATION WITH

THE CENTER FOR ADVANCED RESEARCH IN PHENOMENOLOGY

---

1. F. Kersten: *Phenomenological Method.* Theory and Practice. 1989 ISBN 0-7923-0094-7
2. E. G. Ballard: *Philosophy and the Liberal Arts.* 1989 ISBN 0-7923-0241-9
3. H. A. Durfee and D.F.T. Rodier (eds.): *Phenomenology and Beyond.* The Self and Its Language. 1989 ISBN 0-7923-0511-6
4. J. J. Drummond: *Husserlian Intentionality and Non-Foundational Realism.* Noema and Object. 1990 ISBN 0-7923-0651-1
5. A. Gurwitsch: *Kants Theorie des Verstandes.* Herausgegeben von T.M. Seebohm. 1990 ISBN 0-7923-0696-1
6. D. Jervolino: *The Cogito and Hermeneutics.* The Question of the Subject in Ricœur. 1990 ISBN 0-7923-0824-7
7. B.P. Dauenhauer: *Elements of Responsible Politics.* 1991 ISBN 0-7923-1329-1
8. T.M. Seebohm, D. Føllesdal and J.N. Mohanty (eds.): *Phenomenology and the Formal Sciences.* 1991 ISBN 0-7923-1499-9
9. L. Hardy and L. Embree (eds.): *Phenomenology of Natural Science.* 1992 ISBN 0-7923-1541-3
10. J.J. Drummond and L. Embree (eds.): *The Phenomenology of the Noema.* 1992 ISBN 0-7923-1980-X
11. B. C. Hopkins: *Intentionality in Husserl and Heidegger.* The Problem of the Original Method and Phenomenon of Phenomenology. 1999 ISBN 0-7923-2074-3
12. P. Blosser, E. Shimomissé, L. Embree and H. Kojima (eds.): *Japanese and Western Phenomenology.* 1993 ISBN 0-7923-2075-1
13. F. M. Kirkland and P. D. Chattopadhyaya (eds.): *Phenomenology: East and West.* Essays in Honor of J. N. Mohanty. 1993 ISBN 0-7923-2087-5
14. E. Marbach: *Mental Representation and Consciousness.* Towards a Phenomenological Theory of Representation and Reference. 1993 ISBN 0-7923-2101-4
15. J.J. Kockelmans: *Ideas for a Hermeneutical Phenomenology of the Natural Sciences.* 1993 ISBN 0-7923-2364-5
16. M. Daniel and L. Embree (eds.): *Phenomenology of the Cultural Disciplines.* 1994 ISBN 0-7923-2792-6
17. T.J. Stapleton (ed.): *The Question of Hermeneutics.* Essays in Honor of Joseph J. Kockelmans. 1994 ISBN 0-7923-2911-2; Pb 0-7923-2964-3

Contributions to Phenomenology

IN COOPERATION WITH

THE CENTER FOR ADVANCED RESEARCH IN PHENOMENOLOGY

---

18. L. Embree, E. Behnke, D. Carr, J.C. Evans, J. Huertas-Jourda, J.J. Kockelmans, W.R. McKenna, A. Mickunas, J.N. Mohanty, T.M. Seebohm and R.M. Zaner (eds.): *Encyclopedia of Phenomenology*. 1997 ISBN 0-7923-2956-2
19. S.G. Crowell (ed.): *The Prism of the Self.* Philosophical Essays in Honor of Maurice Natanson. 1995 ISBN 0-7923-3546-5
20. W.R. McKenna and J.C. Evans (eds.): *Derrida and Phenomenology.* 1995 ISBN 0-7923-3730-1
21. S.B. Mallin: *Art Line Thought.* 1996 ISBN 0-7923-3774-3
22. R.D. Ellis: *Eros in a Narcissistic Culture.* An Analysis Anchored in the Life-World. 1996 ISBN 0-7923-3982-7
23. J.J. Drummond and J.G. Hart (eds.): *The Truthful and The Good.* Essays in Honor of Robert Sokolowski. 1996 ISBN 0-7923-4134-1
24. T. Nenon and L. Embree (eds.): *Issues in Husserl's* Ideas II. 1996 ISBN 0-7923-4216-X
25. J.C. Evans and R.S. Stufflebeam (eds.): *To Work at the Foundations.* Essays in Memory of Aron Gurwitsch. 1997 ISBN 0-7923-4317-4
26. B.C. Hopkins (ed.): *Husserl in Contemporary Context.* Prospects and Projects for Phenomenology. 1997 ISBN 0-7923-4469-3
27. M.C. Baseheart, S.C.N.: *Person in the World.* Introduction to the Philosophy of Edith Stein. 1997 ISBN 0-7923-4490-1
28. J.G. Hart and L. Embree (eds.): *Phenomenology of Values and Valuing.* 1997 ISBN 0-7923-4491-X
29. F. Kersten: *Galileo and the "Invention" of Opera.* A Study in the Phenomenology of Consciousness. 1997 ISBN 0-7923-4536-3
30. E. Ströker: *Husserlian Foundations of Science.* 1997 ISBN 0-7923-4743-9
31. L. Embree (ed.): *Alfred Schutz's "Sociological Aspect of Literature".* Construction and Complementary Essays. 1998 ISBN 0-7923-4847-8
32. M.C. Srajek: *In the Margins of Deconstruction.* Jewish Conceptions of Ethics in Emmanuel Levinas and Jacques Derrida. 1998 ISBN 0-7923-4953-9
33. N. Rotenstreich: *Synthesis and Intentional Objectivity.* On Kant and Husserl. 1998 ISBN 0-7923-4956-3
34. D. Zahavi (ed.): *Self-awareness, Temporality, and Alterity.* Central Topics in Phenomenology. 1998 ISBN 0-7923-5065-0

Contributions to Phenomenology

IN COOPERATION WITH

THE CENTER FOR ADVANCED RESEARCH IN PHENOMENOLOGY

---

35. R. Cristin: *Heidegger and Leibniz*. Reason and the Path. 1998 ISBN 0-7923-5137-1
36. B.C. Hopkins (ed.): *Phenomenology: Japanese and American Perspectives*. 1999 ISBN 0-7923-5336-6
37. L. Embree (ed.): *Schutzian Social Science*. 1999 ISBN 0-7923-6003-6
38. K. Thompson and L. Embree (eds.): *Phenomenology of the Political*. 2000 ISBN 0-7923-6163-6
39. O.K. Wiegand, R.J. Dostal, L. Embree, J.J. Kockelmans and J.N. Mohanty (eds.): *Phenomenology on Kant, German Idealism, Hermeneutics and Logic*. Philosophical Essays in Honor of Thomas M. Seebohm. 2000 ISBN 0-7923-6290-X
40. L. Fisher and L. Embree (eds.): *Feminist Phenomenology*. 2000 ISBN 0-7923-6580-1
41. J.B. Brough and L. Embree (eds.): *The Many Faces of Time*. 2000 ISBN 0-7923-6622-0
42. G.B. Madison: *The Politics of Postmodernity*. Essays in Applied Hermeneutics. 2000 ISBN 0-7923-6859-2
43. W. O'Brien and L. Embree (eds.): *The Existential Phenomenology of Simone de Beauvoir*. 2001 ISBN 0-7923-7064-3
44. F. Schalow: *Heidegger and the Quest for the Sacred*. From Thought to the Sanctuary of Faith. 2001 ISBN 1-4020-0036-7
45. T. Toadvine and L. Embree (eds.): *Merleau-Ponty's Reading of Husserl*. 2002 ISBN 1-4020-0469-9
46. J.J. Kockelmans: *Ideas for a Hermeneutic Phenomenology of the Natural Sciences*. Vol. 2: On the Importance of Methodical Hermeneutics for a Hermeneutic Phenomenology of the Natural Sciences. 2002 ISBN 1-4020-0650-0
47. J.J. Drummond and L. Embree (eds.): *Phenomenological Approaches to Moral Philosophy*. A Handbook. 2002 ISBN 1-4020-0770-1
48. D. Fisette (ed.): *Husserl's Logical Investigations Reconsidered*. 2003 ISBN 1-4020-1389-2
49. D. Zahavi, S. Heinämaa and H. Ruin (eds.): *Metaphysics, Facticity, Interpretation*. Phenomenology in the Nordic Countries. 2003 ISBN 1-4020-1754-5

Contributions to Phenomenology

IN COOPERATION WITH

THE CENTER FOR ADVANCED RESEARCH IN PHENOMENOLOGY

---

50. T.M. Seebohm: *Hermeneutics. Method and Methodology*. 2004
ISBN 1-4020-2617-X
51. D. Carr and C.-F. Cheung (eds.): *Space, Time, and Culture*. 2004
ISBN 1-4020-2823-7
52. L. Embree (ed.): *Gurwitsch's Relevancy for Cognitive Science*. 2004
ISBN 1-4020-2891-1
53. M. Endress, G. Psathas and H. Nasu (eds.): *Explorations of the Life-World*. Continuing Dialogues with Alfred Schutz. 2005 ISBN 1-4020-3219-6
54. P.S. Arvidson: *The Sphere of Attention*. Context and Margin. 2006
ISBN 1-4020-3571-3
55. Kwok-Ying Lau and John J. Drummond (eds.): *Husserl's Logical Investigations in the New Century: Western and Chinese Perspectives*. 2007 ISBN 978-1-4020-5757-1
56. C. Painter and C. Lotz (eds.): *Phenomenology and the Non-Human Animal*. At the Limits of Experience. 2007 ISBN 978-1-4020-6306-0

Further information about our publications on *Phenomenology* is available on request.

springer.com

CPSIA information can be obtained
at www.ICGtesting.com
Printed in the USA
LVHW081529180422
716529LV00003B/80

9 781402 063060